HoloLens Beginner's Guide

Join the AR revolution with HoloLens

Jason M. Odom

BIRMINGHAM - MUMBAI

HoloLens Beginner's Guide

First published: April 2017

Production reference: 1260417

Published by Packt Publishing Ltd.
Livery Place
35 Livery Street
Birmingham
B3 2PB, UK.
ISBN 978-1-78646-472-9

www.packtpub.com

Credits

Author

Jason M. Odom

Reviewers

Vangos Pterneas
Michael Washington

Commissioning Editor

Amarabha Banerjee

Acquisition Editor

Larissa Pinto

Content Development Editor

Onkar Wani

Technical Editor

Murtaza Tinwala

Copy Editors

Dhanya Baburaj
Shaila Kusanale

Project Coordinator

Ulhas Kambali

Proofreader

Safis Editing

Indexer

Tejal Daruwale Soni

Graphics

Abhinash Sahu

Production Coordinator

Deepika Naik

About the Author

Jason Odom is a game developer with nearly 20 years of experience working on titles for companies such as Activision and Take 2 Interactive, along with years of game development teaching and mentoring. He is the founder of Thought Experiment, a start-up mixed reality studio, and he is currently working on HoloQuest and CrossTrainMR properties for HoloLens. When he is not making software and applications, he is a loud and proud mixed reality evangelist with a highly active YouTube channel, and a prolific technology blogger for NextReality. You can connect to him on the following:

https://www.youtube.com/playlist?list=PLEjp5Cbksqk4x-3rO_6G8I-k5_vOEX25W

https://github.com/Subere23?tab=repositories

http://www.thoughtexperimentstudios.com/

http://next.reality.news/

I would like to thank my family and friends for being patient with me as I sat locked away from the world working on this project. I would also like to send out a big "Thank you" to James Ashley for his subtle yet meaningful hints at how to make it through your first book, as well as Jesse McCulloch and the HoloDevelopers – Slack Community for being a constant source of great HoloLens information.

About the Reviewer

Vangos Pterneas is helping innovative companies increase their revenue using motion technology and virtual reality. He is an expert in Kinect, HoloLens, Oculus Rift, and HTC Vive.

Microsoft has awarded him with the title of Most Valuable Professional for his technical contributions to the open source community. Vangos runs LightBuzz Inc, collaborating with clients from all over the world. He's also the author of the book *Getting Started with HTML5 WebSocket Programming*, by Packt, and *The Dark Art of Freelancing*.

www.PacktPub.com

For support files and downloads related to your book, please visit www.PacktPub.com.

Did you know that Packt offers eBook versions of every book published, with PDF and ePub files available? You can upgrade to the eBook version at www.PacktPub.com and as a print book customer, you are entitled to a discount on the eBook copy. Get in touch with us at service@packtpub.com for more details.

At www.PacktPub.com, you can also read a collection of free technical articles, sign up for a range of free newsletters and receive exclusive discounts and offers on Packt books and eBooks.

https://www.packtpub.com/mapt

Get the most in-demand software skills with Mapt. Mapt gives you full access to all Packt books and video courses, as well as industry-leading tools to help you plan your personal development and advance your career.

Why subscribe?

- Fully searchable across every book published by Packt
- Copy and paste, print, and bookmark content
- On demand and accessible via a web browser

Customer Feedback
Thanks for purchasing this Packt book. At Packt, quality is at the heart of our editorial process. To help us improve, please leave us an honest review on this book's Amazon page at "Amazon Book URL".

If you'd like to join our team of regular reviewers, you can e-mail us at customerreviews@packtpub.com. We award our regular reviewers with free eBooks and videos in exchange for their valuable feedback. Help us be relentless in improving our products!

Customer Feedback

Thanks for purchasing this Packt book. At Packt, quality is at the heart of our editorial process. To help us improve, please leave us an honest review on this book's Amazon page at `https://www.amazon.com/HoloLens-Beginners-Guide-Jason-Odom-ebook/dp/1786464721`.

If you'd like to join our team of regular reviewers, you can e-mail us at `customerreviews@packtpub.com`. We award our regular reviewers with free eBooks and videos in exchange for their valuable feedback. Help us be relentless in improving our products!

For Aaron,

"Next door the TV's flashing blue frames on the wall.

It's a comedy of errors you see.

It's about taking a fall."

Table of Contents

Preface

Microsoft HoloLens is on par with a modern-day wonder. It is the world's first untethered, head mounted computer capable of projecting holograms into the world around us. This new technology enables forms of interaction that we have not even been able to imagine yet. New ideas are coming to the surface every day.

As this new device and its conceptual successors are further iterated upon, becoming more powerful and smaller, we will see a shift away from the 2D displays that we have had in place for the last 90 years. Even the pocket computers we use daily now will likely fall away into shared experiences that are projected through glasses, and maybe even one day contact lenses.

This book is here to get those interested in being on the front end of the coming wave up to speed with the development process for Windows mixed reality (formerly Windows Holographic), the ecosystem that Microsoft has created in parallel with Windows 10 for their new class of devices.

What this book covers

Chapter 1, *Welcome to the New World*, will introduce Microsoft HoloLens and its capabilities, as well as introduce and install the tools we will use to develop software for the device.

Chapter 2, *HoloWorld*, outlines how to build our first basic application. It will include the entire process from start to running on HoloLens.

Chapter 3, *I Am in Control*, covers the pillars of HoloLens input, Gaze Gesture, and Voice. We will also get into some of the elements of Unity development, such as Prefabs.

Chapter 4, *User-Friendly Interface*, takes you through C# scripting at a high, and teaches you to use what you have learned to build some interactive user interface elements. We then get to see these elements at work.

Chapter 5, *Now That Is How It Should Sound*, teaches you to take the knowledge accrued in the earlier chapters and begin your book project. We then learn about sound: AudioSources, AudioListener, and Spatialized Audio.

Chapter 6, *Not So Blank Spaces*, covers one of the major elements that help HoloLens create the magic that it is capable of--spatial mapping. We then use the spatial map in the context of our project so that we can learn how to move objects around our spatial map.

Chapter 7, *The Tools of the Trade*, focuses on the World Anchor, World Anchor Manager, and World Anchor Store. These important elements of persistence are a must-know. We then create a simple in-game debug output to help us track down problems.

Chapter 8, *Share What You Have Got*, explains the Holographic Sharing service that Microsoft provides as part of the HoloToolkit. This service allows us to create multiuser experiences for HoloLens.

Chapter 9, *Putting It All Together*, takes some of everything we have learned and brings it together to help us round out our project and make a playable game.

Chapter 10, *Fixing Problems*, showcases what debugging and profiling options exist within the confines of our tools, Unity and Visual Studio, and there are many.

What you need for this book

You require either a Windows 10, compatible PC and a HoloLens, or a PC with Windows 10 Pro and the HoloLens Emulator.

Who this book is for

If you are a developer new to Windows Universal development platform and want to get started with HoloLens development, this is the book for you. No prior experience of C# programming or of the .NET framework is needed to get started with this book.

Conventions

In this book, you will find a number of text styles that distinguish between different kinds of information. Here are some examples of these styles and an explanation of their meaning.

Code words in text, database table names, folder names, filenames, file extensions, pathnames, dummy URLs, user input, and Twitter handles are shown as follows: "Run vs_community. exe and complete the installation process."

A block of code is set as follows:

```
public void OnGazeRectStart()
    {
        if (!selected)
        {    rend.material.color = Color.green;
            gazed = true;
        }
```

New terms and **important words** are shown in bold. Words that you see on the screen, for example, in menus or dialog boxes, appear in the text like this: "In the **Camera** component, click on the **Clear Flags** and select **Skybox** drop-down menu"

 Warnings or important notes appear in a box like this.

 Tips and tricks appear like this.

Reader feedback

Feedback from our readers is always welcome. Let us know what you think about this book-what you liked or disliked. Reader feedback is important for us as it helps us develop titles that you will really get the most out of.

To send us general feedback, simply e-mail feedback@packtpub.com, and mention the book's title in the subject of your message.

If there is a topic that you have expertise in and you are interested in either writing or contributing to a book, see our author guide at www.packtpub.com/authors.

Customer support

Now that you are the proud owner of a Packt book, we have a number of things to help you to get the most from your purchase.

Downloading the example code

You can download the example code files for this book from your account at http://www.packtpub.com. If you purchased this book elsewhere, you can visit http://www.packtpub.com/support and register to have the files e-mailed directly to you.

You can download the code files by following these steps:

1. Log in or register to our website using your e-mail address and password.
2. Hover the mouse pointer on the **SUPPORT** tab at the top.
3. Click on **Code Downloads & Errata**.

4. Enter the name of the book in the **Search** box.
5. Select the book for which you're looking to download the code files.
6. Choose from the drop-down menu where you purchased this book from.
7. Click on **Code Download**.

Once the file is downloaded, please make sure that you unzip or extract the folder using the latest version of:

- WinRAR / 7-Zip for Windows
- Zipeg / iZip / UnRarX for Mac
- 7-Zip / PeaZip for Linux

The code bundle for the book is also hosted on GitHub at `https://github.com/PacktPubl ishing/HoloLens-Beginners-Guide`. We also have other code bundles from our rich catalog of books and videos available at `https://github.com/PacktPublishing/`. Check them out!

Downloading the color images of this book

We also provide you with a PDF file that has color images of the screenshots/diagrams used in this book. The color images will help you better understand the changes in the output. You can download this file from `http://www.packtpub.com/sites/default/files/downl oads/HoloLensBeginnersGuide_ColorImages.pdf`.

Errata

Although we have taken every care to ensure the accuracy of our content, mistakes do happen. If you find a mistake in one of our books-maybe a mistake in the text or the code-we would be grateful if you could report this to us. By doing so, you can save other readers from frustration and help us improve subsequent versions of this book. If you find any errata, please report them by visiting `http://www.packtpub.com/submit-errata`, selecting your book, clicking on the **Errata Submission Form** link, and entering the details of your errata. Once your errata are verified, your submission will be accepted and the errata will be uploaded to our website or added to any list of existing errata under the Errata section of that title.

To view the previously submitted errata, go to `https://www.packtpub.com/books/conten t/support`and enter the name of the book in the search field. The required information will appear under the **Errata** section.

Piracy

Piracy of copyrighted material on the Internet is an ongoing problem across all media. At Packt, we take the protection of our copyright and licenses very seriously. If you come across any illegal copies of our works in any form on the Internet, please provide us with the location address or website name immediately so that we can pursue a remedy.

Please contact us at copyright@packtpub.com with a link to the suspected pirated material.

We appreciate your help in protecting our authors and our ability to bring you valuable content.

Questions

If you have a problem with any aspect of this book, you can contact us at questions@packtpub.com, and we will do our best to address the problem.

1
Welcome to the New World

We live in very exciting times. Technology is changing at a pace so rapid that it is becoming near impossible to keep up with these new frontiers as they arrive; they seem to arrive on a daily basis now. Moore's Law continues to stand, meaning that technology is getting smaller and more powerful at a constant rate. As I said, very exciting.

One of these new emerging technologies that finally is reaching a place more material than science fiction stories is Augmented or Mixed Reality. Imagine a world where our communication and entertainment devices are worn, and the digital tools we use, as well as the games we play, are holographic projections in the world around us. These holograms know how to interact with our world and change themselves to fit our needs. Microsoft has led the charge by releasing such a device: the HoloLens.

The Microsoft HoloLens changes the paradigm of what we know as personal computing-- we can now have our Word window up on the wall (this is how I am typing right now), we can have research material floating around it, and we can have our communication tools, such as Gmail and Skype, in the area as well. We are finally no longer trapped by a virtual desktop, on a screen, sitting at a physical desktop; we aren't even trapped in the confines of a room anymore.

What exactly is the HoloLens?

The HoloLens is a first of its kind head-worn, standalone computer with a sensor array, which includes microphones and multiple types of camera, a spatial sound speaker array, a light projector, and an optical waveguide.

The HoloLens is not only a wearable computer, it is also a complete replacement for the standard 2D display. It has the capability of using holographic projection to create multiple screens throughout an environment and fully 3D-rendered objects. With the HoloLens sensor array, these holograms can fully interact with the environment you are in.

The sensor array allows the HoloLens to *see* the world around it, to see the input from the user's hands, and for it to hear voice commands. Although Microsoft has been very quiet about what the entire sensor array includes, we have a good general idea about the components used in the sensor array; let's take a look at them:

- **One IMU**: The **Inertia Measurement Unit (IMU)** is a sensor array that includes an accelerometer, a gyroscope, and a magnetometer. This unit handles head orientation tracking and compensates for the *drift* that comes from the Gyroscope's eventual lack of precision.
- **Four environment understanding sensors**: These together form the spatial mapping that the HoloLens uses to create a mesh of the world around the user.
- **One depth camera**: This is also known as a structured light 3D scanner. This device is used for measuring the 3D shape of an object using projected light patterns and a camera system. Microsoft first used this type of camera inside the Kinect for the Xbox 360 and Xbox One.
- **One ambient light sensor**: Ambient light sensors or photosensors are used for ambient light sensing and proximity detection.
- **2 MP photo/HD video camera**: This is used for taking pictures and video.
- **Four-microphone array**: These do a great job of listening to the user and not the sounds around them. Voice is one of the primary input types with HoloLens.

Putting all of these elements together forms a Holographic computer that allows the user to see, hear, and interact with the world around them in new and unique ways:

What you need to develop for the HoloLens

The HoloLens development environment breaks down into two primary tools, **Unity** and **Visual Studio**. Unity is the 3D environment that we will do most of our work in; this includes adding holograms, creating user interface elements, adding sound and particle systems, and other things that bring a 3D program to life.

Visual Studio on the other hand is the glue that makes everything work. Here, we write scripts or machine code to make our 3D creations come to life and add a level of control and immersion that Unity cannot produce on its own.

Unity

Unity is a software framework designed to speed up the creation of games and 3D-based software. Generally speaking, Unity is known as a game engine but the more apparent the holographic world becomes, the more we will use such a development environment for different kinds of applications.

Unity is an application that allows us to take 3D models, 2D graphics, particle systems, and sound to make them interact with each other and our user. Many elements are dragged and dropped and plugged and played; what you see is what you get. This can simplify the iteration and testing process. As developers, we most likely do not want to build and compile little changes we make in the development process forever. This allows us to see the changes in context to ensure that they work; then once we hit a group of changes, we can test them on the HoloLens ourselves. This does not work for every aspect of HoloLens-Unity development, but it does work for a good 80%-90%.

Visual Studio community

Microsoft Visual Studio Community is a great, free **Integrated Development Environment** (**IDE**). Here, we use programming languages, such as C# or JavaScript, to *code* changes in the behavior of objects, and generally make things happen inside of our programs.

HoloToolkit - Unity

The **HoloToolkit-Unity** is a repository of samples, scripts, and components to help speed up the process of development. This covers a large selection of areas in HoloLens development, such as the following:

- **Input**: Gaze, gesture, and voice are the primary ways in which we interact with the HoloLens.

- **Sharing**: The sharing repository helps allow users to share holographic spaces and connect to each other via the network.

- **Spatial Mapping**: This is how the HoloLens sees our world. A large 3D mesh of our space is generated and give our holograms something to interact with or bounce off of.

- **Spatial Sound**: The speaker array inside the HoloLens does an amazing job of giving the illusion of space. Objects behind us seem like they are behind us.

HoloLens emulator

The **HoloLens emulator** is an extension to Visual Studio that will simulate how a program will run on the HoloLens. This is great for those who want to get started with HoloLens development but do not have an actual HoloLens, yet. This software does require the use of **Microsoft Hyper-V**, a feature only available inside the Windows 10 Pro operating system. Hyper-V is a virtualization environment, which allows the creation of a virtual machine. This virtual machine emulates the specific hardware, so one can test without the actual hardware.

Visual Studio tools for Unity

This collection of tools adds IntelliSense and debugging features to Visual Studio; if you use Visual Studio and Unity, these are a must have:

- **IntelliSense**: An intelligent code completion tool for Microsoft Visual Studio. This is designed to speed up many processes when writing code. The version that comes with Visual Studios tools for Unity has Unity-specific updates.

- **Debugging**: Before this extension existed, debugging Unity apps proved to be a little tedious. With this tool, we can now debug Unity applications inside Visual Studio, thus speeding the bug squashing process considerably.

Other useful tools

The following are some the useful tools that are required:

- **Image editor**: Photoshop and Gimp both are good examples of programs that allow us to create 2D UI elements and textures for objects in our apps.
- **3D modeling software**: 3D Studio Max, Maya, and Blender are all programs that allow us to make 3D objects that can be imported in Unity.
- **Sound editing software**: There are a few resources for free sounds on the Web. With that in mind, Sound Forge is a great tool for editing those sounds, layering sounds together to create new sounds.

Installing the software

Now, we will get our development environment installed and set up so that we can start building the next killer app for HoloLens. We will start with our main tools, Visual Studio and Unity HoloLens technical preview, and then add the extensions that will help speed things along.

Installing Visual Studio

Microsoft has made the installation process for Visual Studio very simple. Just be warned that it can take a while to download and install it:

1. Navigate to `http://www.visualstudio.com/en-us/visual-studio-homepage-vs.aspx`.

2. Click on **Download Community 2015**; this is a free version of Visual Studio that works well with Unity and the HoloLens environment. By default, you should be installing at least Visual Studios 2015 Update 3.

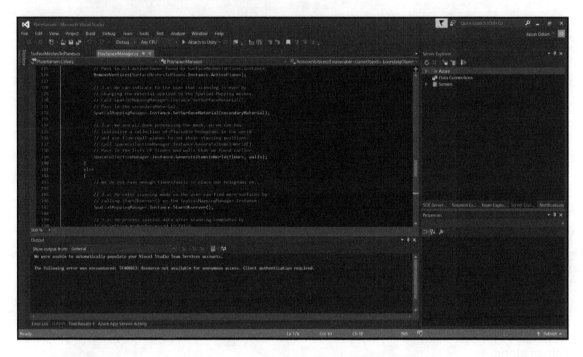

3. Run `vs_community. exe` and complete the installation process.
4. Create a Microsoft Developers account (this is a requirement for the HoloLens development).
5. The first time you run VS2015, you will be prompted to input your account credentials.

Unity HoloLens technical preview

Now, we will install Unity HoloLens technical preview. At the time of writing this, version 5.4. 0f 3 is the most recent and stable version. This is a custom version of Unity made to work specifically with HoloLens. As a result, it does automate a few processes for HoloLens developers:

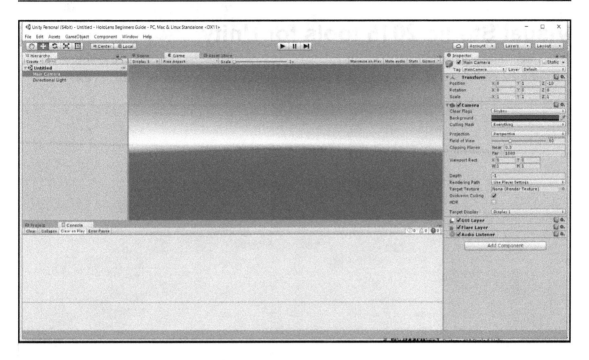

To install Unity HoloLens technical preview, we will need to perform the following steps:

1. Go to `https://unity3d.com/partners/windows/hololens`.
2. Scroll down to the bottom of the page.
3. Click on the **Unity Download Assistant**.
4. Follow the instructions to complete the installation process.
5. You will need to create an account with Unity.

Visual Studio 2015 tools for Unity

In your web browser, go to `https://visualstudiogallery.msdn.microsoft.com/8d26236e-4a 64-4d64-8486-7df95156aba9`. Later, click on the **Download** button and run `vstu2015.exe`:

HoloLens emulator

To install the HoloLens emulator, perform the following steps:

1. Go to `http://go.microsoft.com/fwlink/?LinkID=823018`.
2. Run `EmulatorSetup.exe` once it finishes downloading.
3. Install the emulator.

This will not install if you do not have Windows 10 Pro installed on your development PC.

4. This installation process can take a while.

HoloToolkit-Unity

To install HoloToolkit-Unity, perform the following steps:

1. Enter `https://github.com/Microsoft/HoloToolkit-Unity` in your browser.
2. Click on **Clone or download**.
3. Click on **Download ZIP**.
4. Once the ZIP file is downloaded, unzip the file to your desktop; we will copy this into our project later.

Unity3d quick overview

In the Unity3d quick overview, we will have a quick, very general overview of Unity. In the next chapter, we will begin the first stages of our project. With the following overview, what you will learn in the chapter will stick a little bit better:

1. Click on the **Unity HoloLens** icon to run Unity, as follows:

2. If you have a Unity account, enter your account name and password, otherwise you will need to create a new account before you can move forward.

3. Type the name of the project--HoloLens Beginners Guide--into the **Project name** input field.
4. Ensure that you have 3D selected as the project type and click on **Create project**.

The main view

When the project is created and the program finishes loading, you should see the following default view:

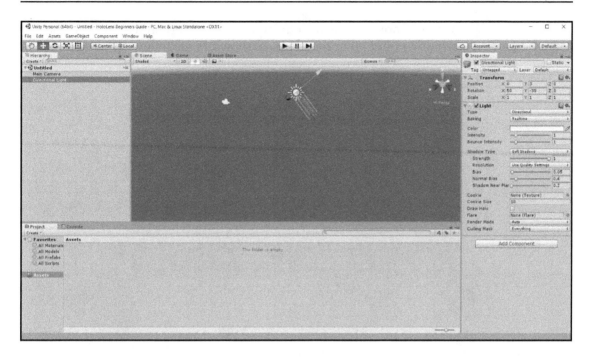

Here, we can see our main work areas:

- **Scene**: This is where we view our scene and can make certain types of changes.
- **Hierarchy**: This is a list of all objects currently in the scene.
- **Project Window**: Here, we have all the assets of the project. This will list our 3D models, scripts, textures, materials, sounds, prefabs, and all other elements of the programs.
- **Inspector**: When an object is selected, we will be given many changeable details about that object.

You may notice a few in at the upper part of certain windows. These windows offer other functions, as shown in the following screenshot:

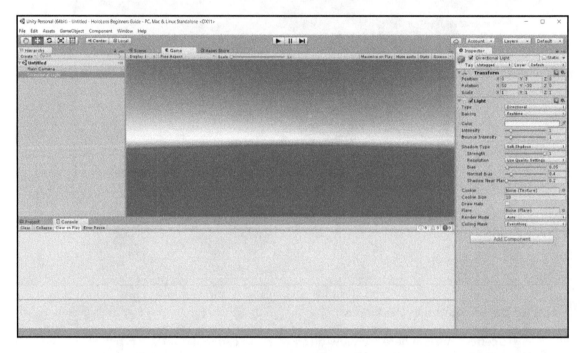

- **Console**: Here, we can have the debug information presented to us. This allows us to test certain parts of a program to ensure that it is working.
- **Game View**: When we test our project on our development computer, this is the window that our program will appear in; this is the main camera view.

Summary

In this chapter, we got to know a little bit about the HoloLens. We have installed and set up the development environment, so we can begin our journey into this new world. Here the only limitations are our imaginations.

2
HoloWorld

In this chapter, we will take a look at all the steps necessary to get your first Holographic app from just an idea to a hologram. This being the first tutorial, we will spend a good deal of time detailing each and every step. As the book progresses, certain knowledge will become assumed or referenced back to previous chapters.

Here, we will open a fresh project and ensure that our scene is HoloLens ready. We will also cover the following topics:

- How to set up the camera so that the HoloLens can use it
- The basic concepts of a scene
- Basics of object creation and components
- How to move, rotate, and scale objects
- Touch on the basics of Materials
- Create 3D text and apply physics to the objects
- Building our project and seeing it in action

Hello World!, as its customary

A long held tradition in programming is to write a simple program called "Hello, World!" as your very first program. This program normally prints the words "Hello, World!" on the screen, and is used as a starting point to understanding the basics of a new programming language or development environment. This is a tradition that dates back to at least 1972, but potentially even further back to 1967.

Here, we will create a "Hello, World!+". We will use it to further familiarize you with Unity, beyond the basic layout of the preceding chapter. In an effort to avoid repeating steps, we will build onto this project throughout the rest of the book.

The layout of a HoloLens project

The most basic Unity project is made up of at least one scene. Any new scene will contain a *directional light* and *main camera*. The HoloLens uses this camera as the user's point of view, so we will need to make a few changes to the default starting scene to suit our needs.

Here, we will set up our main camera, so our program will work correctly with HoloLens:

1. Select the object in the Hierarchy view named `Main Camera`.
2. Look at the right side of the screen in the **Inspector** view.
3. In the **Camera** component, click on the **Clear Flags** and select **Skybox** drop-down menu, as follows:

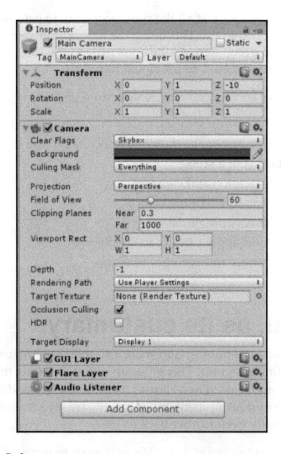

4. Select **Solid Color.**

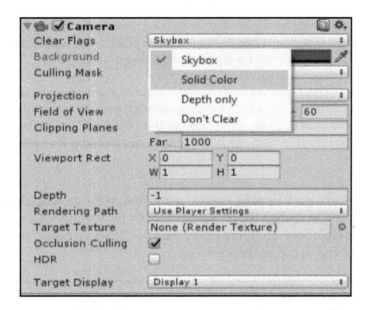

5. Ensuring that **Main Camera** is still selected, click on the **Background** color box (which is currently a deep blue); this will bring up the **Color Picker** dialog box:

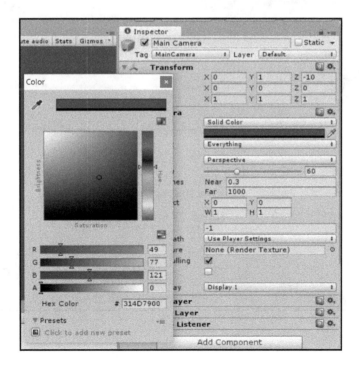

6. In the numeric input fields, change the numbers to R=0, G= 0, B=0, and A= 0 and close the color picker. With the HoloLens a black color with 0 Alpha transparency is needed for a perfectly transparent 3D background.

The HoloLens uses the background color to determine its transparency. Black is completely transparent. If you use black on objects throughout your project, you will run into problems with see-through objects. Also, using colors other than black for the background can block the users' view of the world, which can be extremely disorienting and dangerous for the user.

7. Next, look for the **Clipping Planes** option and its input field labeled **Near.** Here, we will need to change the default 0.3 to the recommended 0.85. Due to the nature of HoloLens, anything closer than 0.85 meters causes the user to cross their eyes and, it can be disorienting.

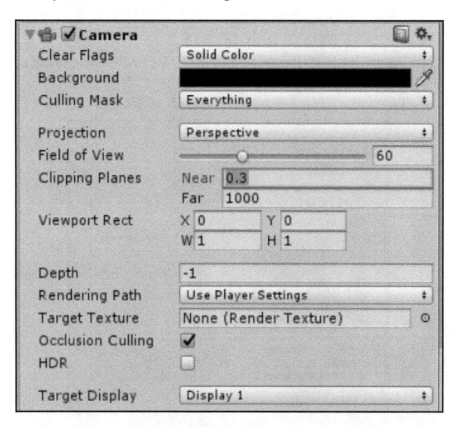

8. With the **Main Camera** still selected, look at the **Transform** component. The first option in that box is labeled **Position**. You will notice **X**, **Y**, and **Z** input fields; change the **Z** element from its default of −10 to 0.

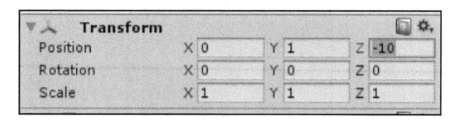

Unity directory structure

We have completed all the steps for our default scene, and now we need to save it. With organization being an important factor as projects get larger and more complex, we need to create the appropriate directories for the different elements and assets that comprise our project. These will include textures, materials, scripts, prefabs, sounds, and--what we are dealing with at this moment--scenes.

Having directories for each type of asset makes quickly sorting and finding a specific object a breeze. For now, since we only have a scene file, we will create a directory to save it in:

1. In the **Project** window in the left-hand corner of the screen, click on **Assets**:

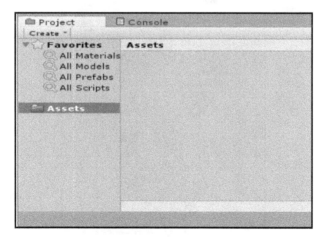

2. Click on the **Create** button near the top of the window, under **Project**.

3. A large menu of options will appear; click on the **Folder** option that is at the top of that menu:

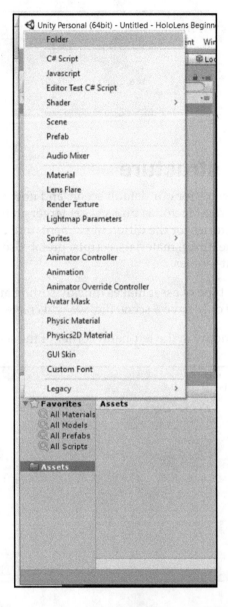

4. A folder named New Folder will appear; do not click on anything just yet:

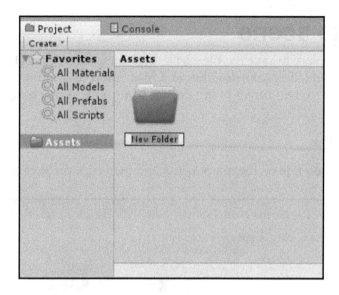

5. Rename the folder to Scenes:

Saving the scene

Now that we have a place to save the files, let's save our scene. A project in Unity is often made up of many scene files. Knowing this, and in an effort to avoid repeating the starting steps many times, I save two copies of my default scene. I name one as `default` and the other as `main`.

Here is how to do that:

1. First, click on **File** on the main menu, and then click on **Save Scene**:

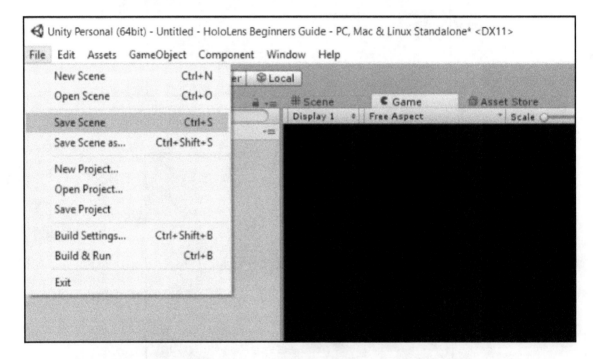

2. The **Save Scene** dialog will appear. In the **File name** field, enter `default`; then, click on the **Save** button:

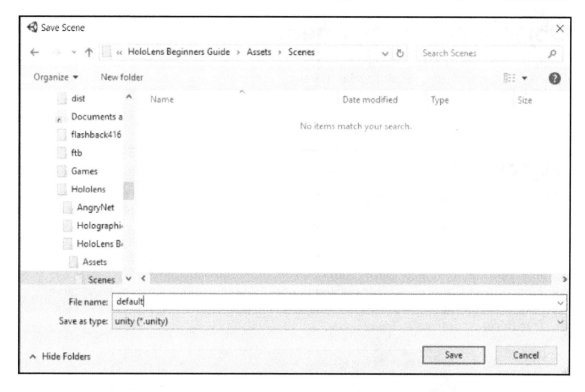

3. Now, you would want to click on **File** one more time. Type main into the **File name** input field and click on the **Save** button again. If everything went according to the plan, the bar across the top of the window should look like this; the name of your project--HoloLens Beginners Guide--and the name of your scene--main.unity--should both be present.

OK, now we are ready to go; but, let's first talk a bit about what we will be using throughout the rest of the chapter.

Objects and components

Before we get to the heart of building our project, let's take a few minutes to talk about objects and components. I wish I had understood some of these ideas much earlier on; it would have sped up my overall understanding of Unity. We will only lightly touch on these subjects for now. We will go into greater detail in later chapters.

Objects

Objects or **GameObjects** are what make up nearly everything in Unity. The characters, camera, 3D text, and lights are all a very basic-level GameObjects. Everything you see in a Unity-developed project is either GameObjects, or connected to them.

It should be pointed out that some things that you cannot see are GameObjects as well. A common practice is to create empty GameObjects so that we can apply scripts or other components to it. These objects are created to perform a function, such as to keep game scores or to handle network traffic. The one common element that all GameObjects share is the **Transform** component:

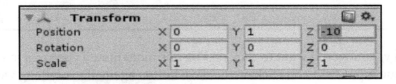

Components

Components add additional functionality to a GameObject. These components come in many forms. Here are some of the components we already have or will see in this chapter:

- **Transform**: The job of this component is to define the *position, rotation,* and *scale* of each GameObject in a scene. This is the minimum defining element of a GameObject, so all GameObjects have one.
- **Camera component**: We have seen this component when we set up the camera earlier in this chapter.
- **Mesh renderer**: This handles details of lighting and materials.

- **Rigidbody**: This component allows you to control how the GameObject reacts to physics.
- **Box collider**: This component adds a way to detect and react to collisions in the program.

As a point of reference, a simple cube is made up of five components. First we have the Transform component, whose job it is to set the **Position**, **Rotation**, and **Scale** of the object it is attached to. Another component is **Box Collider**, which provides the unity system with the ability to know when the object hits another object.

We also have the **Mesh Renderer**, here we can set certain properties involving materials and lighting. We can tell the object whether we want it to cast or receive shadows, we can change the materials applied to the 3D object as well.

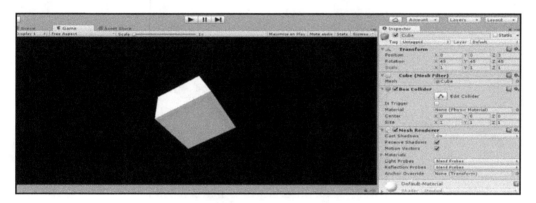

First project

Now that we have a basic understanding of objects and what they are made of, we will begin the creation of our first project with a series of GameObjects.

For this step in our `"Hello, World!+"` project, we will need to create a platform for the words `Hello, World!` to hover over, using the following steps:

1. Click on the **Hierarchy** tab inside the Unity Editor, and then click on the **Create** button. This will bring up the **Create** menu:

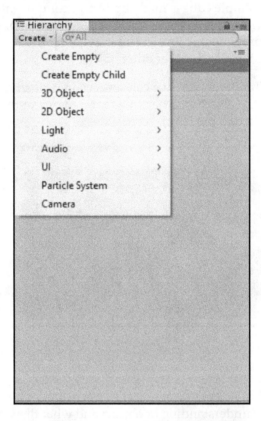

2. Now, with your mouse, hover over the **3D Object** label. A submenu will pop up. Click on **Cube**:

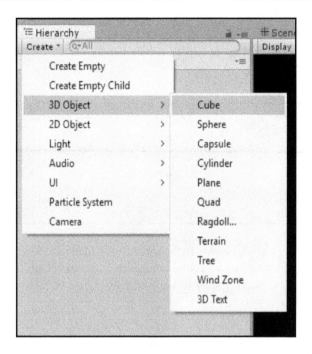

Our cubism period

Now, we have a blank cube in our scene and, we are ready to have some fun. However, where is it? Here, we will use the transform component to change this cube into our platform and move it into view:

1. With Cube selected, look at the **Inspector** tab.

2. First, we want to change the name of our new object to something more appropriate. Click on the input field and change the name from Cube to Platform:

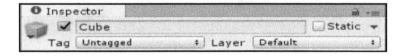

3. In order to move the object into the position we need it in, select Platform in the Hierarchy View, look down to the Transform component. Change the Position to X :0, Y: -2, and Z: 4

4. Now, change the **Scale** field to X: 10, Y: 0.1, and Z: 5. After you finish making changes to your **Transform** component for the platform object, it should look like this:

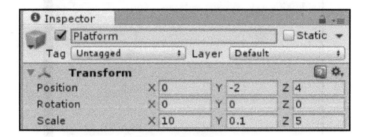

If you are looking at this preceding example and have suddenly become scared that you need to know a bunch of math just to place objects in the work, don't worry. Although this is the most accurate way, it is not the only way of moving objects in a scene. You will learn other options later in this chapter.

Adding a little color

Now, we have a platform. However, it is just a boring white platform at the moment; let's fix that. We will now create a material and drag it onto the platform in our scene view:

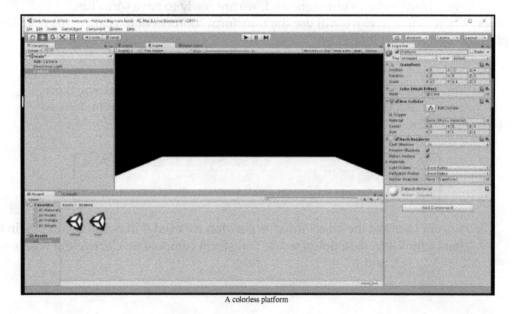

A colorless platform

Let's fix that!:

1. In our **Project** tab, right-click on the **Assets** folder. Hover over the **Create** option at the top of the menu, and click on the **Folder** option in the submenu:

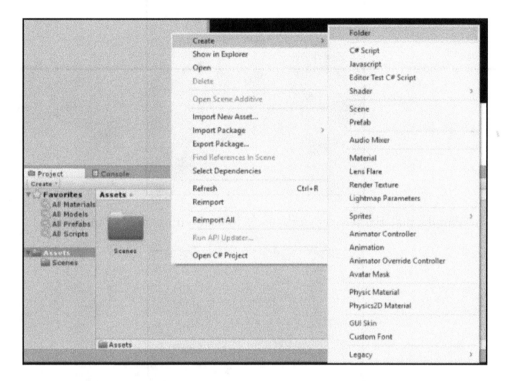

2. Name this folder **Materials**.
3. Select the **Materials** folder in the left panel of the **Project** view.
4. With this folder selected, click on the **Create** button.
5. Select **Materials** from the pop-up menu.
6. When the new material appears, the name text is highlighted, letting you know that you should name it. Name the new material Platform.

> We now have a new material waiting for us to change from the boring default white. There is quite an intimidating number of properties to control for a first-time developer. For now, though, we will keep this simple and change the color only.

7. Ensure that the **Platform** material is selected:

8. With the material selected, let's take a look at our material in **Inspector**:

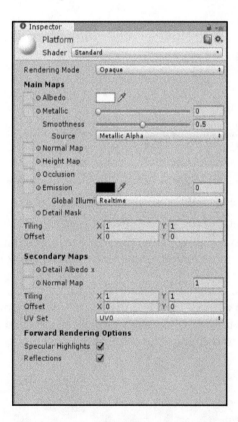

9. Click on the Color Box next to the heading **Albedo** (the one with the icon of the dropper next to it), as follows:

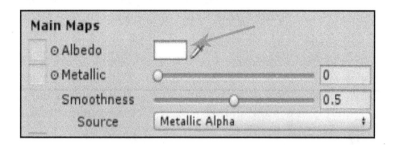

10. When the Color Picker dialog appears, change the RGB values to R= 25, G= 40, and B= 248. This will change the color we are using to deep blue:

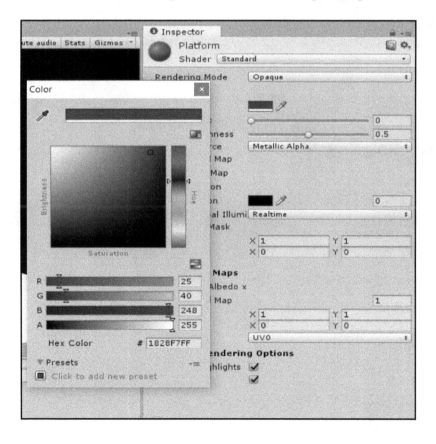

Material plane

Now that our blue material is created, we can move forward to applying that material to the object. In order to do that, let's learn a little bit about the real-time interaction of the **Scene** view.

Let's take a quick look and find the **Scene** view tab, and select it to bring it forward, if it is not already. This view allows real-time interaction and the ability to see our project space from different angles easily. If you click on your mouse wheel/middle button anywhere in this view, you can pan the view around. If you right-click anywhere in this view, you can rotate the view:

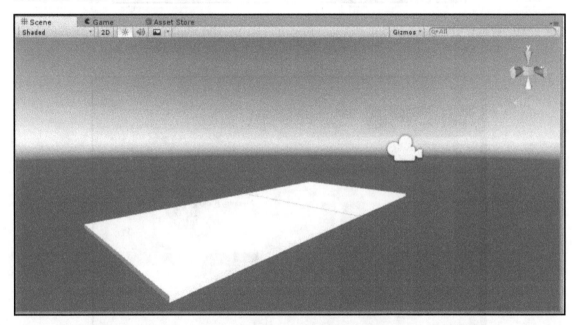

Now, let's apply the material we have just changed to our platform GameObject:

1. In our project window, left-click on the **Platform** material.

2. Without releasing the left-click, drag the mouse pointer to the platform object in the **Scene** view:

Simple enough, right? After you finish those steps, your platform should look something similar to this:

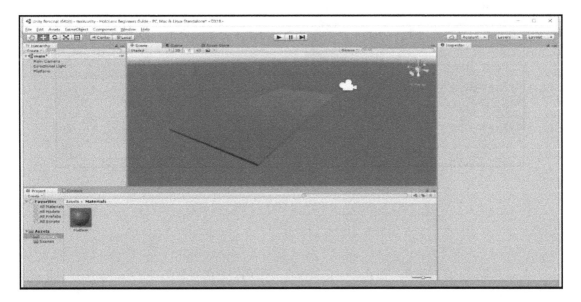

Creating the text

Now, it is time to get into the heart of a `Hello World` project and create `Hello, World!`. With our recent experience of creating objects in the preceding section, this should be a rather simple task.

We will create two separate objects here: one will be `Hello`, and the second will be `World`.

We will be performing the following steps to create the objects:

1. In the **Hierarchy** panel, click on the create button, mouse over the **3D Object** menu option, and choose **3D Text** from the submenu.
2. Ensuring that the object is selected, look at **Inspector**:

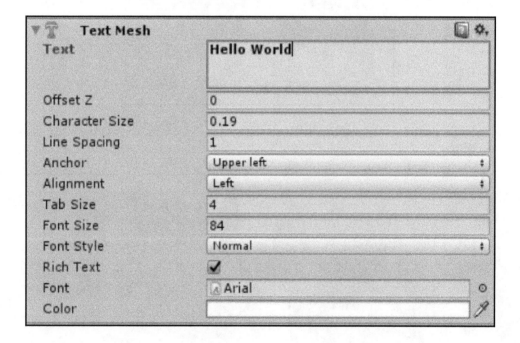

3. You may notice--if you take a look at the **Text Mesh** component--that the words Hello World are the default for a 3D text object. Click on the box, add a comma (,) after Hello and delete the word World from the object.

4. Select **New Text** in the name box, and change the name to Hello.

5. Go to the Transform component and change the Position to X: -4.3, Y: 2 and Z: 5. This will put the object where we need it in the camera view:

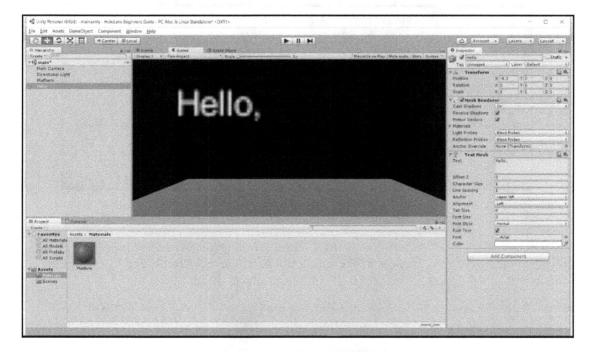

6. Now, you may notice a blurry /blocky effect on the word; let's fix it. In the **Text Mesh** component, look for the filed **Character Size** and change it to 0.19.

7. In the **Font Size** field, change the font size from 0 to 84:

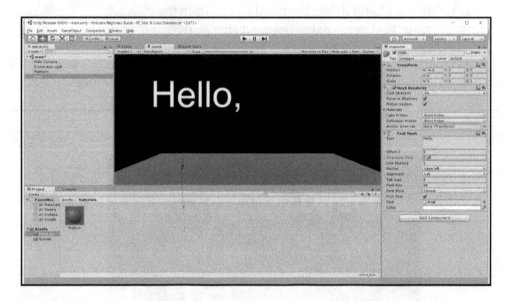

Now `Hello,` should look clear and ready to go. Let's move on to the next word.

We will now duplicate the previous word, make a few changes instead of repeating all the steps from the preceding section. Work smart, not hard they say, but if you do both, well you are probably amazing. Perform the following steps to do it:

1. In the **Hierarchy** panel, right-click on the `Hello` object and select **Duplicate**.
2. In the **Inspector** panel, change the name of the object to `World`.
3. Move down to the **Text Mesh** component and in the **Text** box change the text to `World!`.
4. Now, go to the **Transform** component like before, and change the **X Position** to `-0.2`.

With that, we should now have a scene that looks very similar to this; if that is the case, great work!:

Physics simulations

In this section, you will learn what Unity has to offer in terms of a *physics engine*.

Also known as **physics simulations**, these engines have been an integral part of 3D and game engines for some time, but rarely are they as easy to get into as with Unity.

A physics engine is a basic physics simulation that allows the developer to add physical properties to GameObjects, such as weight, gravity, bounce, and other factors that allow these GameObjects to act and react in different ways:

1. Select the `Hello` object in the **Hierarchy** panel.
2. Click on the **Add Component** button in the **TextMesh** component in the **Inspector** panel.

3. Click on the **Physics** category:

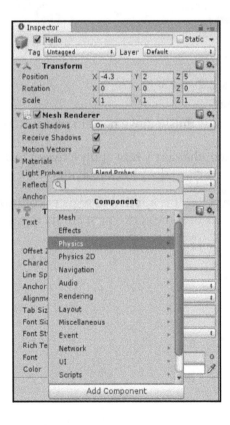

4. Then, select **Rigidbody**:

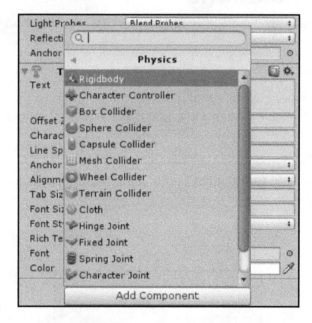

5. Now, repeat steps 1, 2 and 3.
6. Select **Box Collider**.
7. Now, the first word is finished; we need to repeat steps 1-6 for the `World` object.

The **Rigidbody** is a component that lets Unity apply physics to an object. You can change many of the ways the object reacts to the physical changes.

The **Box Collider** allows the object it is applied to register collisions with other objects. The object must also have a collider of some sort. There are six types of 3D physics colliders, including sphere, capsule, and mesh for complex objects.

Now, that we have our physics components on our objects, let's set up the scenes gravity. Here, we will lighten the gravity a bit and apply a different amount of drag to each object so that they fall differently. Let's perform the following steps to do this:

1. Click on the **Edit** menu option, and select the **Project** settings near the bottom of the menu:

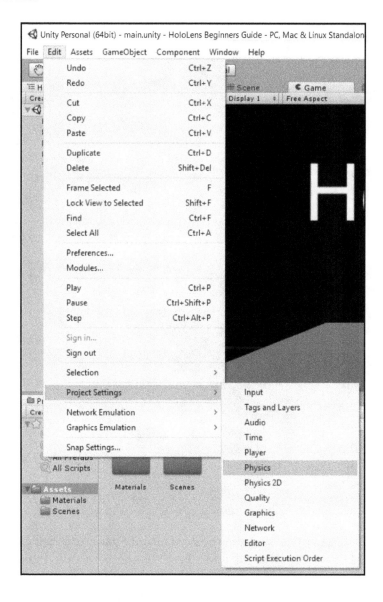

2. Click on the **Physics** option. This will bring up the **Physics Manager** in the **Inspector**:

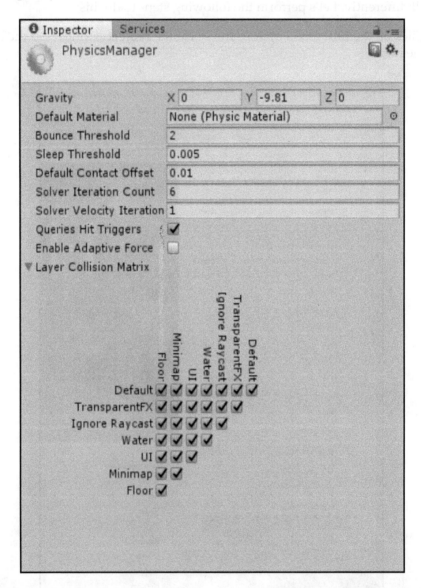

Look at the first field, **Gravity Y** is our vertical axis. Unity has a constant gravity of -9.81 by default. 0 would be no gravity at all, and a positive number would make objects move upward.

Select the number in the **Gravity Y** axis and change it from -9.81 to -6.

Now, we will make a couple of changes on a per-object level so that the physics reactions are different:

1. Select the Hello object in the **Hierarchy** panel.
2. Look for the **Inspector** and scroll down to the **Rigidbody** component.
3. Find the **Drag** heading and change the number to 2.
4. Change the number in **Angular Drag** to 1:

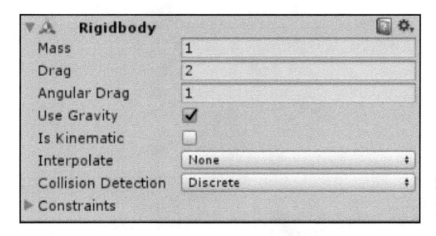

Now, we will make a similar change to the World text object:

1. Select World in the **Hierarchy** panel.
2. Again, look for the **Inspector** and scroll down to the **Rigidbody** component.
3. Change the **Drag** setting to 3.
4. Change **Angular Drag** to 2.
5. Now, let's save our scene by pressing *Ctrl + S*.

Building the project in Unity

We are quickly coming to the fun part. Now that we have our Hello World project constructed, we will learn how to build, compile, and deploy the project. This will allow us to test it on our HoloLens or in the HoloLens emulator. When you begin a new project, the steps given in the subsequent section only have to be done the first time you build and compile. There are quite a few steps; do not let it intimidate you.

Build settings

Before we can start the building process, we will need to set up Unity's build settings so that we get the correct output to compile. The building is a word used to say that Unity will take all of the assets that we have put together and break it down into a format that Visual Studio can understand:

1. Click on **File** and move it to **Build Settings** or press *Ctrl + Shift + B:*

   This will bring up the **Build Settings** window. Unity can output a project to many different platforms; but we need to set it up for HoloLens.

2. Click on the **Add Open Scenes** button to add our current scene to the **Build** register:

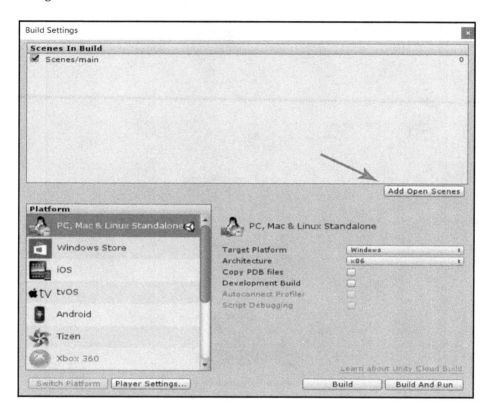

3. Under **Platforms**, select **Windows Store** and click on the **Switch Platform** button below it. The Unity icon will appear next to **Windows Store** to let you know that it is selected.
4. On the right-hand side of the window under **Windows Store**, search for the **SDK** drop-down box and select **Universal 10**.
5. Select the **UWP Build Type** drop-down and change it to **D3D**.
6. Check the box next to **Unity C# Projects**.

This is how our **Build Settings** window should look now:

Player settings

Here, we will learn about a few important HoloLens-specific settings, such as **Capabilities**. Here, we can turn off and on certain features that may or may not be needed on HoloLens projects:

1. In the **Build** Settings window, click on the **Player Settings** button at the bottom.
2. Now, click on the **Other Settings** section in the **Inspector** panel:

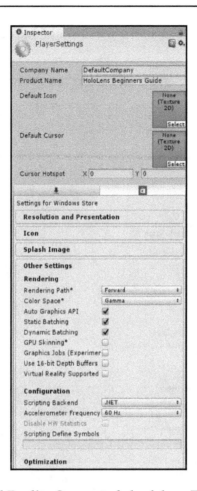

3. Click on the **Virtual Reality Supported** check box. This will automatically select **Windows Holographic** as the default VR platform:

4. Click on the **Publishing Settings** box.

Publishing Settings

5. Scroll down to the bottom of the window and look under the **Capabilities** section:

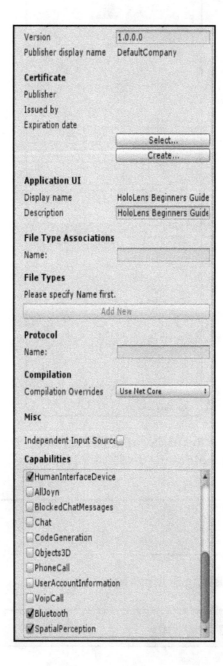

6. Select **Microphone, HumanInterfaceDevice, Bluetooth**, and **SpatialPerception.**
7. Back in the **Build Settings** window, click on the **Build** button:

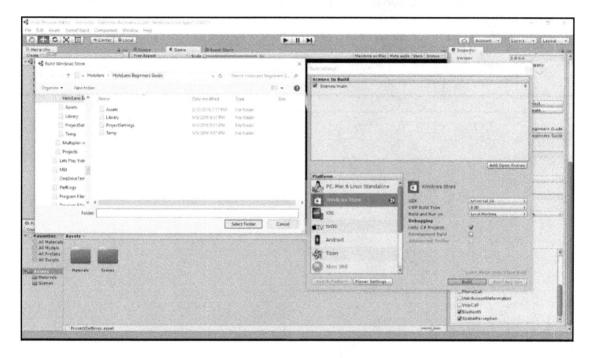

8. When the windows explorer **Select Folder** box shows up, right-click on the main area under the Temp folder, move it to **New**, and select **Folder**.
9. Name this folder **App**.
10. With this newly created folder selected, click on the **Select Folder** button.

Now, Unity will go through an exporting process creating scripts and other elements that Visual Studio can understand. On a modern computer, the process can take a few minutes. When it is complete, a Windows Explorer window will pop up with the App directory selected.

Compiling our project

To compile our project now, we will open our project in Visual Studio; Visual Studio is the program that allows us to turn the assets and code that Unity produced into a format that the HoloLens can use. In order to do so, perform the following steps:

1. First, we need to make sure that the Windows Explorer has appeared and then double-click on the App folder; this is what you should see:

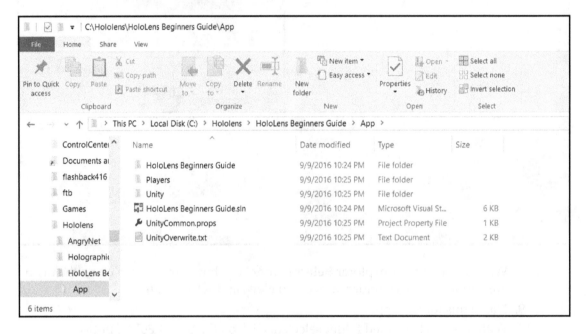

2. Double-click on **HoloLens Beginners Guide.sln**. This will load Visual Studio Community 2015 and the newly built project.

Setting Up Visual Studio

To set up Visual Studio, we have our primary programming environment. Now, we need to set up Visual Studio to compile our code and deploy it to the HoloLens (or emulator).

Let's perform the following steps for deployment:

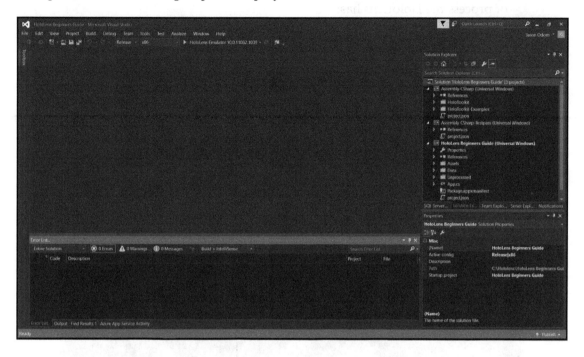

1. On the right-hand side of the screen, **Solution Explorer** should have **HoloLens Beginners Guide (Universal Windows)** selected, exactly like the preceding screenshot. If it is not, select it.
2. Now, click on the **Debug** drop-down menu and select **Release**. This is the Solution Configurations selection.

3. Select the next dropdown that currently says **ARM** and select **x86**; this is the type of process the HoloLens has:

4. Click on the small down arrow next to **Device** and select **Remote Machine** (if you have the HoloLens hardware).

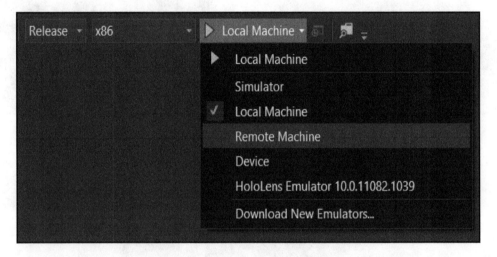

This will bring up the Remote Connections window. At this point, we want our HoloLens on and running. If it is, you should see its name and IP address show up under the Auto Detected area. If not, you will have to manually put the address in the Address box in the Manual Configuration section.

To manually add your IP address, put your HoloLens on and ensure that it is up and running:

1. Say "Hey Cortana, what is my IP address?" Cortana should tell you. Write it down.
2. Put that address in the **Address Box** and click on **Select**.

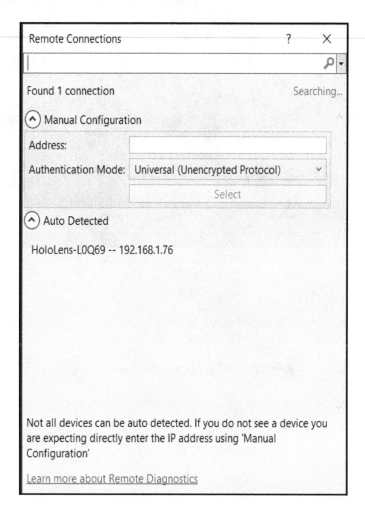

Using the HoloLens emulator

If you are using the emulator instead of selecting Remote Machine from the **Device** drop-down menu, select **HoloLens Emulator 10.0.11082.1039**. Depending on when you go through this book the number proceeding HoloLens Emulator will likely be different.

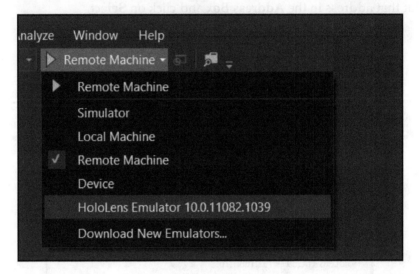

Compilation time

Now, we will let Visual Studio turn everything we have done so far into the code it needs to run on the HoloLens:

1. On the menu, click on the **Build** option and select **Deploy HoloLens Beginners Guide:**

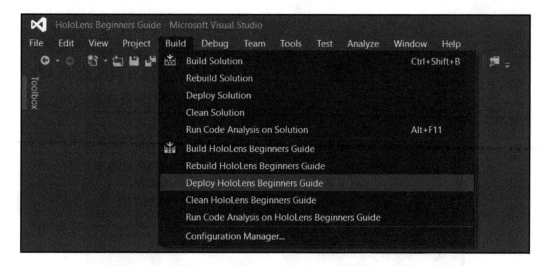

It will begin going through the compilation process; but because this is our first time connecting to our HoloLens, we will need to set up security for remote connections. Shortly after clicking on the **Deploy** option, the following box will appear in your compilation PC:

2. With the HoloLens on, navigate to the **Settings** menu:

3. Select **Update;** here, we will get access to developer options:

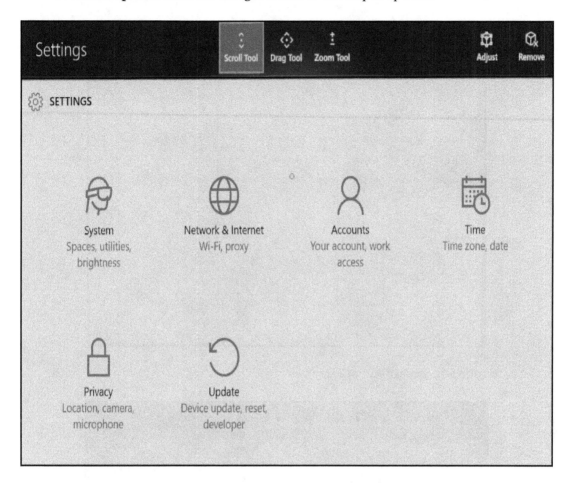

4. Select and hit the **Pair** button:

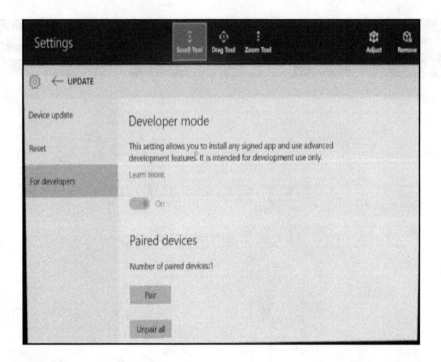

5. A code will appear on your device:

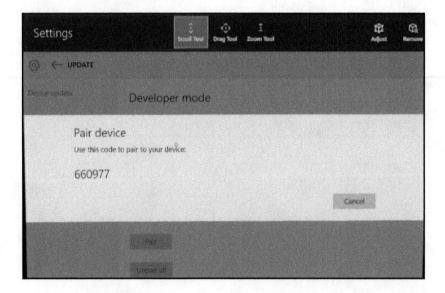

6. Put that number in this input field and click on **OK:**

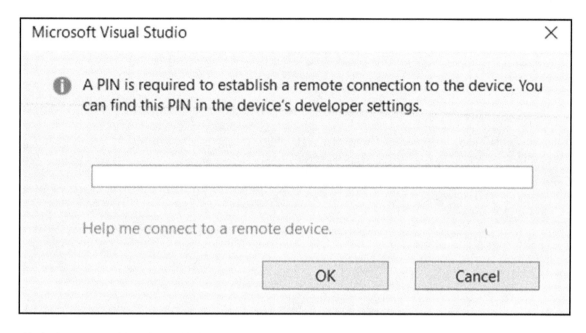

With that, Visual Studio will deploy to your device or emulator. Now load it up.

Congratulations, you have finished your first Holographic program!

Summary

In this chapter, you learned what makes up the basic elements of a 3D program using Unity and Visual Studio and about GameObjects and how to create them. Then, we explored components, which are extensions to GameObjects and added new functions to them. There are many components, such **Transform**, **Camera**, **Rigidbody**, **Colliders**, and **Mesh Renderer**.

After building the scene and a little setup in Visual Studio, we built and compiled our first holographic program and were able to experience for the first time the pleasure of being able to create it in this new environment.

3
I am in Control

In this chapter, we will cover the ways we can interact with HoloLens using the input system. This device has been designed around three pillars of control: **Gaze**, **Gesture**, and **Voice** (**GGV**). Although traditional controllers, such as a keyboard, mouse, and even game controllers, will work with the HoloLens, in most cases, GGV should be the go-to solution for the problems that we, as developers, need to solve.

Before we get there, we will start using the HoloToolKit in this chapter. In order to be successful, we will need to look at a couple of related Unity design concepts that we will use repeatedly, such as **prefabs** and **parent/child relationship**.

As we collect user input, we need to show a change to let the user know that their input was received. To help facilitate this need, we will learn some of the basics of Unity's animation system. We will expand our knowledge of materials and learn about textures as well.

Prefabs

Imagine that you have been hired to build a holographic corporate team-building exercise for an upcoming weekend event. The idea is to create a scavenger hunt to find a cute robot and you have a large group of mean robots trying to stop everyone. The event is a gamified first-person shooter/scavenger hunt. The winning team will get the real robot to help in their office. It will be fun; let the team get some tension out and repair some troubled relationships in the company. From the word go, you will be using prefabs.

A prefab is a Unity asset type that acts as a blueprint or a template. In our preceding example, something as simple as the bullets for the weapons or as complex as the large collection of really mean robots that are trying to stop the entire company from achieving their goals could also be prefabs.

Fundamentally, a prefab is a hierarchical collection of GameObjects and their associated components. Using a parent/child relationship very similar to the file folder system of a computer. A developer can create a complex object made out of many objects, and then copy that object in memory. This is a process known as instantiation, but can easily be understood as cloning.

The benefit of this process is when you need to create 15 robots for a robot game, at any given time you will get more efficient use of memory. Without instantiation and prefabs, each of those robots will take up their own space in memory and potentially start to bog the system down. With this cloning process, these objects that acquire space of memory and therefore use far less memory.

Let's save the HelloWorld

First, we will need to ensure that we load the project from Chapter 2, *HoloWorld*. We will make a copy of the scene to save time; work smart, not hard, they say:

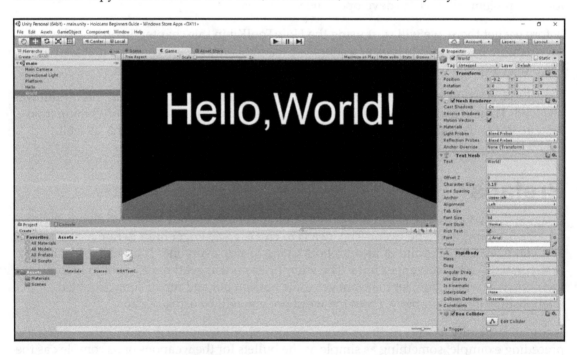

Let's look at the steps we will need to carry out:

1. Click on **File** on the main menu.
2. Click on **Save Scene As**....
3. Navigate to the Scenes folder.
4. Type Chapter2 into the **File name** field and click on the **Save** button.
5. Now, repeat steps 1-3.
6. This time, type Chapter3 into the **File name** field and click on the **Save** button.

If you complete all the preceding steps correctly, you should see Chapter3.unity across the top bar and Chapter3 directly under the **Create** menu in the **Hierarchy** panel:

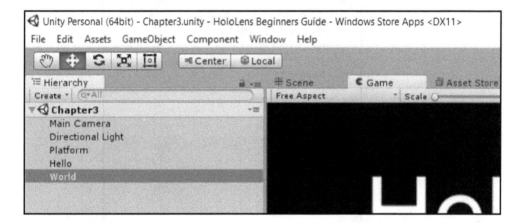

Parent/Child relationship

Before we make our first prefab, a concept that is both useful and important is parentage. In our Hierarchy view, we can have GameObjects with other GameObjects attached to them in a Hierarchy. We call the **primary objects** as **parents**, and the **secondary objects** are called **children**. When these hierarchies exist, there are many benefits from an organizational standpoint as well as for practical application.

Where there is a series of objects connected together in such a manner, if something on the parent object is changed--such as being moved, rotated, or scaled--all the attached objects do the same in relation to the parent.

Parenting is something that also applies to prefabs. With that in mind, we will parent our objects in the scene together and make a prefab from them; let's perform the following steps:

1. Take a look at our **Hierarchy** view; we should still have **Platform**, **Hello**, and **World**:

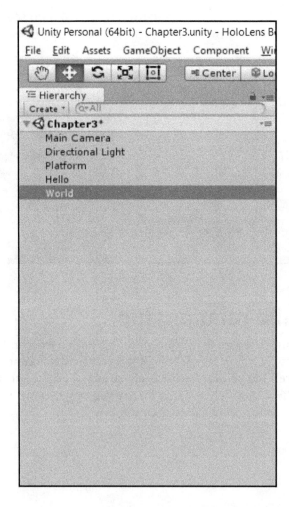

2. Select **Hello** and drag it up onto **Platform** until you see a light blue oval over the destination. Then, release the mouse button:

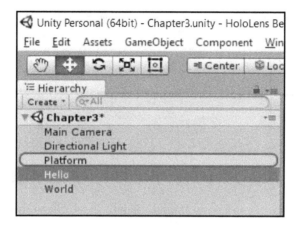

3. Now, do the same thing for the **World** object. After you are done, you should see this in your **Hierarchy** view; your **Hello** and **World** objects are now *children* of **Platform**:

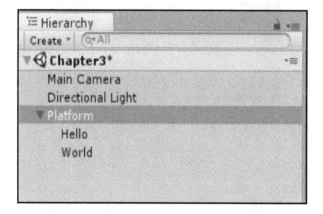

If you click on the **Play** button now to test your app, even after parenting the **Hello** and **World** objects, they will fall onto the **Platform**.

Here's a quick test to see the effect on the children when we transform the parent. Let's look at the following steps:

1. With **Platform** selected, move your mouse to the **Transform** component in the **Inspector**. Click in the Z-axis box. Change the number in the field to 4:

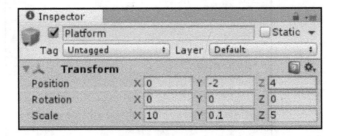

2. Now, click on and drag the Z axis left and right to move the platform:

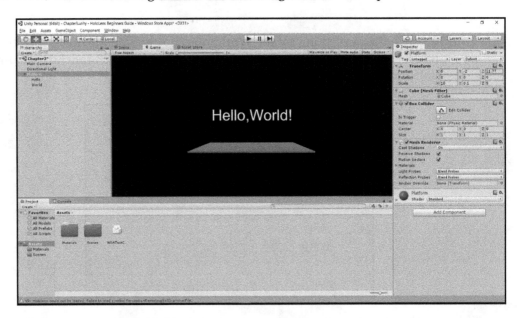

As you can see, the words follow along without any issue. If you were to do the same thing to the scale on the X axis, it would squeeze and expand.

Creating prefabs

Now that we have a bit of an understanding of the preceding concepts, we will take our Platform and 3D text object and create a prefab from them. We will do this twice to see the multiple ways in which this task can be accomplished; let's take a look at the steps we need to carry out:

1. First, let's look at the **Project** view. Using the process from the preceding chapter, create a folder called Prefabs, as a subfolder of Assets.
2. Select the Prefabs folder from the left side of the **Project** view.
3. Right-click in the open area on the right-hand side of the **Project** view, slide your mouse pointer over **Create**, and click on **Prefab**:

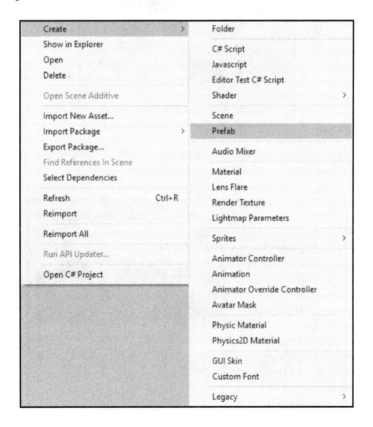

4. A white square should appear in **Project** view with a highlighted name **New Prefab**; name this one `Test One`.

5. In the **Hierarchy** view, click on the **Platform** object and drag it down to the `Test One` prefab. When this is accomplished, your `Test One` prefab will look something like this:

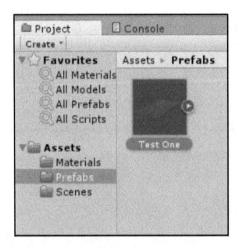

6. If you click on the arrow on the right-hand side of the prefab, you will be able to view the other objects in the `Prefabs`folder:

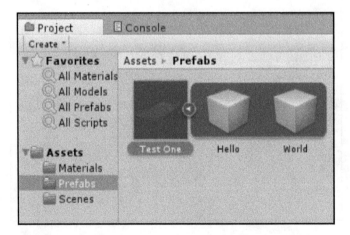

7. In an effort to distinguish prefabs from non-prefabs in the **Hierarchy** view, prefab names are colored blue:

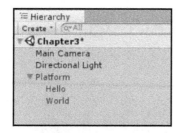

8. Now, delete the Test One object from the **Project** view. You may note that the prefab in the **Hierarchy** view has turned red. This is to let the designer know that master Prefab has been deleted.

9. This time, we will click on the red **Platform** object in the **Hierarchy** view and drag it down to the now empty space in the **Project** view.

10. The same Prefab object will appear again; this time, though, the name of the prefab is the name of the parent object:

Installing the HoloToolkit

Now that we have a basic understanding of prefabs out of the way, we will need to install the **HoloToolkit (HTK)** in our project in order to get into user input. The HTK is a collection of useful tools and examples of how to implement them. Many of the tools that have been designed for the HoloLens are in this very useful repository. The group contributing to the HTK are very active and major changes happen weekly; it is highly recommended that you keep up with the ongoing changes:

1. First, you will need to find the HoloToolkit ZIP file that you downloaded (or download it now from https://github.com/Microsoft/HoloToolkit-Unity) and extract it to your desktop or to a temporary directory.

2. Open the directory that you extracted the files to and double-click on the Assets folder.

3. Select all the files in that directory either with your mouse or using *Ctrl + A*.

4. Split the screen between your **Unity** window and your extraction directory:

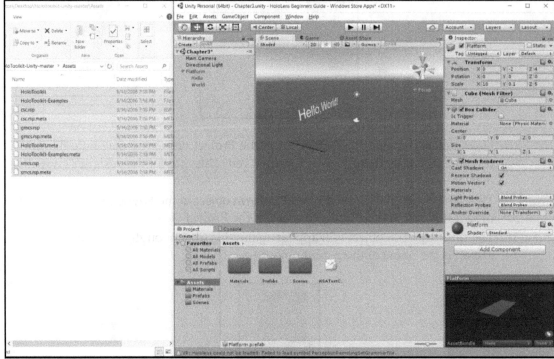

Screen split between Unity window and directory

5. Click on the selected files and drag them down to the Assets folder in the Unity **Project** view:

6. This process can take some time to complete, so be patient. On completion, your `Assets` folder should have these new additions:

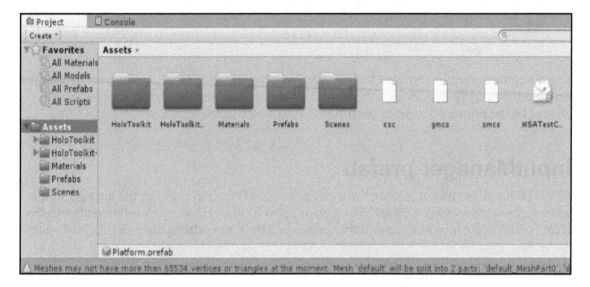

7. We are nearly ready to begin the next section of our project. However, first select the Platform object from the **Hierarchy** view and press the *Delete* key.

8. Now, press *Ctrl + S* to save the scene.

User Input overview

The HoloLens is a unique device, and the control scheme that it has been designed around is equally unique. Instead of your standard keyboard, mouse, or even touch screen, the HoloLens comes with three primary forms of input:

- **Gaze**: Here, you move a cursor with the direction of your head. A cursor is projected straight out and selects what you are looking at.

- **Gesture**: The sensor array is watching for certain hand movements. The *Airtap*, as well as *Airtap and Hold*, are the primary forms of interaction.

- **Voice**: The *Cortana artificial intelligent part* of the *Windows 10* and *Windows Holographic experience*, as well as the *Windows Voice Recognition system*, allow the user to simply say their commands out loud and the system is really good at understanding even those with thick accents.

After some fairly extensive experiments, I have learned that even using fake words or gibberish will control the HoloLens. For instance, *Rodbotter*--a word that I just made up, as you will see later in this chapter--can be used to illicit change. As long as the words are pronounced correctly, the voice recognition system will understand and obey.

Together, these various forms of interactions have been labeled GGV. HoloLens has been designed around these user input types, which, as previously mentioned, should almost always be the primary source of control for holographic applications.

InputManager prefab

The HTK handles most of the hard work of getting GGV going, through the *manager scripts* such as the Gaze Manager, Input Manager, or Speech Input Handler. Recent changes to the HoloToolkit make it so that most of this is handled by simply dropping a prefab into your scene.

Let's look at the following steps:

1. In the **Project** view, find the `InputManager` prefab in the `HoloToolkit>Input>Prefabs` directory.

2. Select the `InputManager` prefab, drag it into the **Hierarchy** view, and release it.

Now, we have our `InputManager` object and nearly all the scripts we need for GGV to work.

New Camera prefab – updated HoloToolkit

During the course of writing this book, the HoloToolkit had a few major revisions. One such major revision was the HoloLens Camera prefab. In the last chapter, we made our own camera from scratch. While this still works technically, the new prefab allows much easier testing inside Unity. Let's set it up real quick:

1. Delete the `MainCamera` object from the **Hierarchy**.
2. In the same directory as the `InputManager` prefab in the previous section, there should be the `HoloLenCamera` prefab.
3. Drag it from your **Project** view into your **Hierarchy** and drop it.

Cursor

With our knowledge of prefabs to guide us, we will grab one from the HoloToolKit that will work as our cursor throughout the rest of the book. This one is premade to help speed up the development process:

1. In the **Project** view, double-click on the `HoloToolKit` directory.
2. Search for the `input` directory and double-click on it.
3. Now, select and double-click on the `Prefabs` directory.
4. Now, select the `Cursor` prefab from the directory and drag it up to the **Hierarchy**window:

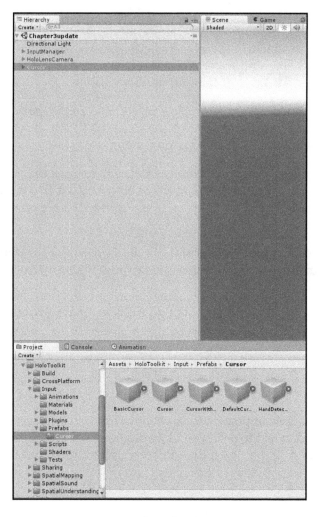

Gaze

Simply put, Gaze is the HoloLens equivalent of a mouse. Now, instead of moving your hand to move the cursor around, you move your head. HoloLens uses the wearer's head position and orientation to cast a ray. At the end of that ray is the cursor. When the user moves their head, the cursor moves accordingly. As the cursor moves over or touches holograms, you can combine Gaze with the other members of GGV to interact with objects.

Now, let's start setting up the manager object and the cursor we need to start the most basic interaction.

Gesture

If Gaze is the mouse movement, Gesture is the left-click. Microsoft has done a great job of keeping this control scheme simple yet powerful. There are a few gestures that the HoloLens understands: **Air-tap**, **Air-tap and hold**, and **Bloom**.

Bloom has a reserved purpose: to *exit applications* and *to open* the main menu system. Due to this, developers cannot currently do anything else with it. This leaves us with two primary gestures to work with: air-tap and air-tap and hold.

The HoloLens uses its large forward-facing sensor array to track the position of both hands when they are in front of the device. When one or both hands are in viewing range, the HoloLens looks for either hand in a ready state--your index finger pointed upward at a 45-degree angle or higher.

The gestures used are just combinations of these states. Air-tap goes from ready to pressed back to ready in a fluid movement, whereas air-tap and hold goes from ready to pressed and holding.

Soon, using combinations of these states and multiple hands, developers will be able to come up with more gestures and add layers of complexity to their software efforts.

Voice

The last but hardly the least important form of input for the HoloLens is Voice. The Voice component is designed to let the user look at a hologram, see any commands associated with that hologram, and simply say the command out loud to invoke it.

A convention has been laid out for developers. *See it, say it* means that if you have a voice command for the user input, a label with the appropriate button should be visible; for instance, a button that causes robots to destroy a village in a game might say destroy. When the user Gazes at the village and utters the word, he can smile as the army of robots descend on those poor villagers. Oh, the humanity!

Now, apart from voice commands, the Voice system can also be used for taking dictation, as well as communication. Dictation works surprisingly well inside Unity apps, and in the chat room social media-driven world we live in, real-time voice communication is essential.

It should be noted that only one of these modes can be running at a given moment.

Animation

In this section, we will create two objects to be animated. We will go through the basics of the **Animation** and **Mecanim** systems in Unity. Then, in order to turn these animations on and off, we will write a very simple script. Since we will cover scripting in a later chapter, this will be a very cursory look at scripting.

In the past year or so, Unity has added a very powerful tool for animating GameObjects and other properties, called Mecanim. Here, we will go over a few basic elements and animate a few objects. For those with little knowledge of how animation works, here are the big concepts in a short primer.

A quick history

In a traditional hand-drawn animation, normally, a collection of frames played at 24 frames per second, so a minute's animation is 1,440 frames. So, extrapolating 20 minutes of animation adds up to 28,800 frames of animation.

Of course, in most cases, this is way too much work for a single artist. So, a lead artist will draw the signature frames. These might be the superhero's main poses or the sweeping landscapes' endpoints. These important frames called **keyframes**. Once the keyframes are laid out, the junior artists will fill in the frames between these keyframes. This process is known as**in-betweening**, or simply **tweening**.

Keyframing is the single most important concept to learn with regard to animation. I have never in my life seen an animation tool that does not use it. This is how most of the animation is done in the world, whether hand-drawn or electronically rendered.

Nowadays, you are the lead artist setting keyframes. The computer will do the tweening. There are a lot of options to ensure that these frames are correct. For now, we will keep this simple.

Humble beginnings

Before we do any animation, we will need to create a couple of objects to animate. So, let's create some objects:

1. Click on the **Create** button, select **3D Object**, and then select **Cube**.
2. On the right-hand side of the **Transform** component, click on the gear with the down arrow and click on **Reset**; this will fix any positioning, rotating, or scaling issues:

3. Change the **X** position of the **Cube** to -0.5 and the **Z** position to 4.
4. Change the **Scale** of the **Cube** to **X**: 1, **Y**: 0.2, and **Z**: 0.2.
5. Change the name of the object to LeftRect.
6. Now, duplicate LeftRect by selecting it and pressing *Ctrl* + *D*.
7. Change its **X** position to 0.5.
8. Change its name to RightRect.

When you are finished, it should be similar to this:

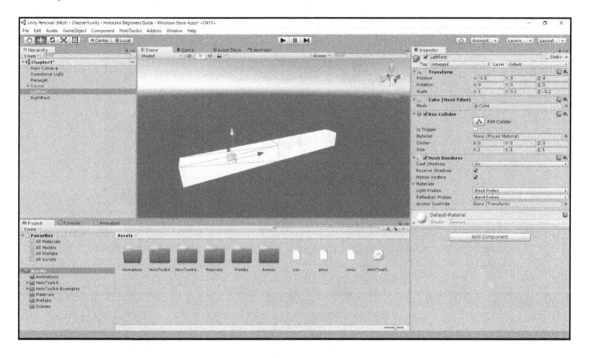

Okay, now we have a couple of objects to animate. Let's add the animation window to our layout:

1. First, click on the **Window** main menu option and move down to the **Animation** option:

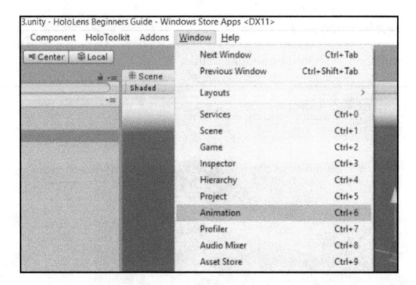

2. The animation window will pop up. Click on the **Animation** tab and move it around until you find a spot that you like. I prefer it to be on my **Project/Console** panel:

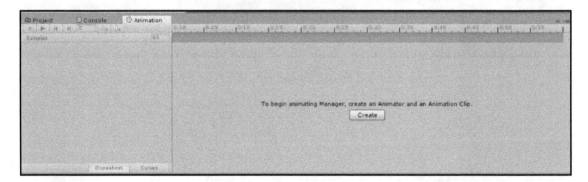

Time to move!

Now, we are ready to animate the two objects we have in our scene. Let's look at the steps required to animate the two objects:

1. Select `LeftRect` in the **Hierarchy** view.
2. Click on the **Create** button in the **Animation** pane.
3. When the **Create New Animation** window pops up, create a folder called `Animations`, name the file `LeftRectIdle.anim`, and click on **Save**.
4. Repeat steps 1-3, substituting the object name with `RightRect`.

This will be the idle position for the object. The idle animation does not need anything to be changed. Now, we will make the animation we need to transition to:

1. With `LeftRect` still selected, click on the bar that says **LeftRectIdle** in the **Animation** window.
2. Click on the **Create New Clip** option.
3. Navigate to the `Animation` folder, and save the file as `LeftRectMove.Anim`.
4. Click on the **Add Property** button; a list of components that can be animated will appear.
5. Click on the arrow next to **Transform**:

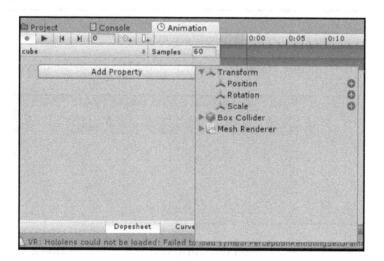

6. Click on the plus symbol corresponding to **Position**.
7. Now, repeat steps 1-6, substituting the object and animation names with `RightRect`.

It's easier than it seems

Now we are ready to animate.

In order to do this, like the classic lead animator, we will set *keyframes*. Then, we will let the junior animators--Unity, in our case--handle everything in between. To keep our first experience in animation simple, we will make a **looping animation**. We will leave the opening and closing keyframes alone so that the animation loops seamlessly.

Creating keyframes is a simple matter of moving the playback head (the vertical red line) to different points on the timeline and changing properties, such as position, rotation, scale, and so many others:

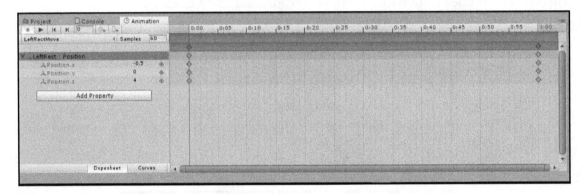

Let us take a moment and see how to create those keyframes.

1. Click on theTimeline at the bar just before **0:20** to move the playback head there:

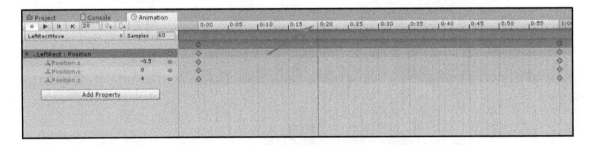

2. Now, when you look at the **Transform** component of LeftRect, you will note that all the Position Input fields are red; this means that this object is in record mode:

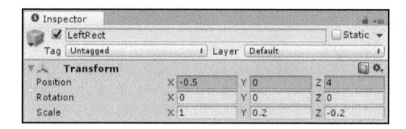

3. Now, change the **Y** position to 0.2.

4. Repeat step 1, substituting the time for 0:40.

5. Change the **Y** position to -0.2.

Now, if you click on the **Play** button, you should see the cube animating. Good work!:

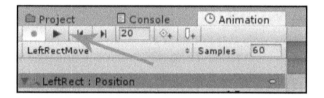

We will follow all the steps for the previous cube object with a couple of minor differences:

1. Ensure that **RightRectMove** is the selected animation that we are working on and click on the **Add Property** button:

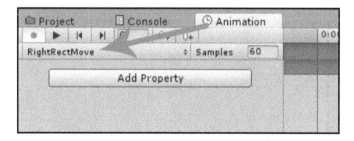

2. Click on **Transform** and then click on the plus symbol next to **Position**.

3. With RightRect still selected, click on the Timeline at the bar just before **0:20**.

4. Now, change the **Y** position to -0.2.

5. Click on the Timeline from the bar just before **0:40**.

6. Change the **Y** position to 0.2.

Mecanim

Now that we have two animated rectangles, we will take a quick look at Mecanim. Mecanim is a state machine-based controller for playing animations or clips. Without getting too deep into this heavily complex animation solution, we can say that this allows us to change an object's animation with simple variables.

For instance, a character can have a speed parameter. This parameter can be set up in our code to be changed based on how far the player pushes up on the game controller. Let's imagine that the speed variable is from 0 to 10. We also have three animations: standing still, walking, and running. If the user is not pushing the game controller up at all, the variable is 0; if they are halfway, then 5; if they are all the way, then 10.

The Mecanim window

Let's take a quick overview of the Mecanim or Animator view. In order to see our Animator view, we need to click on the **Window** menu item and click on the **Animator** option; as shown in the following screenshot.

First, you will notice a large grid area. This is where the various nodes are. These are our various states or animation clips. The orange node is our default state. As this animation controller gets more and more complex, you will have arrows connecting many of these nodes together in a flow chart:

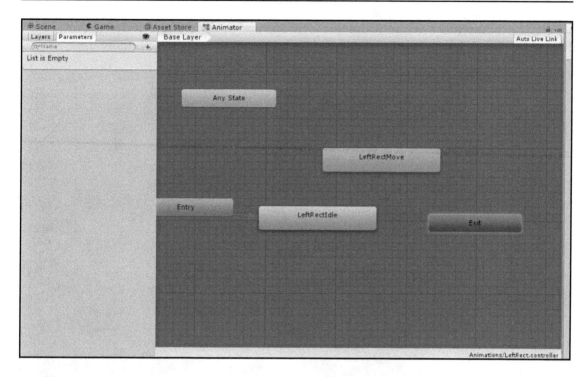

On the left-hand side of the **Animation** view, you will see our **Parameters** list, where we can set the variables we need to let our scripts transition from state to state.

The types of variables we can use are limited to floats, ints, bools, and triggers. These will be explained in a little more in detail later. For now, we will be using bools, which are variables with a true or false result.

Make them interactive

Now that we have two animated rectangles, we will make them interactive with the GGV that we talked about earlier in this chapter. In order to do this, we will first set up our Mecanim nodes and the parameter that we need for them to work.

Once this is done, we will write our first C# script. It will be a very simple script, and since we will not be covering script writing just now, only the very basics will be explained.

If you do not currently have an **Animator** view open, with `LeftRect` selected in our **Hierarchy** view, click on **Window** followed by **Animator** to bring this window up:

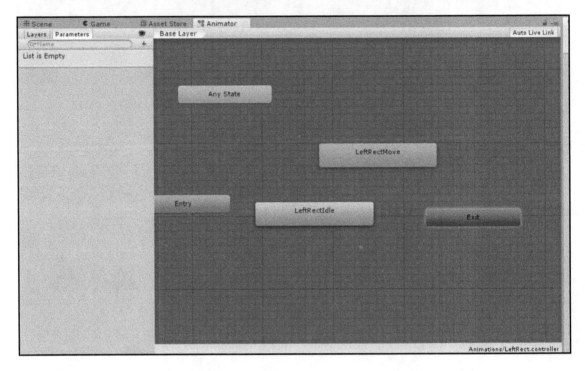

As mentioned in the preceding section, you can see our nodes for the `LeftRect`.GameObject. The green node is our entry point. This node connects directly to **LeftRectIdle**, our default animation. We will be connecting our **Entry** node to our **LeftRectMove** as well. To do so, perform the following steps:

1. First, right-click on the **Entry** node and click on **Make Transition**:

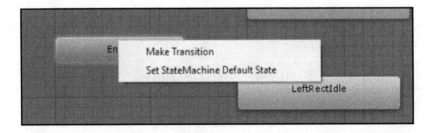

2. A gray arrow and line will appear beneath your cursor. Move your cursor to the **LeftRectMove** node and click on it; the line will darken to let you know that it is set:

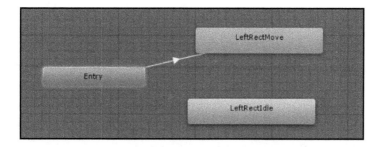

3. Select `RightRect` in the Hierarchy view and repeat steps 1 and 2.

Now, we will need to rename the states. Let's perform these steps:

1. Click on **LeftRectIdle**.
2. In the **Inspector**, change the name to `RectIdle`:

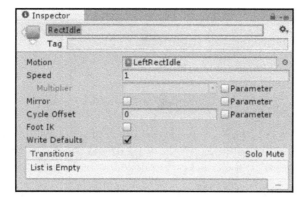

3. Click on **LeftRectMove**.
4. In the **Inspector**, change the name to `RectMove`.
5. Repeat these steps for **RightRect** also.

Simple so far, right?

Now, we need to set up our parameter so that our script can do its job:

1. On the `Parameter` side of the **Animator** view, ensure that **Parameters** is highlighted; click on the plus sign:

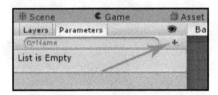

2. When the list of options appears, click on **Bool**.
3. Type in `idle` as the name of the parameter.
4. Then, `idle` will appear in the **Parameters** list with a checkbox next to it. Click on the checkbox and ensure that it is checked:

5. Now, repeat these steps for **RightRect**.

Here is the Game Plan

Before moving ahead, I want to give a quick rundown of what we are doing. We have an object with two animation states: idle and moving. Idle is the default mode. We have created an idle parameter with the checkbox checked, which makes the condition true.

In the next section, we will write a script that has the following two main functions:

- If the object is selected, it changes idle from true to false or vice versa
- In the update function, it checks for two conditions: whether idle is true or false and to play the correct animation

When the application loads, you will see the two boxes; because idle is the default state, nothing will happen until they are selected. Once they are, they will move. If they are selected again, they will go idle once more:

1. With **LeftRect** selected in the **Hierarchy** view, search for the **Inspector** panel, scroll to the bottom, and click on **Add Component**:

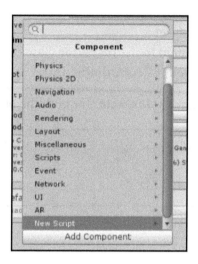

2. Scroll down to **New Script** and select it.
3. Name the new script RectAnim:

4. Click on **Create and Add**.

For the **RightRect** object, we do not have to create a new script; we will use the same one. Since we gave the states for both **RightRect** and **LeftRect** the same names, it will allow this to work with the same script:

1. Select the **RightRect** object.
2. Click on **Add Component** in the **Inspector** view.
3. Click on **Scripts** and select **RectAnim(Script)**.

This is what it should look like in the **Inspector** for both the objects when done:

Our first script

Here, we will take our first steps into Visual Studio's code editing capabilities. As previously explained, this will be a very simple script with some, but with very little, explanation.

Now, double-click on the grayed-out **RectAnim** script to open Visual Studio:

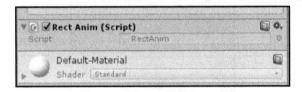

Once it is loaded, your screen should look comparable to this:

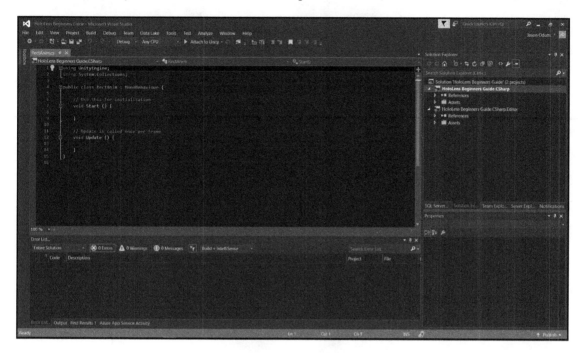

You should see the RectAnim.cs filename highlighted in the left-upper corner. When a developer writes code, this is where we do it. Currently, you will see a couple of namespace declarations, the class name, and a few functions.

The Start() function is called when an object is first instantiated; it is one of the first things that happens. So, it is the setup for a scripted object in Unity.

The Update() function is called for every frame. When you need something to change on a regular basis, it is normally done through Update.

Now, replace all the code in `RectAnim.cs` with the following code:

```csharp
using System.Collections;
using System.Collections.Generic;
using UnityEngine;
using System;
using HoloToolkit.Unity.InputModule;

public class RectAnim : MonoBehaviour, IInputClickHandler {

    Animator anim;
        // Use this for initialization
        void Start () {
         anim = GetComponent<Animator>();
        }
        // Update is called once per frame
        void Update () {

            if (!anim.GetBool("idle"))
            {
                anim.Play("RectMove");
            }
            else if (anim.GetBool("idle"))
            {
                anim.Play("RectIdle");
         }

        }


    public void OnInputClicked(InputClickedEventData eventData) {

        if (anim.GetBool("idle"))
        {
            anim.SetBool("idle", false);
        }
        else
        {
            anim.SetBool("idle", true);
        }
    }
    public void OnSpeechKeywordRecognized(SpeechKeywordRecognizedEventData
eventData)
    {
        var voiceCommand = eventData.RecognizedText.ToLower();

        switch (voiceCommand)
        {
```

```
        case "change color":
        {


            break;
        }
        case "reset":
        {

            break;
        }
    default:
        break;
    }
  }
}
```

The `OnInputClicked(InputClickedEventData eventData)` function is part of the HoloToolKit Input function. When an object is being looked at via Gaze and the user does the air-tap gesture, it will send the `OnInputClicked()` message to the object and run that code.

If we press the Play button:

We can see what appears to be a white bar against a black background:

Now, if we click on the two halves of the bar, we will see them move up and down:

If you see the blocks moving, congratulations on learning the basics of Unity animation.

Materials, textures, and shaders

In this section, we will discuss, you guessed it: materials, textures, and shaders. As we have touched on this subject lightly before, we will dig in a bit deeper this time. Unity's rendering system and lighting model uses **Physically Based Shading (PBS)**, which is a simulation between the materials in the scene and the lights. **PBS**, in many ways, closely imitates how lights and materials work in real life.

Materials

Materials are art assets placed on an object that give various rendering properties. A highly reflective polish job on a smooth, silver surface or a rough and rugged wooden door with moss growing on the bottom are both examples of Materials. Materials are made up of the Material component itself, shaders, and textures.

While the details of shaders are beyond the scope of this book, we do need a general overview. A shader is a small script file that tells Unity how to react to light. In real life, when light hits a surface, it does not just stop there. Elements such as color, reflectivity, and smoothness can determine the way light bounces around a space. In its effort to simulate this, PBS is designed to take these factors into account at, more or less, real-time speed. Shaders help facilitate this in many ways.

Textures are digital images that a material uses to help give the fine details of a surface, such as the reflectivity or roughness. A texture can also simply be a pattern, such as a pattern of rivets to make the back of a robot, or a highly detailed picture, such as, the front of a soda machine placed on the front of a box to create that illusion with very few polygons used.

Combined, these constituents can help to render beautiful, complex, and detailed worlds.

Now let's go back to our project and ensure that we have **LeftRect** selected. If we look at the **Inspector** panel, we should see the **Default-Material** component near the bottom. Click on the little arrow off to the left of that component, as shown:

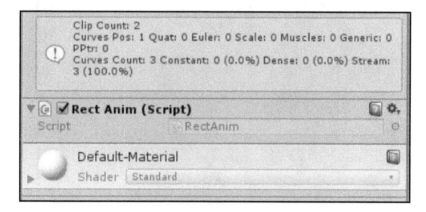

In that case, it should expand outward to look like this:

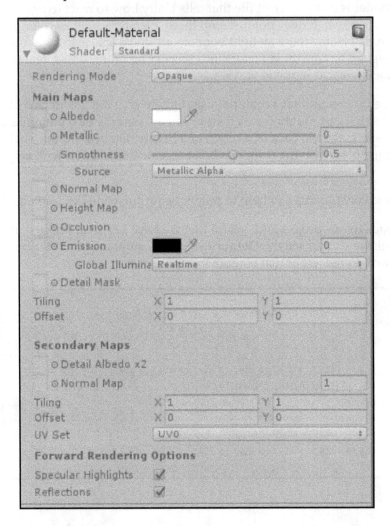

One will assume--after reading what all a material can do--that it is complex; and that is right. With that in mind, we will be touching only parts of the Material overview.

In our **Project** view, let's navigate to the `Materials` folder.

Here, we have the **Platform** material we created in our `Hello World` project. This time, we will make our materials look a bit better. Blue plastic is kind of boring.

Search For It

Now, we will use a great resource to find textures to prototype with: Bing or Google.

For this section, we will need to go to a search engine and type `metal box texture`, or something similar. Once you have made that choice and saved it, we need to type `wood panel texture`. Did you find something you like? Great!

In the Project view, select **Materials** if it is not already selected. Right-click on the **Folder** and click on **Create** and then on **Folder**. Name the folder `Textures`.

Now, we will bring an art asset in a different way:

1. Click on **Assets** in the main menu.
2. Click on **Import New Asset**.
3. Navigate to the folder where you saved your new textures.
4. Select the **Metal** texture.
5. Repeat steps 1-4 for the **Wood** texture as well.
6. Ensure that you have the scene view selected in the main window so that your screen looks like this, and **LeftRect** is the selected object:

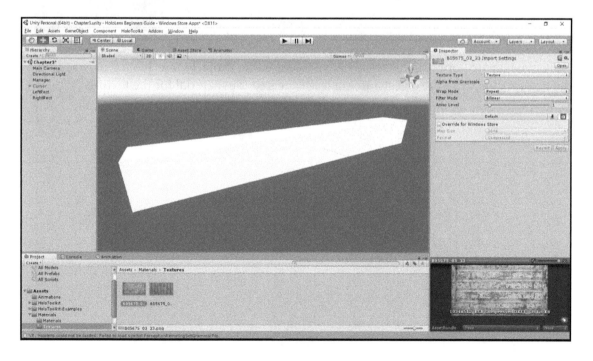

7. Click on your **Metal** texture and drag it to **LeftRect**.
8. When the mouse is over the object, release it:

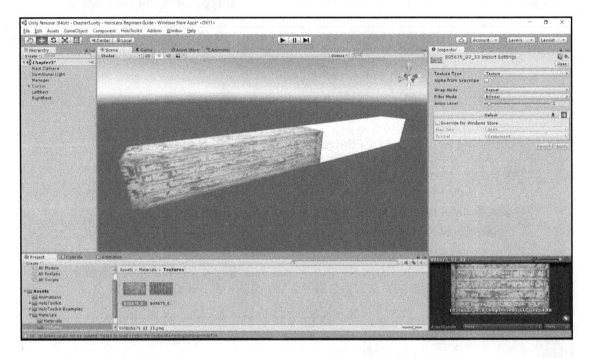

Now, navigate to your original `Materials` folder in the **Project** view. Note that dragging the texture directly to the object automatically created the material for the texture.

In the process, though, it also created another `Materials` directory that is a child of the original `Materials` directory; let's delete that directory to keep our project directories clean:

1. Move to this new directory.
2. Drag the metal material to the original `Materials` folder:

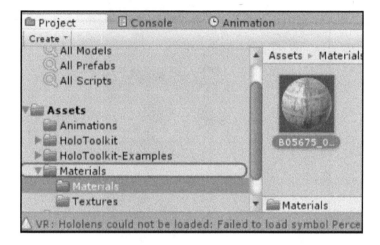

3. Delete the child `Materials` folder by selecting it and pressing the *Delete* key.
4. When the warning box shows up, either click **Delete** or press the *Enter* key.

Now, we can move on and look at some parts of the material that we will use. Select the **New Material** in the **Project** view. In the **Inspector**, you should see this:

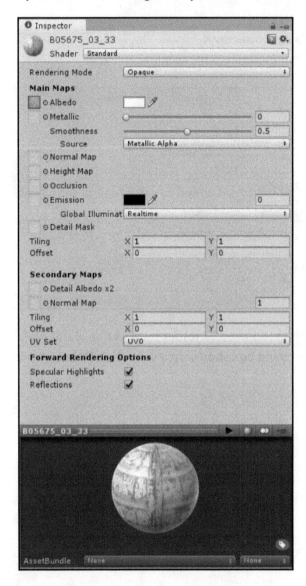

The following is a quick overview of the commonly used areas:

- **Rendering Mode**: This has four options to help objects use transparency and blending; the options are **Opaque**, **Cutout**, **Transparent**, and **Fade**.

- **Albedo**: This is where our color map goes. We can change the overall color by clicking on the color picker and changing it from the default white.
- **Metallic**: Without getting too heavily into the theory, the **Metallic** setting helps determine how *metal-like* the surface is, that is, the reflectivity of the material, or how much of the surrounding environment shows up in the rendering process.
- **Smoothness**: The smoothness slider is part of the **Metallic** parameter.
- **Normal Map**: A **Normal Map** is a type of bump map that is great for creating fine details on a model. These details can make the model appear to be of a far higher resolution than they really are.
- **Height Map**: This is another type of bump map. This version is far less detailed but great for creating depth.
- **Tiling**: In the **X** and **Y** fields of tiling, we can change how often a pattern repeats on an object or adjust a texture map to fit a bit more snugly.
- **Offset**: The offset option allows the developer to line up how the texture is sitting on the object. Changing the **X** and **Y** fields will move the texture around accordingly.
- **Specular Highlights**: This turns the **Specular Highlights** option on and off, which is used primarily for controlling the brightness of **Specular Highlights**. It can also change the color of these highlights.
- **Reflections**: This turns the reflections of the objects on or off.

Adding the details

Now, let's make a few adjustments to our material.

First, we will change the default shader. The HoloToolkit comes with a shader designed to work better with its architecture:

1. Click on **Standard,** which is at the top of the **Inspector**, next to the Shader heading.
2. Scroll down and hover the mouse over HoloToolkit.
3. When the submenu appears, click on **StandardFast**.

The HoloToolkit version has the same options as the Standard, though the shader itself has math that is more geared toward the HoloLens.

While this is not normally how one would use a color map, we will place a copy in the **Height Map** area so that we can see a bump map at work; let's perform the following steps:

1. Click on the circle next to the **Height Map**:

2. When the selected texture box opens, scroll down and search for the texture map that you are currently using for your **Albedo** map:

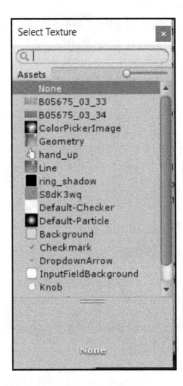

3. Once the map is selected, a slider will appear next to the **Height Map** heading, adjustable from **0** to **1**.
4. If you move this slider, you will note that the texture in the **Scene**, on the object, deepens in accordance with the sliders. Put the slider somewhere that looks good to you.

Now that we have had a good overview of Materials, let's create another material for our second box:

1. In the `Materials` folder, right-click in the empty space in the right section.
2. Hover over **Create** and click on **Material**.
3. Type `WoodPanel` for its name.
4. Again, change its shader type to **StandardFast** from the HoloToolkit.
5. Click on the circle next to **Albedo**.
6. Search for and select the second texture that you chose.
7. Again, in the **Height Map** section, click on the circle and choose the same texture.

It should look something like this at the moment:

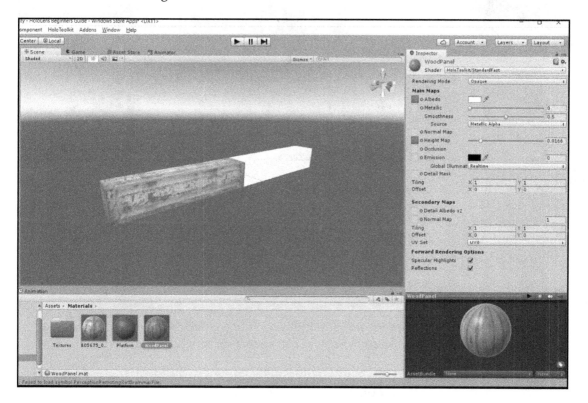

Now, let's drag the texture to the other object in the **Scene**:

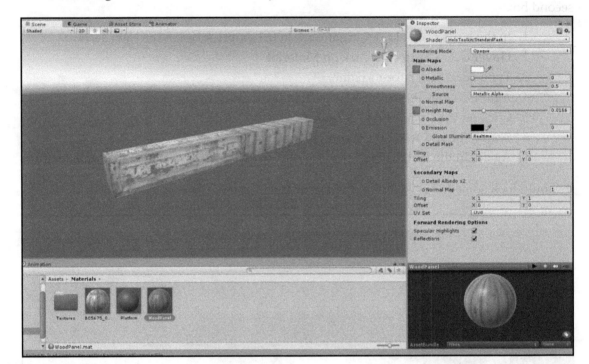

In my case, I am not a big fan of how the vertical stripes are lining up. So, I will adjust my **Tiling** and **Offset** until it fits my liking. Also, I want to play with the Height Map slider to give the crevices more depth and the smoothness slider until it looks more like wood; adjust yours according to your liking.

Changing the color

So, the final lesson in this chapter will add interaction to change the color of our material. Instead of Gaze and Gesture though, we will use a voice command:

1. With **LeftRect** selected, click on the **Add Component** button.
2. Scroll down and click on the **New Script** option.
3. Type ChangeRectColor in the **new script** dialog; then, click on **Create** and then **Add**.

Just like last time, instead of creating a second script for the right side, we will add the same script to **RightRect** using the following steps:

1. Select **RightRect**.
2. Click on the **Add Component** button.
3. Click on **Scripts**.
4. Select **ChangeRectColor** from the list.

This script will be slightly more complex than the previous one. From a scripting standpoint, materials are handled by the Renderer class. So, we get a reference to the renderer that is attached to this object. Then, we create a couple of bools.

We will use the `OnFocusEvent.cs` HTK class attached to an object and with two functions in our ChangeRectColor script, we can change the color of the object with `OnGazeRectStart()` when the user is looking at the object and `OnGazeRectExit()` when the user stops looking at the object. Then, we have two more public functions: `VoiceSelect()` and `ResetColor()`. All of these functions are public so that the `OnFocusEvent` and `Speech Input Handler` can use them; we will learn about this in a few minutes.

Here's a quick run through from the user's standpoint. The program starts and the user sees two boxes. If they look directly at either box, the box will turn green. If the user looks at one of the objects and gives the `VoiceSelect()` command, it will change color to blue. If the user looks at the box object and gives the `ResetColor()` command, the color will reset it to white.

The word select is used by the system as a vocal replacement or equivalent of Air tap. Saying select while looking at an object is exactly the same as Airtapping that object. In the case of this program, saying select causes the objects to start animating.

The following are a few other reserved words you should avoid using:

- Place
- Face me
- Bigger/smaller

Now, let's double-click on the `ChangeRectColor.cs` in the `Assets` folder of the **Project** View so that **Visual Studio** opens up our new file.

Select and copy or type everything in the following code into `ChangeRectColor.cs`. I highly recommend that you type it; when we take the slow route in learning, we often start picking up things that we are not aware of:

```
using UnityEngine;
using System.Collections;

public class ChangeRectColor : MonoBehaviour {

        Renderer rend;
        bool selected;
        bool gazed;


     void Start () {
      rend = GetComponent<Renderer>();
      bool selected = false;
      }

    public void OnGazeRectStart()
    {
        if (!selected)
        {   rend.material.color = Color.green;
            gazed = true;
        }
    }
    public void OnGazeRectExit()
    {
        if (!selected)
        {   rend.material.color = Color.white;
            gazed = false;
        }
    }
    public void VoiceColorChange()
    {
            rend.material.color = Color.blue;

    }
    public void ResetColor()
    {
            rend.material.color = Color.white;
            selected = false;
    }
    public void OnSpeechKeywordRecognized(SpeechKeywordRecognizedEventData
 eventData)
     {
        var voiceCommand = eventData.RecognizedText.ToLower();
```

```
    switch (voiceCommand)
    {
        case "change color":
        {
            VoiceColorChange();
            break;
        }
        case "reset":
        {
            ResetColor();
            break;
        }
    default:
            break;
    }
  }

}
```

Okay, now that we have copied our code, save it by pressing *Ctrl + S*.

OnFocusEvent component

The OnFocusEvent component is set up to handle our gaze. It has two modes: Focus Enter and Focus Lost. Here, we will need to add the component and then set up our object to work with it.

Click on **Add Component** in the **inspector** on the **LeftRect** object. Type in OnFocusEnter and select the OnFocusEnter component:

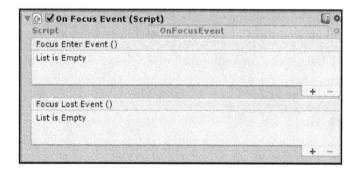

When the `OnFocusEnter` component appears, you will see two boxes with plus and minus signs under them. Click on the plus sign for each box:

Now you will see two boxes appear, looking for GameObjects. Simply drag the **LeftRect** object from the **Hierarchy** view and drop it into each of these empty fields:

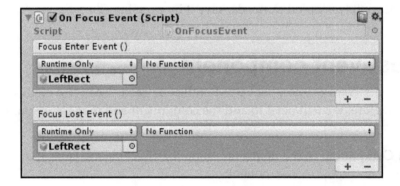

Now, in our **ChangeRectColor** script, we have two methods to work with these two events: `OnGazeRectStart()` and `OnGazeRectExit()`.

Click on the top bar labeled No Function, select `ChangeRectColor`, and then `OnGazeRectStart()`:

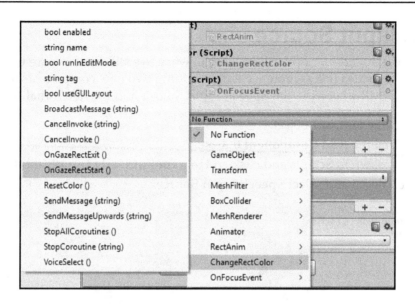

Click on the lower bar labeled **No Function**, select `ChangeRectColor`, and then `OnGazeRectExit()`:

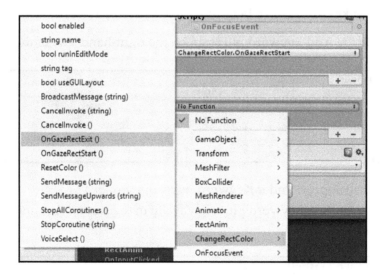

Now follow steps 1 - 7 on the **RightRect** object as well.

Now if you hit the play button in Unity, right-click and move the view around. You should see the object change colors as your cursor moves over them.

Speech Input Source

While our code is already set up for keywords to work, we still need to wire up the keywords to our app. In this section, we will be adding two new components to the **LeftRect** and **RightRect** objects: the **Speech Input Source** and the **SetGlobal Listener**.

1. Select the **LeftRect** object.
2. Click on the **Add Component** button.
3. Scroll down to **Scripts** and click on **HoloToolkit.Unity.InputModule.**
4. Scroll down and select **Speech Input Source**:

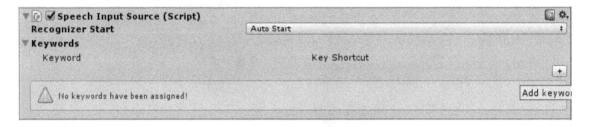

You will see the **No keywords have been assigned!** warning. Let's fix that.

1. Click on the **Add keyword** plus sign on the right-hand side of the component:

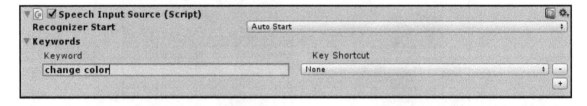

2. A line will appear; under **Keyword**, type change color.
3. Click on the Add keyword plus sign again; in the second line under **Keyword**, type Reset:

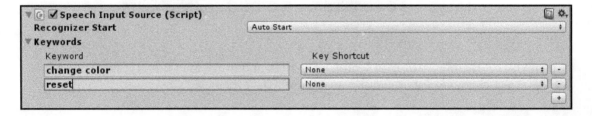

At this moment, were you to go Build Compile and Deploy, you this would function, but let's talk about the code that is handling this from the `ChangeRectColor.cs` file before we do that:

```
public void VoiceColorChange()
    {
            rend.material.color = Color.blue;

    }
    public void ResetColor()
    {
            rend.material.color = Color.white;
            selected = false;
    }
    public void OnSpeechKeywordRecognized(SpeechKeywordRecognizedEventData
eventData)
    {
        var voiceCommand = eventData.RecognizedText.ToLower();

        switch (voiceCommand)
        {
          case "change color":
          {
             VoiceColorChange();
             break;
          }
          case "reset":
          {
             ResetColor();
             break;
          }
        default:
             break;
        }
    }
}
```

I know that we have not covered scripting yet and this may mean little at the moment, but it is important enough to get this functioning; so, we can go through it real quick and you can come back and revisit this once we have covered scripting and switches as well.

The last three methods of this class, that is, `VoiceColorChange()`, `Reset()`, and `OnSpeechKeywordRecognized(SpeechKeywordRecognizedEventData eventData)` handle the work once Speech Input Source recognizes one of our words.

OnSpeechKeywordRecognized receives the `eventData` from **SpeechInputSource** and the first thing it does is to create a variable named `voiceCommand`, and converts the `RecognizedText` in the `eventData` to lowercase using the `ToLower()` method.

The next block of code is a switch statement that will take the information in the `voiceCommand` variable and compare that data with the cases offered in the switch statement, based on which voice command the `change color` or `reset case` is run, and then the `VoiceColorChange()` or `ResetColor()` methods are called.

Time to build and test

Now, let's see this work on HoloLens. We will be repeating most of the exact same steps from the last chapter; I will lighten up on the visual aids this time:

1. Click on **File** and select **Build Settings**.
2. From the **Scenes** In **Build** box, select **Scenes/Main** and press the *Delete* key.
3. Click on the **Add Open Scenes** button.
4. Click on the **Build** button.
5. When the **Build Windows Store** window appears, if you are not already in your app directory, navigate there.
6. Click on **Select Folder**.

Here we are, building again! This will take a few moments, and as before, a Windows Explorer window will pop up upon completion:

1. Double-click on the `Apps` folder.
2. Double-click on the **HoloLens Beginners Guide.sln**.

Now, we wait again as Visual Studio opens up. Ensure that your HoloLens is up and running:

1. In the Solution Explorer, select **HoloLens Beginners Guide (Universal Windows)**.
2. Click on **Build** and select **Deploy HoloLens Beginners Guide**.

When this process is finished, you will see these statements in your output window:

```
========== Build: 3 succeeded, 0 failed, 0 up-to-date, 0 skipped ==========
========== Deploy: 1 succeeded, 0 failed, 0 skipped ==========
```

You are now ready to test out all the hard work you did in this chapter. Bring up your menu, find the **HoloLens Beginners Guide** app, and run it.

Remember your commands:

- **AirTap / Saying Select**: This causes the block being gazed at to move up and down
- **Change Color**: This causes the block being gazed at to turn blue:

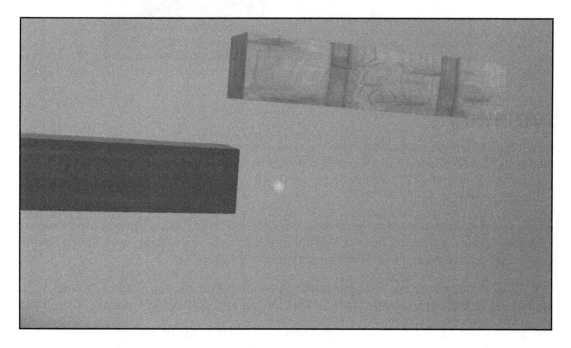

- **Reset**: This causes the gazed-upon block to turn back to the default color

- **Gazing at the Blocks**: This causes them to turn green so that you know the one that is being looked at:

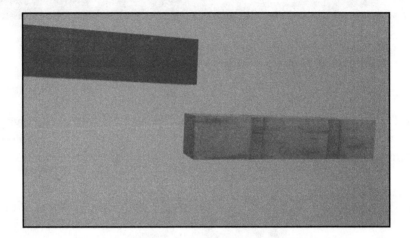

Summary

Wow, congratulations on making it through this chapter! It was a long and tough road, but you persevered. While the main focus of this chapter was HoloLens input and Gaze, Gesture, and Voice, or GGV, we needed to learn a few other things first so that we could see the input happen.

We discussed Prefabs and object templates, which allow us to instantiate and save memory in the process. An important, but not terribly tough concept--parentage--was then covered, because Prefabs are often just a collection of various children.

We took a look at how to use a simple keyframe animation to move an object around. We also learned how to write a basic script so that we can airtap our object to make it animate.

Next, we covered Materials, Textures, and Shaders, and the look of our objects. We learned how to use Voice and keywords to animate/change these materials through script as well.

Finally, we built and compiled this code and ran it on our HoloLens. We used all the various forms of control we scripted and got to see our work in action. Exciting!

Next up, we will start digging into building user interfaces; see you there.

4
User-Friendly Interface

Now that we have an understanding of many of the essentials of Unity, we can begin to learn some of the more exciting elements of HoloLens and Unity development. However, before we can move into UI and its various elements, we need take a while to learn more about how we will make everything we do inside our UI work, by learning and using Unity C#.

Once we have accomplished our goals by learning C# and scripting in Unity, we will go over the basics of interface design, its purpose, and some best practices. This will lead us into HoloLens-specific interface design. We will then break down Microsoft's best practices for creating a comfortable application.

After the UI overview, we will learn a bit about the Unity camera and how it relates to HoloLens.

Upon completion of the best practices and camera lessons, we will then take our new knowledge of C# to begin Unity UI development on the HoloLens. We will expand on what we learned in the last chapter as we explore using 3D objects in our world as a user interface.

Reloading

We are about to dig into a primer on the thick and complex subject of C# scripting. Before we do, we need to get our chapter's Unity scene set up inside the Unity editor; let's perform the steps to do this:

1. First, let's make a prefab out of our `Manager` object by selecting the `Manager` object and dragging it down to the `Prefabs` directory in the Project View.

2. With the Chapter 3, *I Am in Control*, scene still loaded, we need to navigate to Assets/Scene in the Project View and double-click on the Chapter 2.unity scene file.

3. In the Hierarchy view, delete Platform, Hello, and World.

4. Click **File** on the main menu, and click on **Save Scene As...**.

5. Name the file Chapter4 and click on **Save**.

6. To keep a copy of this file in the current state, click on **File**, followed by **Save Scene As...**

7. Name the file Fresh and click on **Save**.

8. In the Assets/Scene folder, double-click on Chapter4 to load it again.

9. Select the Manager prefab and drag it into the Hierarchy view.

10. In the Inspector, in the Keyword Manager component, click on the gear in the upper-right corner.

11. Select **Reset**.

12. In the Project View, drill down to **HoloToolkit** | **Input** | **Prefabs** and drag the cursor object into the Hierarchy view.

Unity C# scripting

Now, it is time to dig into the fun stuff. C# scripting in Unity should simply be considered another component. While it is in some ways very similar to the transform, rigidbody, or collider components, C# scripts new functionality to the object it is attached to. The big difference is that they add nearly infinite possibilities.

What is C#?

C# is a robust and easy-to-learn **Object Oriented Programming (OOP)** language designed by Microsoft. C# fits the **Common Language Infrastructure (CLI)** open specification. If you do the research, you will discover that C# is very similar conceptually to C and C++ and is also very similar to Java.

To begin to understand OOP, we must understand that these programs are built out of collections of data structures and functions called classes. A class is the *blueprint* from which we make an object.

Classes can be something as simple as a cup or as complex as a Tesla Model X, though generally the more complex an object, the more objects that are involved. For instance, a car object would be made up of a chassis object, an engine object, door objects, and so on. Integrating these objects together with their functions would result in a complete car.

Objects use actions or functions to interact with each other. These are referred to as **methods**. With our `Cup.cs` class in mind, let's assume we have two other classes, `fluid.cs` and `hardwoodfloor.cs`. In OOP, we could write a method of the cup class called `SpillCup`. This function could pass a copy of the `Fluid` object to the `Hardwoodfloor` object.

A quick example

Before we dig deep into the theory, let's take some time to make a class and see it in action.

First, we will need to create a sphere in our Hierarchy view:

1. Click on the **Create** button.
2. Hover over 3D object and click on sphere.
3. Name the sphere `Ball`.
4. In the Inspector, make sure that all position elements are 0. Alternatively, you can simply click on the gear icon and select `reset`.
5. With the sphere reset, change its `position.x` to `3.05`, `position.y` to `0.87`, and `position.z` to `4.15`.

Now, we will add a script file to the ball:

1. Click on the **Add Component** button in the Inspector.
2. Scroll down to **New Script** and click on it.
3. Name the script `LaunchBall`; click on **Create** and then on **Add**.
4. Double-click on the `Launchball` script in the Inspector.

Visual Studio should be loading now. Once it is loaded, you should see a blank class called `LaunchBall` with two using statements and two methods, `Start` and `Update`. Now, we will need to copy or type the following code into that class.

Let's take a look at Part 1 of the code for the `LaunchBall.cs` file:

```
using UnityEngine;
using System.Collections;


namespace HoloLensBeginnersGuide
{

    public class LaunchBall : MonoBehaviour {

      // Member Variables

    public Vector3 launchBallHome =
                    new Vector3(0.0f, 0.0f, 4.0f);
    public float lbSpeed;
    public bool checkLBToggle = true;
    private Color lbColor;
    Renderer rend;
    bool lbJump;

    void Start()
    {
        gameObject.transform.position = launchBallHome;
        lbSpeed = 0.1f;
        lbColor = new Color(0.1f, 0.2f, 0.5f);
        rend = gameObject.GetComponent<Renderer>();
        lbJump = true;
    }
```

Let's take a look at Part 2 of the code for the `LaunchBall.cs` file:

```
// Update is called once per frame
        void Update ()
{
        if (lbJump)
{

            TeleportBall();
            ChangeColor();
            rend.material.color = lbColor;
            LaunchBallJump();
        }

        if (checkLBToggle)
        {
            CheckLB();
        }
    }
```

```
//Class Methods
void TeleportBall()
{
    if (transform.position.y >= 2)
    {
        transform.position =
 new Vector3(transform.position.x, -1,
            transform.position.z);
    }

}

void ChangeColor()
{
    float redColor = 0.1f;

    lbColor.r = redColor;
    lbColor.g = Random.Range(0, 1f);
    lbColor.b = Random.Range(0, 1f);
}
void LaunchBallJump()
{
    transform.Translate(Vector3.up *
                        lbSpeed * Time.deltaTime);
}
```

Let's take a look at Part 3 of the code for the LaunchBall.cs file:

```
void CheckLB()
{
    int i = Random.Range(0, 1000);
    if(i < 997)
    {
        lbJump = true;

    }
    else
    {

        lbJump = false;
        transform.position = launchBallHome;
    }

}


}
```

This is what Unity should look like before we test our new class: the offset white ball against a black background. Now, click on **Play** in the Unity editor:

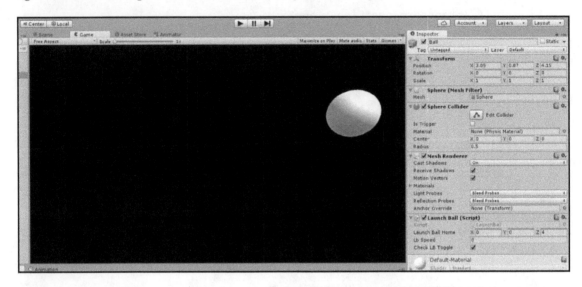

Upon doing so, the ball should move to the lower center and start changing colors. It will move up slowly until a certain condition is met, at which point the ball moves down again:

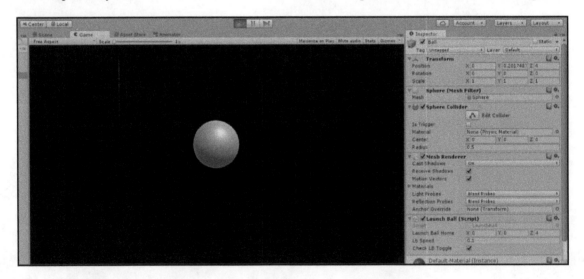

If for some reason your code is not working, double-check the case of the variable and method names. C# is a case sensitive language, which means if you create a variable called LaunchBallHome and then later refer to that variable as LaunchballHome the system will not recognize it as the previously declared variable.

Where to begin

When we write a standard C# program, we would use the Main() function as our starting point. In Unity, we use the Start() and Update() functions as our main sources of flow control; these functions are part of the MonoBehaviour class.

MonoBehaviour is the base class of all Unity scripting. All classes derived from MonoBehaviour are required to be attached to a GameObject to run. MonoBehaviour also has a set of events or functions each script responds to.

We have touched on some of these events in previous chapters:

- Start: This is called on the frame when a script is enabled, often used for setup.
- Update: This is a method that is called every frame.
- OnMouseDown: This is a method that is called when the user clicks the mouse button. This method is tied directly to the MonoBehaviour base class.

The breakdown of a Unity C# class

Let's look at the class we created in this chapter and break it down into easily digestible parts.

Firstly, here is what a basic Unity C# class looks like, broken down to its bare essentials:

```
using UnityEngine;

namespace HoloLensBeginnersGuide
{
    public class LaunchBall : MonoBehaviour
    {   //member variables and properties belong here.

        void Start()
        {

        }
```

```
        void Update()
        {
        }
    }
}
```

Now, we will want to compare that to `LauchBall.cs`. A `Unity C#` class consists of the following:

- **Using declarations**: The `using` directive is primarily used for including namespaces in the application. Defaults in Unity are `UnityEngine` and `System.Collections`:

  ```
  using UnityEngine;
  using System.Collections;
  ```

- **Namespace**: Namespace definitions are designed to prove a way to keep names separate from one another; this helps simplify reusing code later:

  ```
  namespace HoloLensBeginnersGuide
  {
  ```

- **Class declaration**: The name of this `LaunchBall` class, which will normally derive from `MonoBehaviour` in Unity:

  ```
  public class LaunchBall : MonoBehaviour {
  ```

- **Member variables**: These are the variables or data storage for the class; we will talk about this subject very soon:

  ```
      // Member Variables

  public Vector3 launchBallHome =
                  new Vector3(0.0f, 0.0f, 4.0f);
  public float lbSpeed;
  public bool checkLBToggle = true;
  private Color lbColor;
  Renderer rend;
  bool lbJump;
  ```

- **Class methods**: The actions this class can perform:

  ```
  //Class Methods
      void TeleportBall()
      {
          if (transform.position.y >= 2)
  ```

```
    {
        transform.position =
          new Vector3(transform.position.x, -1,
              transform.position.z);
    }

}
void ChangeColor()
{
    float redColor = 0.1f;

    lbColor.r = redColor;
    lbColor.g = Random.Range(0, 1f);
    lbColor.b = Random.Range(0, 1f);
}
void LaunchBallJump()
{
    transform.Translate(Vector3.up *
                          lbSpeed * Time.deltaTime);
}


void CheckLB()
{
    int i = Random.Range(0, 1000);
    if(i < 997)
    {
        lbJump = true;

    }
    else
    {

        lbJump = false;
        transform.position = launchBallHome;
    }

}
```

Here are our MonoBehaviour-specific methods `Start()` and `Update()` at work:

```
void Start()
    {
        gameObject.transform.position = launchBallHome;
        lbSpeed = 0.1f;
        lbColor = new Color(0.1f, 0.2f, 0.5f);
        rend = gameObject.GetComponent<Renderer>();
```

```
                lbJump = true;
        }


        void Update ()
        {
                if (lbJump)
                {
                        TeleportBall();
                        ChangeColor();
                        rend.material.color = lbColor;
                        LaunchBallJump();
                }

                if (checkLBToggle)
                {
                        CheckLB();
                }
        }
```

- **Statements and expressions**: This is where a good deal of the work happens. All statements and expressions must end with a semicolon:

```
gameObject.transform.position = launchBallHome;
transform.Translate(Vector3.up * lbSpeed * Time.deltaTime);
```

Variables

Variables are how we store data for use in other places. Now in the preceding example, we want to change the color of an object. Here, we have a piece of code that would do just that:

```
rend.material.color = new Color(1f, 0.4f, 0.8f);
```

In this example, we hardcoded a new color; this is considered a bad practice and should be avoided.

To help facilitate this, we use variables; a variable is a name given to space in memory or a storage area. A better way to handle the preceding problem would be to declare a variable and initialize it, or give it a value:

```
private Color lbColor;
lbColor = new Color(0.1f, 0.2f, 0.5f);
```

Here, the *data type* is `Color` and the variable name is `lbColor`, and we have stored a collection of floats that make a new color.

Now we can assign this newly initialized variable to the color of the material, as follows:

```
rend.material.color = lbColor;
```

One benefit of using variables is the ability to use `lbColor` anywhere a `Color` data type is needed. Also, we can change `lbColor` as we did in the preceding example.

Camel casing is important. You may note that when declaring a variable, I used a lowercase `m` and an uppercase `B`. This is a highly recommended standard called camel casing, where the first word in a variable declaration is lowercase and all other words are uppercase.

Keep in mind that there are different types of variables, which are determined by their scope. A variable defined in a method will only last for the duration of that method:

```
[data type] [name];
```

Class-scope variables will last as long as the class is active, but will have additional protection as a result; they are called **access modifiers**:

```
[Access Modifier] [data type] [name];
```

Some variables are **standard data types** or what are more commonly referred to as **simple data types.** Combinations of these data types are used to make the more complex types:

```
Floating Point: float lbSpeed;
Boolean: public bool checkLBToggle = true;
Integer: int i = Random.Range(0, 1000);
```

Some variables are **complex data structures**:

```
public Vector3 launchBallHome = new Vector3(0.0f, 0.0f, 4.0f);
Renderer rend;
private Color lbColor;
```

You will notice that some of these variable declarations from the `LauchBall` class start with public or private keywords; these are known as access modifiers.

Access modifiers

In Unity, when declaring class-scope variables, we need to declare an access modifier. The options available are `private`, `public`, or `protected`. If no access modifier is chosen, `private` is assumed. One of the main reasons to make variables in Unity `public` is to be able to access them in the Unity Inspector.

In C#, this means:

- **Private**: This means the access modifier cannot be accessed by other scripts
- **Public**: This means the access modifier can be accessed by other scripts
- **Protected**: This means the access modifier can only be accessed by internal or derived sources

In Unity, this additionally means:

- **Public**: A variable shows up in the editor and can be changed outside of the script
- **Private**: Variables do not show up in the editor
- **Protected**: A variable can only be accessed by internal or derived sources

Class methods

A class method is an action or a function. We have seen a few of these so far. Like variables, class methods can use access modifiers to allow or restrict external use. Using no access modifier is the equivalent to setting a method to private:

```
[Access modifier] [return datatype] [method-name (parameter list)]
{
        Method Body
}
```

This list will give a simple overview of the pseudo-code example above:

- **Access modifier**: `public/private/protected`
- **Return type**: The data type the method returns
- **Method name**: A unique, case-sensitive name
- **Parameter list** (or the signature): Many parameters can be passed into a method; each needs a type and a name
- **Method body**: The instructions needed to accomplish the given task

Declaring a method looks a bit like this:

```
private void ChangeColor(float redcolor)
    {

        lbColor.r = redColor;
        lbColor.g = Random.Range(0, 1f);
        lbColor.b = Random.Range(0, 1f);
    }
```

In the preceding example (a slight modification of the program's version), we have created a method called `ChangeColor`. This simple class receives a float, which gets assigned to the `redcolor` variable. The `void` keyword means that there is no return type for this method. `ChangeColor` will only be accessible from within its own class due to the private access modifier.

`ChangeColor` is a simple method that takes the `lbColor` variable and randomizes the green and blue elements.

Understanding scope

The **scope of a variable** is the *area or length of code* that can be used. In a sense, scope is a variable's lifetime. There are two primary types of scope that we use with regularity in C#:

- **Local scope**: These variables are defined within a method or inside the block of a method. Local scope variables defined within a method are released when the method ends.
- **Class-level scope**: All the names defined inside the current class, aside from local names, are said to be local to that class. This means that the class-level variables live as long as the class is active.

Code blocks are generally the means of defining a scope and are marked with curly braces `{}`:

```
public class ScopeExample: MonoBehavior
    {
        public int dodododo = 3;
        public int mahna = 2;
        public int mahnah = 5;

        void MethodScope(int never, int again)
        {
            int methodScopeVariable;
            methodScopeVariable = (never + again +dodododo +
```

```
          mahna + mahnah);
       Debug.Log(methodScopeVariable);

    }
    void Update()
    {
      MethodScope(mahna, mahnah); // Answer 17
      Debug.Log(dododododo); //answer 3
      Debug.Log(mahna); //answer 2
      Debug.Log(mahnah); //answer 5
      Debug.Log(methodScopeVariable); //error out of scope.
    }
  }
```

As you can see here, we declare three class-scope variables. We also have a method that gets called. During the process, a variable is created. Due to `methodScope`, the variable is limited to the method that created it; so, when `Debug.Log (methodScopeVariable)` is called, we are outside of its scope, which causes an error. Enjoy this earworm!

A lot to take in

Keep in mind that this is just an overview. The subject of Unity scripting could fill books on its own. We will continue to learn more and more about C# throughout the rest of the book but in much smaller portions. Hopefully, with what we have learned here, we will have a good starting point to actually understand what we will be doing throughout the rest of the book.

User interface design

In the world we live in, we are constantly using new and different software. When the newest social media app hits the ground, we want to try it out. Quite often, when we load these new apps, we almost instantly know how they work. This is very much due to **user interface design**.

According to Wikipedia *"user interface design or user interface engineering is the design of user interfaces for machines and software, such as computers, home appliances, mobile devices, and other electronic devices, with the focus on maximizing usability and the user experience."*

Good interface design is both an art and a science, the core being the ability to anticipate the user's needs and design a system that helps nudge the user down the path they are on.

With this understanding, we need to make sure that the necessary elements to accomplish the task are available. These elements can be informational, interactive, or visual in design, or combinations of these. A good interface design is clear, easy to grasp, and feels natural to its user. Ideally, a good interface design is almost invisible to the user; no, this does not mean that the user cannot see it, but that the interface feels so natural that they do not realize they are using an interface.

There are many interface elements that we use every day, and unless you are an interface designer, you likely take them for granted. We have used many of these so far in this book. Here are some of the elements that Unity uses:

- **Buttons**: This lets the user know that there is an action when it is used
- **Input Field**: This allows the user to enter text
- **Toggles**: This is a two-position button; on/off states are common
- **Slider**: A slider allows the user to adjust a parameter by sliding a bar
- **Dropdown**: This is an interface element that allows the user to choose from many options listed in some order

According to the U.S. Department of Health and Human Services, interface elements can be broken down into these categories:

- **Input Controls**: Buttons, text field checkboxes, radio buttons, dropdown lists, list boxes, toggles, and date fields
- **Navigation Controls**: Breadcrumbs, sliders, search fields, pagination, tags, and icons
- **Informational Controls**: Tooltips, icons, progress bars notifications, message boxes, and modal windows

General user interface best practices

User interface is a big subject, and a comprehensive view is well beyond the scope of this book. There are many books on the subject alone. For our purposes, I wish to provide you with some ideas and inspiration. With that in mind, this is a list of best practices:

- **Clarity**: This is one that hits all the lists. A clear and easily understood interface will have them in and out in no time. The user remembers whether an experience was good or bad, though likely not on a conscious level. This can have a direct effect on whether or not a user wishes to return to that interface.

- **Be forgiving /flexible**: The more natural a user interface is, the less likely the user is to actually read what the controls say. As a result, people will make mistakes, even with the best design. Ensure that you are prepared for the user to make these mistakes and fix them when they do happen.
- **Keep it simple**: As mentioned previously, an interface that is barely noticeable wins, hands down.
- **Keep it familiar**: As developers, our purpose is to find solutions to fix problems. Often, the problem we are finding a solution for has already been solved. When this is the case, why would we not use one of the solutions that exist? To learn is a fair answer, but you don't want to reinvent the button or input field, neither does your user want to relearn an entire interface when a common solution would suffice perfectly well.
- **Consistency**: Use similar elements for similar functions throughout your application. Inputs that look similar should also behave in a similar way.

Something new

Due to the HoloLens' unique nature, although user interface design definitely has directions to push us, the HoloLens user interface is ours to explore. There is a growing list of best practices, which will likely evolve into standards, but currently there really are no rules when it comes to UI development on HoloLens. So, if you have an idea, try it; maybe it works, maybe it doesn't. Regardless, the process of trying it will have taught you something.

Microsoft HoloLens best practices

Now, don't take my excitement for something other than an experimental nature. The best practices that Microsoft has laid out for developers are fairly sound:

- **The user is the camera**: We have touched on this in earlier chapters, but it can't hurt to reiterate it. A HoloLens App built from Unity will use the Main camera as the user's viewpoint. This must be taken into account when designing apps for the HoloLens; let the user drive.
- **Avoid head locking**: Having UI elements locked to the user's head movement can be extremely uncomfortable.

- **Try body-locked instead**: There is a forgiveness that comes with having holograms moving with the position and angle of the body as opposed to the head.
- **Keep holograms at least 1-2 meters from the user's head**: Holograms closer than 1 meter cause the user to cross their eyes, which is quite painful after a period of time. 2-5 meters is optimal.
- **Holograms in the real world**: Spatial mapping and spatial understanding allow holograms to really appear to be living in our world. Leveraging this feature for our interfaces can create unique experiences; we will cover these in later chapters.
- **Use gravity**: To further embed the holograms in our world, putting things on the ground can help facilitate new ways to control our world.
- **Lead a horse to water**: Ensure that the user knows where they are going and what they need to do next. Since we are not limited to a 2D plane anymore, we need to make sure that we point our users to their next stop.

The Unity camera and HoloLens

The camera inside a game engine, such as Unity, is designed to capture and display a viewpoint to the player. In the case of the HoloLens, the camera is the user's perspective, much like a first-person game. There is one big difference though: the camera's controller is the user's head. This can be a tough factor to design around for some application types, especially UI.

What this amounts to, when designing an application for HoloLens, we need to think around the camera. We need to place the things that the user will interact with within a reachable distance. User interfaces, as well as the overall experience, will have a very different look and feel from what we have come to expect from a 2D screen. Also, of course, that is the point.

The Unity camera is highly customizable. For HoloLens development, we are fairly limited to what we can use:

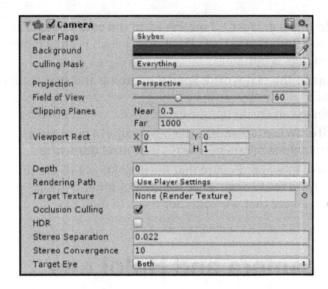

The fields can be explained as follows:

- **Clear Flags**: This will almost always be set to **Solid Color**.
- **Background**: In most cases, the setting for this will be black (r= 0, g = 0, b = 0, a = 0). HoloLens uses the color black to set full transparency. This allows the user to see the world they are in.
- **Field of View**: The default is 60; there is talk on the HoloToolkit of Unity GitHub that it should be 16. For now, we will stick to the default.
- **Clipping Planes**: The recommended setting for this is around 0.85.

Unity UI

Unity has designed a rather robust user interface system, containing just about any traditional user interface element one could need. In addition, Unity's new system is a very smart and expandable system that can easily grow with the developer's needs. It was designed to anticipate, with a good deal of forethought, the needs of new platforms that come along.

In this section, we will use the `launchball` class and build a basic UI to change some parts of that class. Before we do, though, we will have a quick overview of Unity UI and its workflow.

Overview

The Unity UI workflow, being far less programmer centric than Unity's previous effort--,the infamous OnGUI, is highly editable inside the editor; let's take a look.

Load Unity, assuming it is not already running. Also, select the **HoloLens Beginner Guide** from the project list.

Once loaded, it should look similar to this:

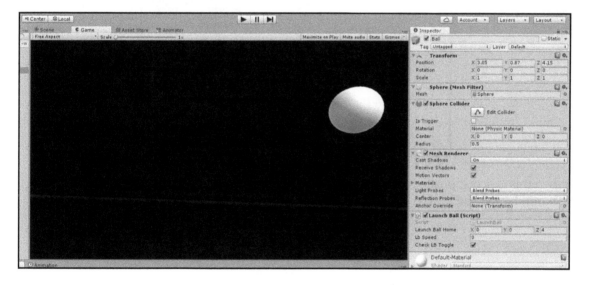

Let's add a UI element so that we can see how it all works. Click on **GameObject** in the main menu. Scroll down to **UI** and select **Button**:

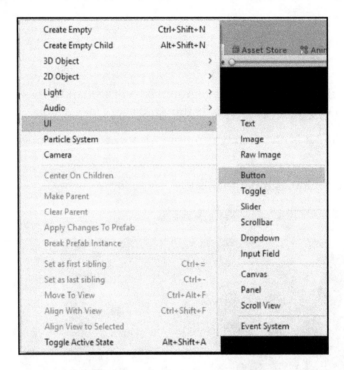

When this is accomplished, you should note a few new things. First, we now have a large rectangular labeled button on the screen:

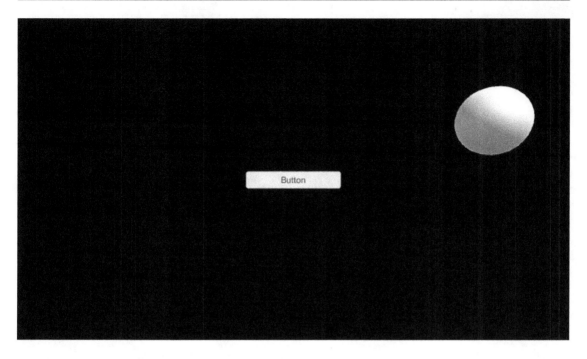

We also now have three new objects in our Hierarchy view: **Canvas**, **Button**, and **EventSystem**:

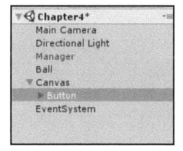

- **Canvas**: The **Canvas** is the heart of the UI system. All elements of our user interface will be children of a canvas.
- **EventSystem**: The **EventSystem** handles input from various sources.

- **Button**: A button is exactly what you think it is. If you select it in the Hierarchy view, you will see another important element of the UI system.
- **RectTransform**: The **RectTransform** component is used to place UI elements on a canvas. It always helps the canvas to be resized for different platforms with little hassle:

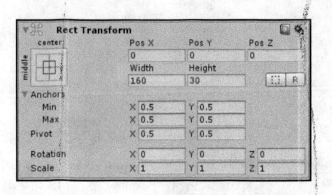

In order to see this new UI in action, we will need to make a few modifications to the `LaunchBall` class.

First, we will need to take a look at our `Update` function :

```
void Update () {

        if (lbJump)
        {
            TeleportBall();
            ChangeColor();
            rend.material.color = lbColor;
            LaunchBallJump();
        }

        if (checkLBToggle)
        {
            CheckLB();
        }
    }
```

Then, we need to change the preceding code to this:

```
void Update () {


    }
```

We need to add the following line to both, our `Start` function and our `ChangeColor` function:

```
rend.material.color = lbColor;
void Start()
    {
        gameObject.transform.position = launchBallHome;
        lbSpeed = 20f;
        lbColor = new Color(0.1f, 0.2f, 0.5f);
        rend = gameObject.GetComponent<Renderer>();
        lbJump = true;
        rend.material.color = lbColor;
    }
```

Also, while we are here, let's add the `public` keyword to the start of the function:

```
public void ChangeColor()
    {
        float redColor = 0.1f;

        lbColor.r = redColor;
        lbColor.g = Random.Range(0, 1f);
        lbColor.b = Random.Range(0, 1f);
        rend.material.color = lbColor;
    }
```

Rename the `TeleportBall` method to `ResetBall` and change the code to match this:

```
public void ResetBall()
    {

    transform.position =
                new Vector3(transform.position.x, -1,
        transform.position.z);


    }
```

We also need to add the `public` keyword to the `LaunchBallJump` method as well.

If we go back to Unity and click the Play button, the ball will now move to center of the screen and turn blue. These changes are defined in the `Start()` function, while everything else that was previously happening was in the `Update()` method, which is now empty.

With that out of the way, we can now make our ball do things in an interactive fashion.

Interactivity

Here, we will make a few buttons, rename them, and assign them to the functions of our `LaunchBall` class:

1. Look at the Hierarchy view and search for the **Button** child of **Canvas**:

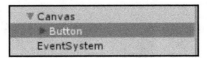

2. Click on the arrow next to the **Button** object to expand it, and select the child of **Button** labeled **Text**:

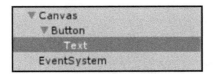

The Button text object

3. Now, take a look in the Inspector at the **Text** component. Here, we have a wide variety of ways to change the text that is on the button:

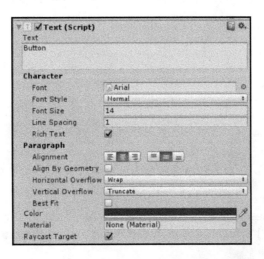

4. Select the word `Button` in the **Text** box. Press the *Delete* key and type `Change Color`.

5. Back in the Hierarchy view, select **Button**.

6. In the **Inspector**, change the object's name to `ChangeColorBtn`:

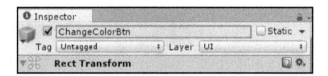

Now, we will wire a function to this button. Earlier in the chapter, we added the `public` keyword to the class methods to make this work. With that keyword, the following step would not work.

Take a look at the following **Button** component. Make a note of all the options that you see. We will go over some of these soon. For now, we will use the **On Click ()** box to assign our function to our object:

1. In the **On Click ()** box, click on the + symbol:

The Button component

2. Now, the **On Click ()** box should look like this:

3. In the Hierarchy view, select the **Ball** object and drag it to the **None (Object)** slot.
4. Click on the drop-down bar labeled **No Function**. Move down to **LaunchBall** and select **ChangeColor()** from the list:

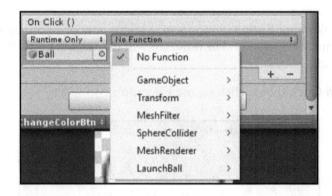

5. In the **Button** component, click on the highlighted color and select color-picker box. Change the RGB values to 0, 255, and 12. This will produce a neon green mouse-over affect that will help you see that you have the button selected.

Great work!

Now, run the application by clicking on the Play button. Again, the ball should now be seen in center itself; in addition, we now have a button that says **Change Color**. Go ahead; and click on it:

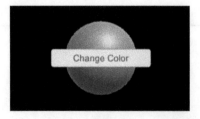

You will see a new color:

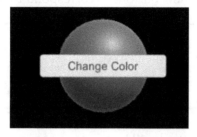

For each click, you will see a new color:

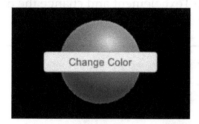

Now that we have finished one button, we will make two more and give them each different functions. After that, to keep them in a uniform pattern, we will use a Layout group.

Let's perform the following steps:

1. Right-click on the **ChangeColorBtn** object in the Hierarchy view.
2. Select **Duplicate** from the menu.
3. Select the new Button, `ChangeColorBtn(1)`, and change the name to `ResetBallBtn`.
4. Duplicate `ResetBallBtn` and change the name to `LaunchBallJumpBtn`:

Now we have three buttons. Now that we have duplicated the button, we need to change the **On Click ()** box for the two new buttons to correspond to their names:

Teleport BallBtn's `OnClick` function will be `LaunchBall.TeleportBall()`, and `LaunchBallJumpBtn` will be `LaunchBall.LaunchBallJump()`. When going through this process, remember to open the Text element and change the displayed name to something similar.

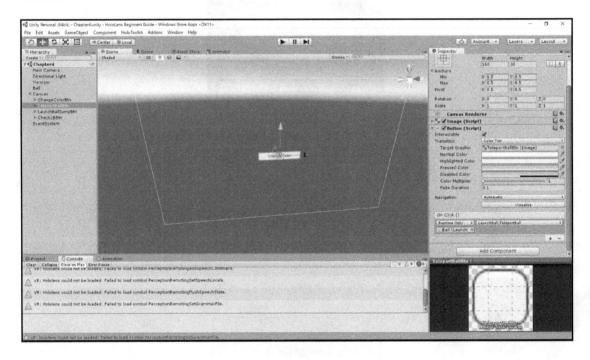

As you can see in the Scene view, we only see one button. Let's fix that with Layout groups. These canvas components automatically and evenly space out UI elements on a canvas. These are the center of how the new Unity UI system can work uniformly from platform to platform:

1. Select the **Canvas** object in the Hierarchy view.
2. From the Inspector, click on the **Add Component** button.
3. Select the **Layout** subcategory.
4. Select **Vertical Layout Group** from the list.

Now we have three buttons taking up the entire view:

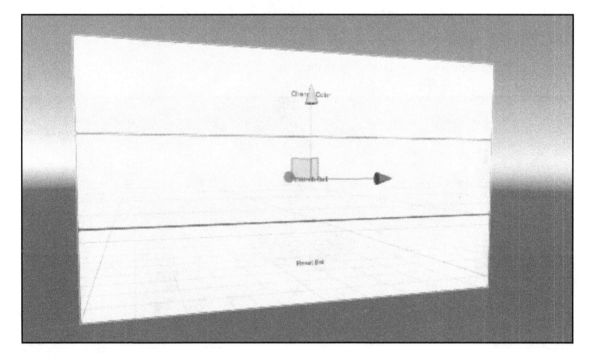

If you look at the **Vertical Layout Group** component that we have just added and open the padding section, you will see four directions we can add padding. Let's make these buttons work better for our needs:

1. In the **Right** input field, change it from 0 to 800:

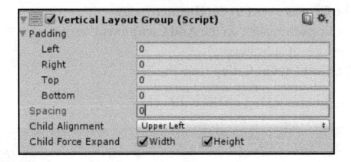

2. In the **Spacing** box, change it from 0 to 100:

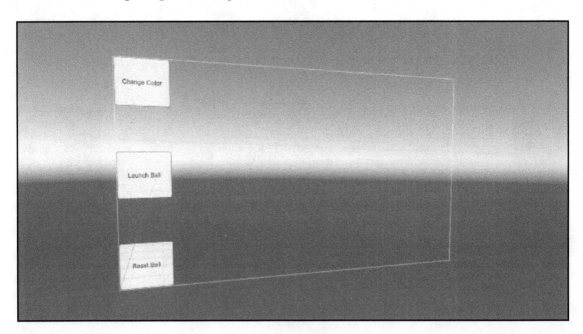

Now we have something that looks very different; it's time to press Play and check it out:

As before, **Change Color** will do exactly that, with the addition of the LaunchBallJump and the ResetBall functions.

HoloLens UI

Now, we will take this same menu system and make it work with the HoloLens. To make this happen, first we will need to make the canvas visible to the user. Then, we need to add a few components of the HoloToolKit so that they function in a manner befitting the holographic best practices.

A visible canvas

Here, we will add a panel object to the Canvas to make the whole thing visible to the user instead of a few floating buttons.

Let's remove the **Vertical Layout Group** from the **Canvas** object by performing the following:

1. Select the **Canvas** in the Hierarchy view.

2. In Inspector, delete the **Vertical Layout Group** component, as follows:

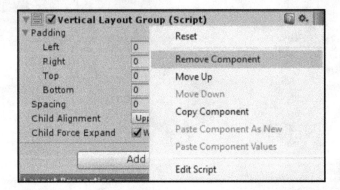

3. Click on the gear in the upper-right corner to get to this menu.
4. Right-click on **Canvas** in the Hierarchy view, slide the mouse pointer over UI, and select **Panel** from the menu:

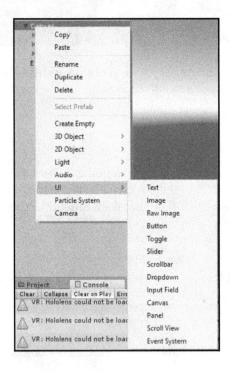

5. Select the three button objects in the Hierarchy view, drag them to the **Panel** object, and release them:

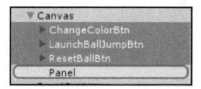

6. Select the **Panel** object and click **Add Component;** select **Layout** and again add a **Vertical Layout**. The setting should match the following screenshot:

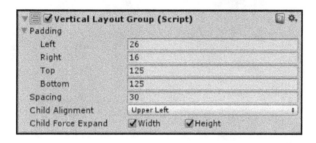

Setting for the Panel Verticle Layout Group

7. Select the Canvas and look at the **Rect Transform**. Change the setting to match this screenshot:

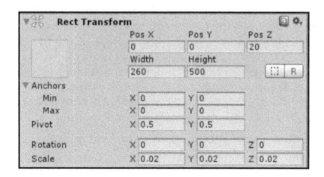

Settings for the Canvas Rect Transform

This is how our canvas should look on completing these steps:

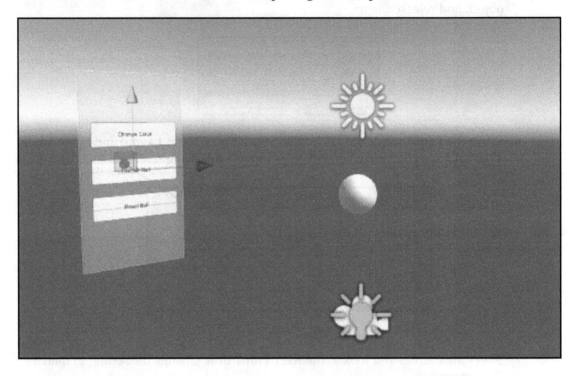

With the visual changes accomplished to work with HoloLens, now it is time to make the technical changes. The canvas has something called a **Render Mode**. Its default setting is **Screen Space-Overlay**, which lays the canvas on top of the screen. We need to change that option to **World Space**. This allows the menu to move around in 3D space.

Now, we will need to add a couple of components from the HoloToolkit:

1. With canvas still selected, click on the **Add Component** button, then on Scripts, on `HoloToolKit.Unity`, and finally select **Tagalong**.
2. Repeat everything in the preceding step, instead adding Billboard.
3. In the Tagalong setting, change the Tagalong distance to 22:
    - **Tagalong**: It's a class that keeps the selected object within view of the user without it locking to their head
    - **Billboard**: This keeps the object facing the user at all times

Now, we need to select the **EventSystem** and click on **Add Component** and type `Holo` in the search field. Select the HoloLens Input Module; this will allow the HoloLens system to interact with the UI elements.

Now it's time to build again

As we did in the last few chapters, we need to build again. Before we do that, we must make sure that this scene is in the build setting; let's carry out the following steps:

1. Press *Ctrl + Shift + B* to open the build settings window.
2. Click on the `Scenes/Chapter3` entry.
3. Press *Delete*.
4. Now, click on the **Add Open Scenes** button.

If you see `Chapter4` appear in the window, you are ready to go. Click on **Build**, and follow the process previously laid out.

Once the build is complete and deployed onto your HoloLens, run `HoloLens Beginners Guide`.

You will initially see the menu and the ball in front of the menu. If you move your head to the left or right, the menu should move as well. Once you can see your menu, look at the buttons; when they are green, you can airtap to activate them.

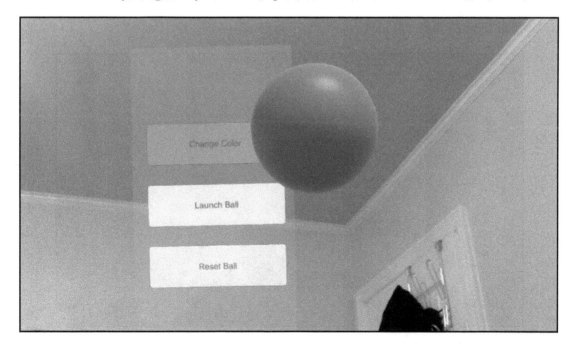

Change Color will obviously change the color of the ball:

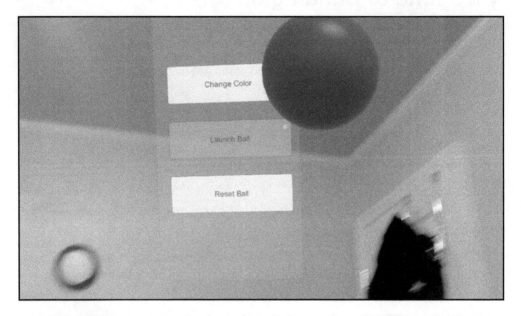

Air tapping **Launch Ball** will move the ball upward:

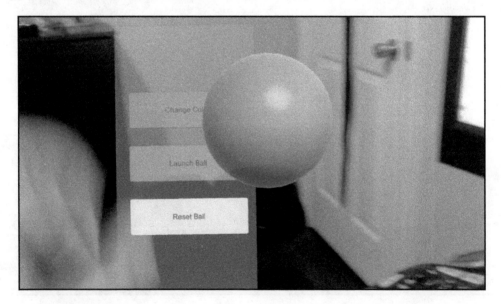

Reset Ball will move the ball back down near the bottom.

Nicely done!

With a basic understanding of Unity UI, we have one more quick item to go over in the topic of User Interfaces.

Any object can be an interface object

We are not limited to the Unity UI to make interfaces in Unity, and to prove that point, we will use the ball object itself to affect the scene. While we have seen this in the past, this lesson is worth repeating:

1. Select the **Ball** object and click on **Add Component**.
2. Select **NewScript** and type `PowerSwitch` into the **NewScript** dialog.
3. Click on **Create** and then on **Add**.

Here is the code for that script file; either type it out or copy and paste it and name the file `PowerSwitch.cs`:

```
using UnityEngine;
using System.Collections;

public class PowerSwitch : MonoBehaviour {

    public GameObject go;

    void OnSelect()
    {

        if(go.activeSelf)
        {
            go.SetActive(false);

        }
        else
        {
            go.SetActive(true);

        }

    }
}
```

This code uses a single public `gameobject` called `go`. This `gameobject` is public, which means that you will see it in the editor.

It then calls `OnSelect`, which is a method called by the HoloToolkit when the cursor and objects are intersecting and an airtap occurs. The code then checks whether the object is currently active (`go.activeSelf`). If it is active, it turns the object off; otherwise, it turns the object on. This simple piece of code would work with any object in the scene, but we will use it on the Canvas object.

First, we will need to pick our Game Object and put it in the **Go** box of **Power Switch (Script)**:

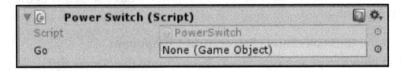

In the Hierarchy view, select the **Canvas** object and drag it to the **Go** object of the **Power Switch (Script)** class seen previously; then, release the mouse:

This is how your **Power Switch (Script)** should look when finished.

That is it. Now, it is time to rebuild and deploy. We have our menu and our ball, as usual:

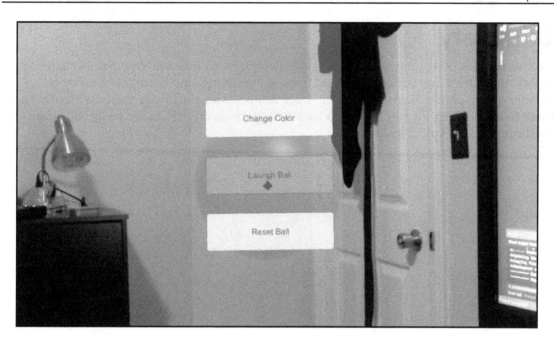

Now what happens when you airtap the ball? The menu disappears, as shown in the following image; tap again, and it comes back.

Summary

I know, this has been a massive chapter. I think it really should be two separate chapters. In reality, there are many books offered on Unity C# scripting, and there could easily be a chapter or two on HoloLens-specific interface design. Somehow, we covered a bit of both of those heavy subjects in one chapter. What I have presented here should be a solid start. Next up, we will explore sound.

5
Now That Is How It Should Sound

Sound is an element of entertainment and interactive software that is often ignored or overlooked by newcomers to the field. As Microsoft often explains, holograms are made up of light and sound. Now, whether this is an even 50/50 is splitting hairs, but sound is a crucial factor.

If you look at film as a medium, sound is one of the primary qualities that gives one a truly immersive experience. Directors such as David Lynch, Alfred Hitchcock, David Fincher, and the Coen brothers have all made films with some of the best sound design ever.

With that in mind, we will not approach recreating Eraserhead in a mixed reality setting, but we do want to think about what we can add to an experience to bring it to life.

In this chapter, we will explore the various ways to produce sound in the HoloLens. We will work with both stereo sound that travels with you and 3D spatialized sound that lives in the space around you. Also, we will layer these types of sounds together to create the illusion of a real environment.

Audio overview

A sound is emitted from a source, for instance a speaker or perhaps a vehicle in a Unity game. Sound is received by a listener in the real world, maybe a user's ears or a microphone.

Since we have two ears, just by listening to sound, we can tell many details about it:

- What was the weight of the object that emitted the sound?
- In what direction did the sound come from?
- Was it hollow or solid?
- What type of environment produced the sound?
- Is it a real or synthesized sound?

These details help us in our daily lives. They allow us to communicate verbally; they let us know if someone is trying to contact us, if our lunch is ready, and often they warn us of danger.

Unity has designed its audio system around these core principles with two primary components: the Audio Source and the Audio Listener.

The Audio Source is a component that is attached to GameObjects. A sound is assigned to the Audio Source, and it is either played on a constant loop or is triggered to play when certain conditions are met.

After the sound is emitted, it is received by the Audio Listener, which then transmits those sounds to the player through their speakers or headphones.

Before we get any deeper into the sound element of things, we need to reveal the project that we are going to start in this chapter and will be working on throughout the rest of the book.

Here is what it is all about

Now that we have made it through the basics in the previous chapters and are getting into the more mid-level subjects, it is time to learn how we will put together all the elements we are learning. I went for a simple idea that incorporated everything we learned; Skeeball was the idea that came to my mind:

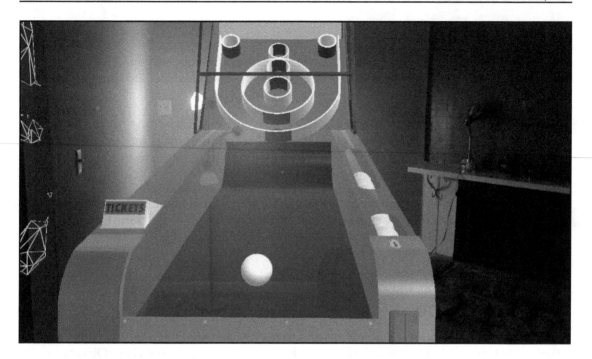

The view in the screenshot is temporary for now; throughout the rest of this book, everything we do will add to this project, or we will learn about something to add to this project.

Here are some of the things we will use for this project:

- Input to control the angle and strength of the ball being thrown
- UI menu system and scorekeeping
- Sounds for scoring, atmosphere, and action
- Spatial mapping for object placement
- World Anchors for persistence and sharing

The art and sound assets, as well as a version of the HoloToolkit, will be stored at `https ://www.packtpub.com/books/content/support`.

Unity audio components

In this section, we will break down Unity's audio components to the degree that we will be needing throughout the project. These components are the Audio Listener, the Audio Source, and the Audio Mixer.

Audio Listener

The **Audio Listener**, simply put, is a component designed to work exactly like a pair of human ears. Its purpose is to hear the sounds in the application world and transmit that to the user, through their speakers.

Much as your head can only be in one place at a time, in Unity, there can only be one active Audio Listener at a time. There may be times when doing sound tricks may require multiple listeners turning on and off. In those cases, if you have more than one Audio Listener active at the same time, you will get an error.

The Audio Listener is a component that is automatically created and attached to the Camera object on its creation. Generally speaking, you will never move this from the Camera object. Also, due to its simplicity of purpose, the Audio Listener component does not have any options to change.

Audio Source

An **Audio Source** is a component that is used to play back sound in the application space. Attached to GameObjects, Audio Sources can be moved along with the GameObjects to create the effect of moving sound. Imagine that a car is coming down your street with its horn held down. If you were standing outside on the street as it went by, you would be able to determine that the horn was in the front of the vehicle. If someone runs their fingernail down a chalkboard--assuming you are not completely freaking out from the sound--you would be able to see and hear that the sound was coming from where the fingernail touches the chalkboard. The sound sources have an obvious point of origin.

The same applies to the **Audio Source** component. In a game, every single sound would have an associated **Audio Source**. Often, the sources are attached to the objects emitting the sounds. In the fingernail and chalkboard example, the **Audio Source** will be connected to the finger. In the car horn example, the **Audio Source** component is attached to the horn itself.

Unlike the Audio Listener component, this component has many changeable parameters as you can see in the following screenshot; some of these parameters are options such as **Loop**, **Pitch**, or **Spatial Blend**:

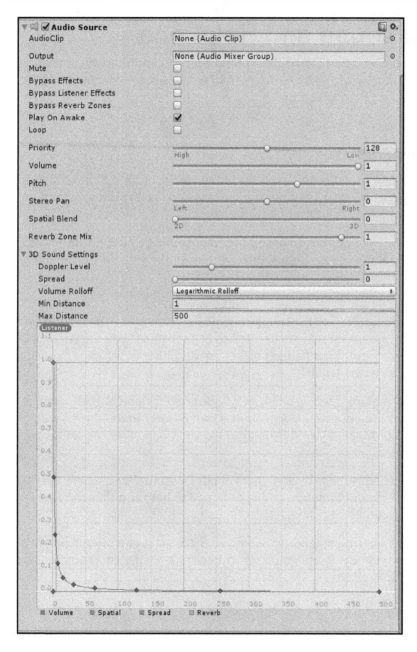

We will get into the options that we need in just a minute, but, for now, we need to get some details about spatial sound.

Spatial sound and HoloLens

In this section, we will first learn what spatial sound is and then about the types of sounds we will use in our project. From there, we will create a sound landscape to create an atmosphere for our Skeeball game.

Spatial sound

Simply put, spatial sound is how we hear in the world. Although most of us are never quite aware of it, sounds tell us a lot about the space we are in. We interpret and incorporate this information quickly without ever being aware of it.

Objects emit sounds in the world around us, and sounds reflect off the surfaces and give us information about the space. For instance, you most likely could tell the difference between a carpeted and a hardwood floor in a space without seeing it. You could likely tell whether a room has a high vaulted ceiling or a much lower drop ceiling.

Our brain can interpret even the smallest details in the sound. The amount of time between a sound reaching your left ear versus your right ear can tell you tons of details about your space; subtle noise and shifts that get picked up and filtered through those sounds in the movement tell us other details.

One of these important filters is what we call **Sound Occlusion**. If an alarm is going off two rooms away, through multiple doors, as you move closer to the source with fewer obstacles occluding, or filtering, the sound from your ears, not only does the sound gets louder, but it also sounds fuller.

For HoloLens, Microsoft has created the **MS HRTF Spatializer**, where **HRFT** stands for **Head-Related Transfer Function** and is designed to help simulate the elements of real-world spatial sound.

With that very loose understanding behind us, because if you are reading this you likely do not want to learn to be a sound engineer yourself, we need to start a new scene and set up our MS HRTF Spatializer.

As before, open the `Chapter2` scene, delete the `Platform`, `Hello`, and `World` objects from the Hierarchy and save it as `Chapter 5`.

We now need to go to our audio setting and change the spatializer to the MS HRTF Spatializer, as follows:

1. Click on the **Edit** option on the main menu. Move down to **Project Settings** and click on the **Audio** option:

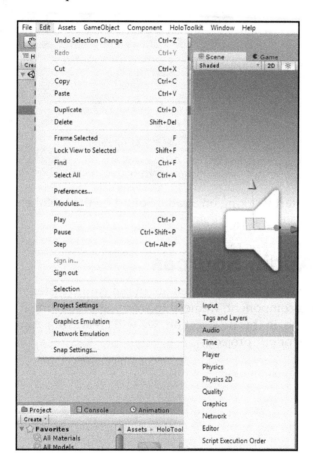

2. In the Inspector, look for the Spatializer plugin, click on **None**, and select the **MS HRTF Spatializer**:

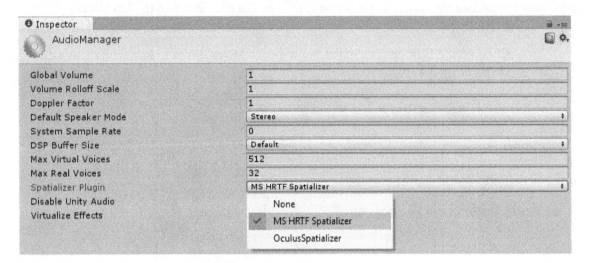

Now, we are ready to start working on Spatial Sound on the HoloLens.

Setting up Audio Sources

Setting up Audio Sources previously talked about the Audio Listener being part of the camera, so that is not a component, we need to worry about setting it up. Again no parameters to change. So, in this next section, we will create four Audio Sources to build the ambiance of an arcade for our project.

The Audio Sources will be at four different corners of the space, so we can create a layered soundscape:

1. In the Hierarchy panel, click on the **Create** button, click on **Audio,** and then click on **Audio Source**:

2. Rename this Audio Source **Layer 1** and change its position information to x = 2, y = 0, and z = 2:

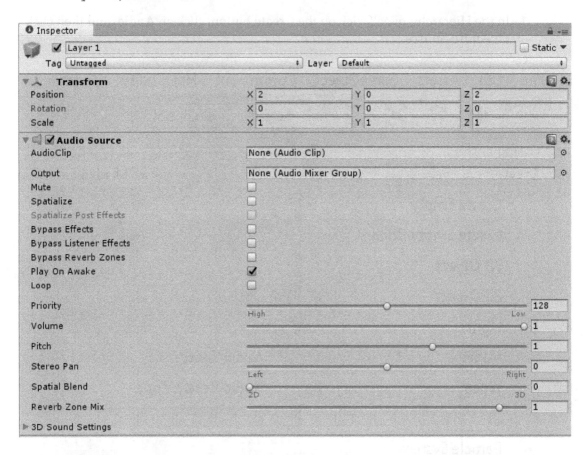

3. Now, with the **Layer 1** object selected and the Hierarchy view active, press the *Ctrl + D* key three times to create three copies of this layer. Name these new copies **Layer 2**, **Layer 3**, and **Layer 4**.

4. Set the positions of these new layers according to these positions:

```
Layer 2: X= -2, Y = 0, Z = 2
Layer 3: X = 2, Y = 0, Z = -2
Layer4: X= - 2, Y = 0, Z = -2
```

5. When you are finished, your view should look similar to this:

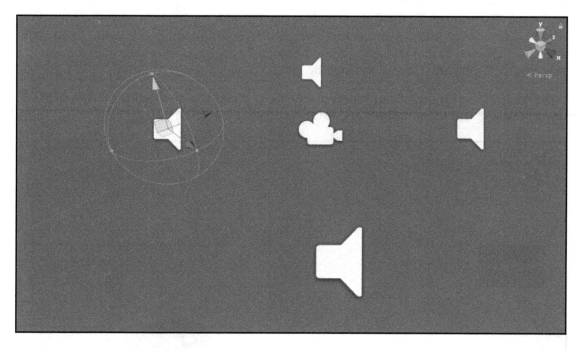

There should be a camera with four Audio Sources in the shape of a square.

Now, we just need some sounds to fill the space in; that is what we will be handling in the next section.

Building a soundscape

For the Skeeball-MR project, we want our sounds to recreate the environment that we are going to place our Skeeball machine in--an arcade. To recreate this type of atmosphere, we will need to break down what sounds you might hear in an arcade:

- Skeeball machine
- Pinball machines
- Video games
- People talking and laughing
- Coins being put into the machines

Finding sounds

So, one obvious way to get the sounds that we need for this project is to grab a handheld recorder, go to an arcade (if you can find one), and record the sounds manually. The benefit in doing it this way is that you can control the sounds you get to some degree and make sure that the layers are what we are looking for.

I will not be going through that process in this book. Instead, we will use a website called www.freesound.org to hunt down and find sounds that will fit our needs:

First, we will need to go to www.freesounds.org in our web browser. Once there, we need to create an account by clicking on the **Register** button in the top-right corner.

Once our account is created, we need to log in. We can't download any sounds unless all of this is done.

Now, we are ready to do some searching for sounds by typing the word arcade into the search bar and pressing *Enter*--you should see a list that looks similar to this; of course, your results may vary:

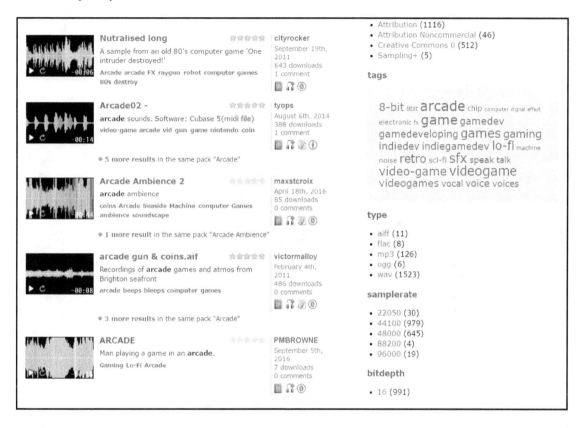

Now, go through and listen to some of the sounds and pick out the ones that you like. If you would rather, I will list the ones I ended up choosing:

- Arcade, Mr. mayo
- Penny Arcade, nlm
- Arcade Machine, Harry Peaks
- Trevor Webb Arcade Ambience, bleachbear

Although it is outside the scope of this book, if you have the means, I would highly recommend that you convert these sounds to MP3. These are much smaller and will save you a lot of time in the compiling and testing phases.

Importing our sounds into Unity

We will now import the sounds in either MP3 or wave format into our project.

As we have done before, we will need to create a Sounds folder in the **Project** panel. Once we have that, we are ready to begin importing:

1. In the **Project** panel, right-click on the newly created Sounds folder and select **Import New Asset**:

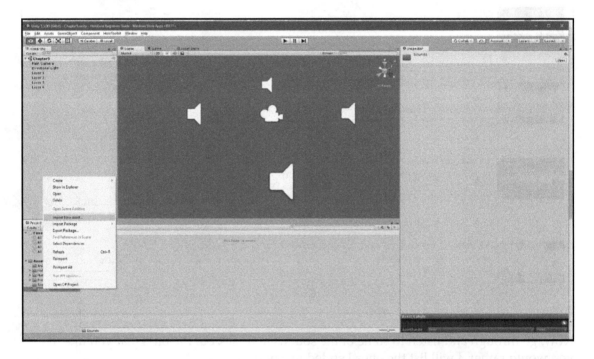

2. When you click on **Import New Asset**, an explorer window will open. Navigate to the directory where you stored your downloaded sound files (most likely your `Downloads` folder) and select the first one:

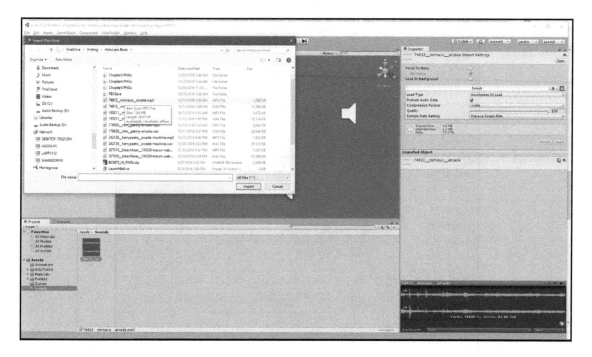

3. Click on **Import**.

Once the sound file is imported, repeat steps 1-3 for the other three files.

Now, we are ready to assign sounds to our Audio Sources. Before we do so, let's pull that Audio Source component and go over some of the options we will be looking at:

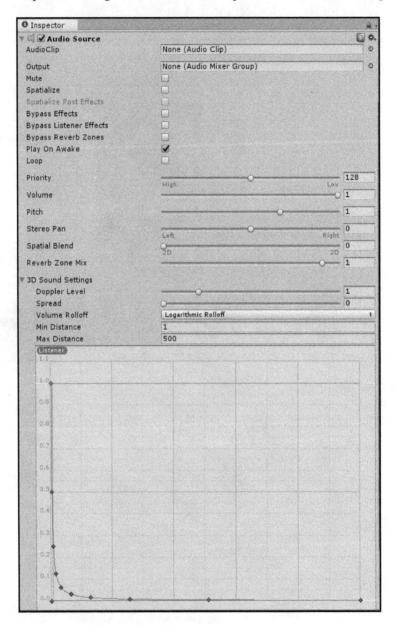

Audio Source options

The Audio Source has a lot of options, but don't get intimidated by them. Also, if you pay close attention, you will note that this version of the Audio Source looks a little different than the one mentioned previously in the chapter; that is due to the MS HRTF Spatializer plugin being used.

Now, let's take a look at the options we need to worry about for this chapter:

- **AudioClip**: This will be where our sound clip goes.
- **Spatialize**: This one is probably self-explanatory at this point, but just in case, this will force the sound we use to be spatialized for the MS HRTF plugin.
- **Play On Awake**: If this is selected, this will start playing as soon as it loads. If it is not selected, you will have to trigger this sound using a script.
- **Loop**: This forces the sound to start again from the beginning when it ends in an infinite loop.
- **Volume**: This is a volume slider ranging from 0.0 to 1.0.
- **Spatial Blend**: This is a slider bar ranging from 2D to 3D. We will stick to the 3D option for now.

For our purpose, these will be the options we use; on that note, let's begin.

Using our sounds

We will now go through the steps of getting one of our sounds into **Layer 1** and then setting all the necessary options to get our arcade atmosphere working:

1. In Hierarchy view, make sure that **Layer 1** is selected. In the **Inspector**, click on the tiny donut on the far-right side of the **AudioClip** input field:

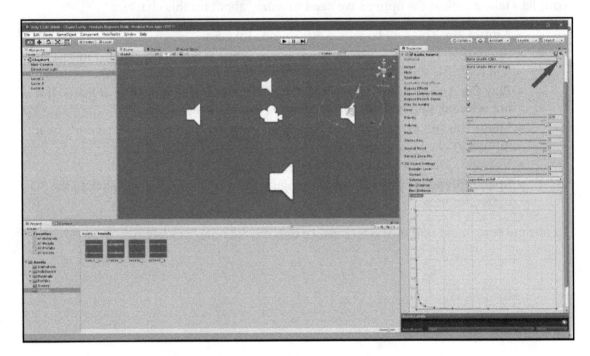

2. A window labeled **Select Audio Clip** will appear. This lists all of the sounds we
   have available for us to choose from; select our first imported sound from the list:

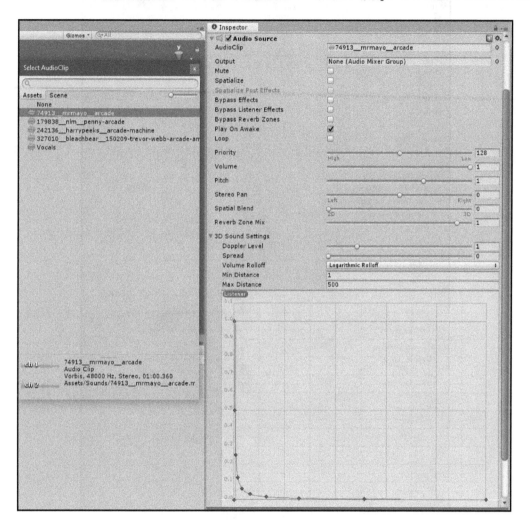

3. Now, in the Inspector, set the following options:
   - **Spatialize**: Checked
   - **Play On Awake**: Checked
   - **Loop**: Checked
   - **Spatial Blend**: 1 (fully 3D)

This is shown in the following screenshot:

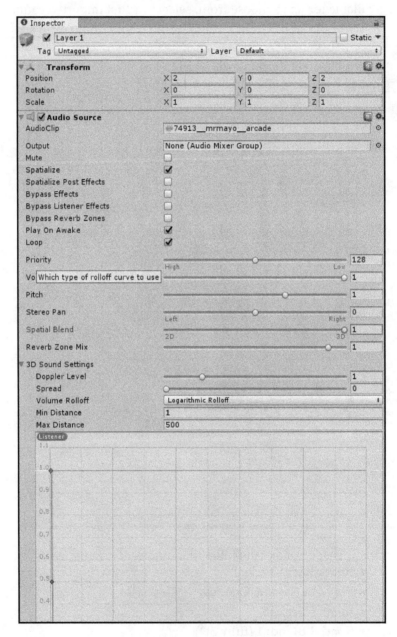

That is it; now, repeat the exact process for Layers 2–4. Once we are done, we will compile and test out our atmosphere.

Let's listen to our work

I won't walk you through the build process again. But I would remind you to make sure that you have the `Chapter 5` scene added to your **Scenes in Build** list.

Alright, once everything is built, compiled, and deployed, load it up on your HoloLens and walk around. You should hear the various collections of sounds getting louder as you move from one area to the other.

One experiment you might want to try, especially if you are working with limited space, is to change the positions of the Audio Sources from a 2-meter square to a 1-meter square.

Summary

In this chapter, you learned about sound and its effect on the overall experience. We looked at the Unity-specific approach to sound and the MS HRTF Spatializer. You learned how to search for some sounds to use for our tests and how to implement them.

6
Not So Blank Spaces

In this chapter, we will start filling up our space. We will be talking about Spatial Mapping, an essential element in creating a mixed reality experience. We will begin adding new elements to the sounds we created in the preceding chapter and start filling out our Skeeball game. Once we create our input manager and spatial map, we will learn how to place our Skeeball machine in the play space.

We will set up a voice command and text that instruct the user what to say.

Spatial Mapping

When working with the HoloLens flavor of mixed reality, the very element that makes it mixed reality is that the holograms understand where your walls, ceiling, and floor are. They can, if coded to do so, even distinguish between a chair and a table. They can hide behind walls or in other rooms. They can even physically react to surfaces in simulated ways, that appear authentic.

This illusion is created primarily with Spatial Mapping, a mesh representation of your surroundings. This is the main reason that your HoloLens has all those sensors. So, to say we are in the heart of the process would be a fair assessment.

Occlusion is what allows holograms to be hidden. The purpose of occlusion is to tell the HoloLens, based on the spatial map, when to draw a hologram and when it is hidden or occluded from view.

As we will see in this chapter, the spatial map also simplifies object placement, using the various surfaces as a point of reference.

Let's get into this

Here, we will do some initial setup so that we can get into this chapter. After ensuring that we are synced up with the preceding chapter's scene file, we will bring in a few necessary Game Objects in the form of the input manager, basic cursor, and HoloLens camera. Then, we will import some new assets into Unity.

If you followed the tutorials in `Chapter 5`, *Now That Is How It Should Sound*, this is roughly what your Unity screen should look like; if that is the case, then follow the pattern we have used in the previous chapters and save this scene as `Chapter6.unity`.

This will be our starting point:

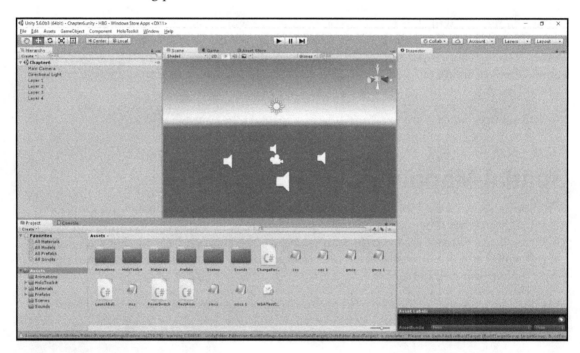

All right, now for some quick clean up:

1. Right-click in your **Assets** window and select **Create**. Click on folder and name that folder `Scripts`:

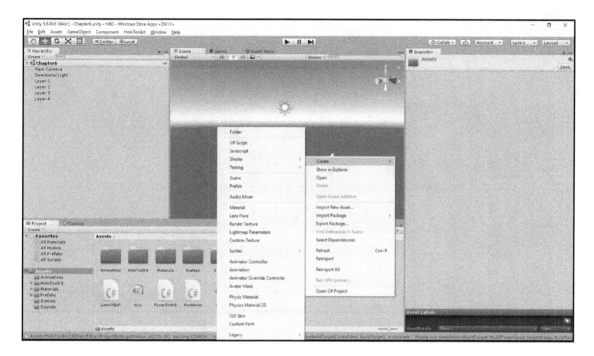

2. Select each script file that is in the root `Assets` folder and drag it to the `Scripts` folder; this is what your Unity window should look like when this is done:

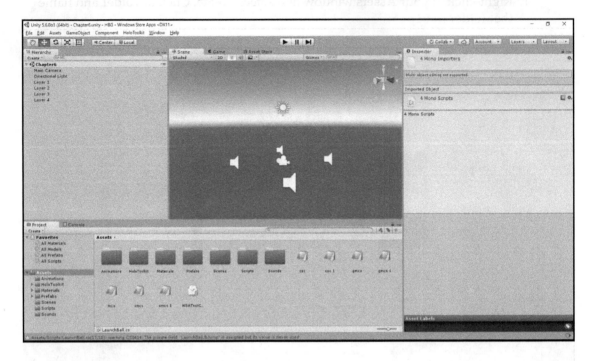

So, before we can really get into the Spatial Mapping, we will need to set up our input manager and cursor, like we did in the past. So, let's perform the following steps:

1. Drill into the **HoloToolkit** | **Input** | **Prefabs** directory in your Project View:

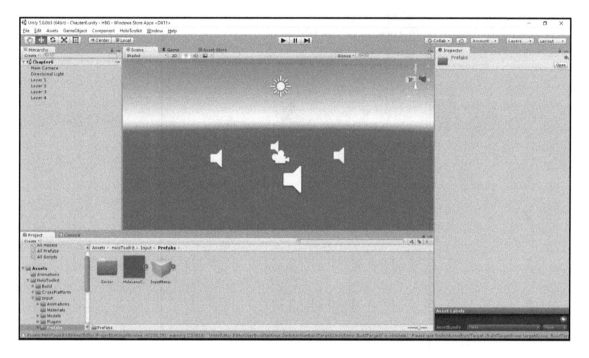

2. Select both the `InputManager` and the `HoloLensCamera` prefabs and drag them to our Hierarchy view.
3. Delete the `MainCamera` object in the Hierarchy view.
4. Now, double-click on the `Cursor` folder in the Assets view.
5. Drag **BasicCursor** in the Hierarchy view.

3. When you have completed these steps, your Hierarchy view should look like this:

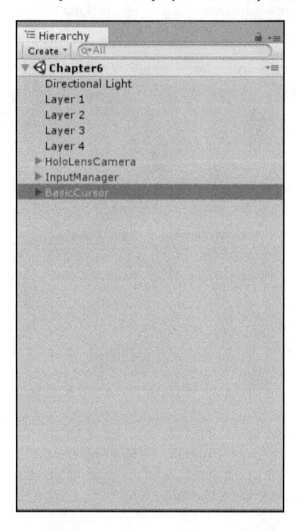

So, for the next section, we will import our Skeeball machine and a spatial map to work with inside Unity. This will dramatically speed up the testing process.

Importing the essentials

Now, ensuring that you have the `Chapter6downloads.zip` file, extract that file to somewhere you can easily reach; this file should contain `skeeballmachine.unity` and `spatialmapping.unity`:

1. Click on **Assets** on the top menu and select **Import Package** | **Custom Package...**:

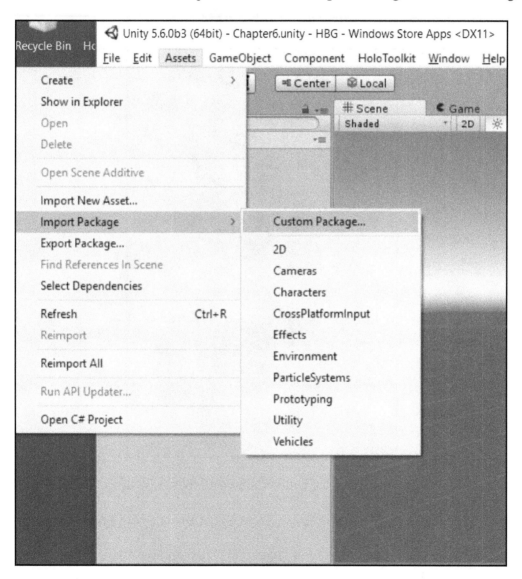

2. Find and select `skeeballmachine.unitypackage`. The **Import Unity Package** window will open up and will look like this:

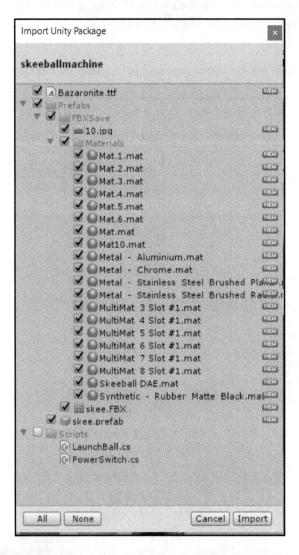

3. Click on the **Import** button. Unity will pull all those files in and place them where they need to go.
4. Repeat steps 1 to 3 for the `spatialmapping.unitypackage` file.

Now, we have the important parts of this chapter in Unity, and we are ready to go.

Spatial Mapping in practice

Here, we will put the Spatial Mapping prefab into our application and set up the Spatial Mapping model that we imported in the preceding section. This will allow us to see Spatial Mapping at work inside the Unity Editor without having to go back and forth to the HoloLens.

In your Project View, go to the **HoloToolkit** | **Spatial Mapping** | **Prefabs** directory and click on the **Spatial Mapping** prefab and drag it to the Hierarchy view and release it.

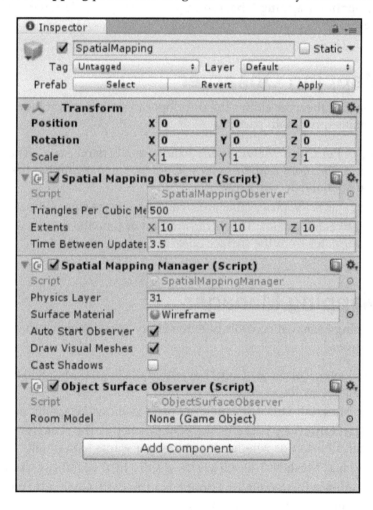

Spatial Mapping can be broken down into two primary parts:

- **Spatial Surface Observer**: This component allows us access to the Spatial Mapping surface information created by the HoloLens sensor array.
- **Spatial Surface**: The surface information or mesh data that is created by the sensor array on the HoloLens. Simply put, this is a collection of all the surfaces that can be seen by the HoloLens, converted into triangles.

If you look at the Inspector now, you should see a Game Object with three main components: the **Spatial Mapping Observer**, **Spatial Mapping Manager**, and **Object Surface Observer**.

Spatial Mapping Observer

The **Spatial Mapping Observer** allows the developer to set how often the spatial map is updated and contains three main parts:

- **Triangles Per Cubic Meter**: This is exactly as the name states. The higher this number is, the more triangles you will get, but also the higher the performance hit your spatial map will cause.
- **Extents**: This is the observable area from the camera's position.
- **Time Between Updates**: This is the amount of time the system waits for before it accepts updates from the surface observer.

Spatial Mapping Manager

The **Spatial Mapping Manager** controls how the Unity application handles surface data from multiple sources.

- **Physics Layer**: This is the Unity Layer that the Spatial Map will be set to automatically by the system.
- **Surface Material**: This is the material used to show the spatial map.
- **Auto Start Observer**: This tells the system whether the observer should automatically start or whether the developer wants to manually control that.
- **Draw Visual Meshes**: This allows the user to turn visibility on or off.
- **Cast Shadows**: By default, this option is turned off. Generally, you do not need your spatial map casting shadows, as it already does that naturally.

Object Surface Observer

Finally, we have the **Object Surface Observer**. This is simply a solution to allow Unity users to have a spatial map that they can use inside the editor.

The Game Object that is a mesh of the space you want to test in is called the **Room Model**.

Let's take a quick minute to go ahead and put the spatial map that we imported earlier into the **Object Surface Observer**:

1. Click on the root `Prefabs` folder.
2. Click and drag the Spatial Mapping model to the Room Model field, as follows:

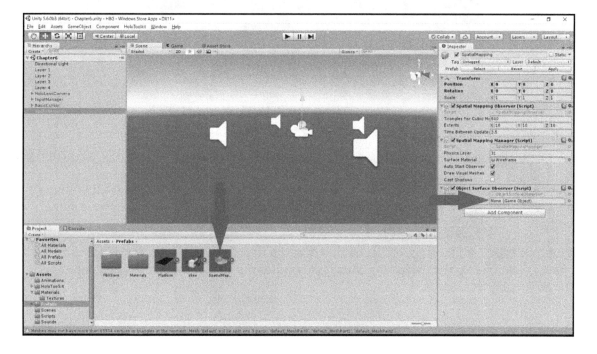

3. Now, drop it as shown here:

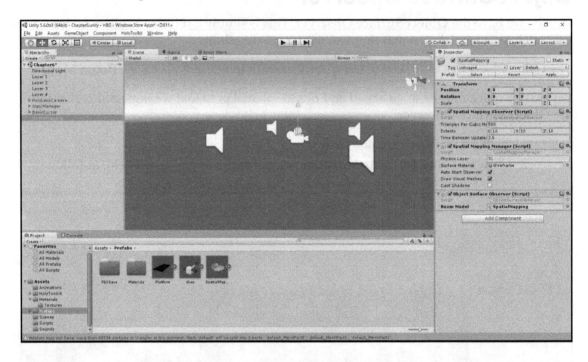

Now, if you click on the play button to test out our application, you should see this spatial map mesh. If you are wondering, yes this is my apartment. You can use the mouse along with the *W*, *A*, *S*, and *D* keys to move around and see the mesh.

You could also build, compile, and deploy this app to your HoloLens now to see your spatial map. The **Spatial Mapping Manager** handles the spatial map to be used based on the device that is running it.

It should be noted that the mesh is rather ugly at the moment. Mesh processing, such as gap closing, mesh smoothing, or even adding fancy shaders, is an option, but can be an expensive option for the HoloLens processors. As a result, it is not handled automatically. Also, since we do not need a pretty spatial map for our project, we will not address it in this book.

Now that we have the spatial map in and working, it is time to move on to creating our application manager and learning a little about design patterns.

Our new Skeeball machine

So, who would not love a Skeeball machine in their living room? Well, aside from the sheer space it would take up, that is. Those things are big! Well, when we are done with this book, we will mostly have a working Skeeball machine that does not take up the entire living room. It does not even require being put away afterward.

In this section, we will create our application manager to handle everything that we need going on in the scene. We will bring the Skeeball machine into our scene and set it up so that it can be placed on the spatial map.

Application management

This is not the first time we have used a manager object. However, this one will do a bit more than what we did in the past. It will also give me an opportunity to talk a bit about programming design patterns.

Design patterns

A design pattern is a software solution that can be used over and over due to its ability to fix a common problem. There are a few different types of design patterns, such as creation, behavioral, and structural. Knowing and understanding a variety of design patterns can not only dramatically increase the speed at which you can code but also help in keeping your code readable for others who may have to jump into it.

This is a subject that is covered already by many books and is well outside the scope of this book. I bring it up because firstly we will be using one of the more popular design patterns: the **Singleton**, and secondly because I really wish someone had broached the design pattern subject a long time before they did.

There can be only one

The primary point of the singleton pattern is to instantiate a single object of a specific class. The instanced object will check whether it would create a conflict when another exists and destroy itself if it does. It is notable that many of the classes that we are working with from the HoloToolkit are singletons. The input manager and the Spatial Mapping Manager are perfect examples of singletons that are active in our project right this moment.

The reason for its popularity and criticism comes down to how simple it is to understand and get working with. This simplicity means that many people use it and often in places where another pattern would work better. Often, games use a singleton pattern by creating a single managing system that runs everything else; that is exactly what we will do in this game.

Creating our application manager

Here, we will create an empty Game Object and attach a script to that object. We will add our Skeeball machine, and then we will set up our app manager to handle all the assets we currently have in place. Let's perform the following steps to do this:

1. Ensure that you have nothing selected in the Hierarchy view. Click on the **Create** button just under the word Hierarchy and then click on **Create Empty**:

2. In the Inspector, name that Game Object **AppManager**.

3. Now, in the Project View, select **Assets | Prefabs directory**. Select the **skee** prefab and drag it under the `AppManager` object in the Hierarchy view:

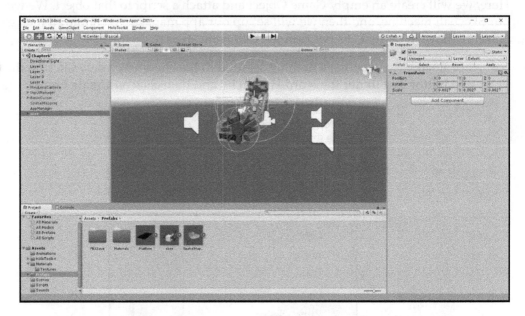

4. With the **skee** object selected, select the enable check mark next to the object name to disable it:

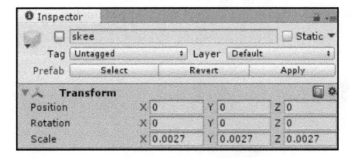

5. Click on the **Apply** button in the **Inspector**:

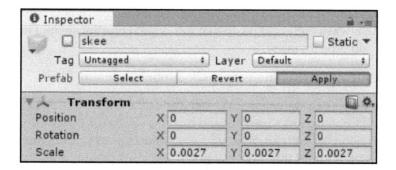

6. Now, in the Project View, go to the `Scripts` folder, and right-click on the open space. Click on **Create** and then on C# **Script**:

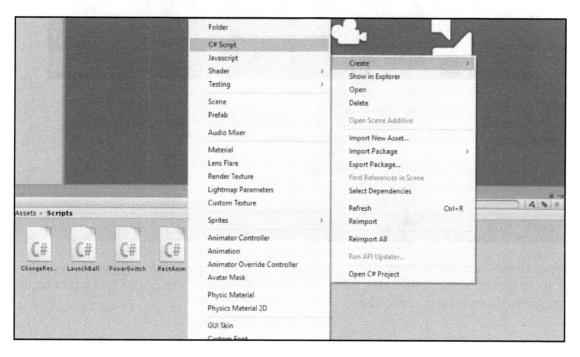

7. Name this file `ApplicationManager` (case matters).

The ApplicationManager code

Inside the `Chapter6Downloads.zip` file, you will find the `ApplicationManager.cs` file. Of course, you can always copy and paste that into Visual Studio; again, I highly recommend that you type it yourself.

Here, we will go through each section and walk through the entire file.

First up, we have the `Using` statements. We have added a few: `HoloToolkit.Unity`, `HoloToolkit.Unity.SpatialMapping`, and `HoloToolkit.Unity.InputModule`. As I had mentioned previously, both `SpatialMapping` and `InputManager` are singletons and could not be accessed without these statements:

```
using System;
using System.Collections;
using System.Collections.Generic;
using UnityEngine;
using HoloToolkit.Unity;
using HoloToolkit.Unity.SpatialMapping;
using HoloToolkit.Unity.InputModule;
```

Here is where we make our own singleton out of the application manager. `HoloToolkit.Unity` has a declaration of Singleton instead of having to create one ourselves.

Of course, we have our input interfaces here, `IInputClickHandler` and `ISpeechHandler`:

```
public class ApplicationManager : Singleton<ApplicationManager> ,IInputClickHandler, ISpeechHandler
```

Next up, we have our variable declarations. We have five references to objects where we want to control whether they are enabled or disabled, and the three `bool` that I am using as simple switches for this application:

```
public GameObject soundLayer1;
public GameObject soundLayer2;
public GameObject soundLayer3;
public GameObject soundLayer4;

public GameObject skeeballmachine;

public bool spatialMapSet = false;
public bool skeeBallMachinePlacementSet = false;
public bool toInit = true;
```

Here is our start event and our first call to another singleton object--note `InputManager.Instance` as a sign of that.

Here, we are setting the `InputManager` to a **modal mode** so that when the user finishes scanning the room they can airtap or say done to move to the next part:

```
void Start () {

        InputManager.Instance.PushModalInputHandler(this.gameObject);

}
```

Speaking of parts, here we have our `Update` function, which is called by every frame. Here, we have an `if` statement looking at the `spatialMapSet` bool, which defaults to false:

```
// Update is called once per frame
void Update () {
    if (spatialMapSet)
    {
        skeeballmachine.SetActive(true);
        if (toInit)
        {
            //this is the first time through only
            skeeballmachine.transform.position = Camera.main.transform.position;
            skeeballmachine.transform.position += new Vector3(skeeballmachine.transform.position.x, -1.25f, 3.0f);
            //we have finished the initiallization of the skeeball machine set the toInit flag to false
            toInit = false;
        }
    }
}
```

If the statement becomes true (which happens after the user airtaps or says done), the Skeeball machine is set to active. Now, if this is the first time we have been through this part of the code, another `If` statement happens to check whether it needs to initialize Skeeball machine's position.

By default, the answer is `yes`, and so it gets the position of the camera and sets the Skeeball machine there and then moved it to `3.0f` or 3 meters in front of and down `1.25f`.

Once we are done positioning the Skeeball machine, we will set the `toInit` to `false` so that we are not continually positioning it.

If `spatialMapSet` is not true, the `skeeBallMachine` stays disabled:

```
else
{
        skeeballmachine.SetActive(false);
}
```

If the `skeeBallMachinePlacementSet` is `true`, then turn all of your sounds on; otherwise, they should be off. This is set when the user places the machine on the spatial map:

```
if (skeeBallMachinePlacementSet)
{
        soundLayer1.SetActive(true);
        soundLayer2.SetActive(true);
        soundLayer3.SetActive(true);
        soundLayer4.SetActive(true);
}
else
{
        soundLayer1.SetActive(false);
        soundLayer2.SetActive(false);
        soundLayer3.SetActive(false);
        soundLayer4.SetActive(false);
}
}
```

Here, we have our illustrious input interface implementation.

If `OnInputClicked` gets called, it calls the `SetSpatialMap` function, as follows. If the word done is recognized, the exact same thing happens. However, it is a slightly different version of that function. You will note that `eventData` is passed to the function and then to the `SetSpatialMap()`; this event data is the word that the **Keyword Manager** recognized:

```
public void OnInputClicked(InputClickedEventData eventData)
{

    SetSpatialMap();

}

public void OnSpeechKeywordRecognized(SpeechKeywordRecognizedEventData eventData)
{
    switch (eventData.RecognizedText.ToLower())
    {

        case "done":
            SetSpatialMap();
            break;

    }

}
```

The `SetSpatialMap` function sets `spatialMapSet` to `true`. Then, we turn off drawing the spatial map mesh and remove the `ModalInputHandler` with a pop.

The second version of the function calls the first if the word that was recognized is *done*:

```
void SetSpatialMap()
{

    spatialMapSet = true;
    SpatialMappingManager.Instance.DrawVisualMeshes = false;
    InputManager.Instance.PopModalInputHandler();

}

public void SetSpatialMap(string command)
{

    switch (command.ToLower())
    {

        case "done":
            SetSpatialMap();
            break;

    }

}
```

That is all there is for us to do to our application manager currently. It is simple right now. It will become a bit more complex as the rest of the chapters come to pass.

Attaching our application manager and wiring it up

Now, we need to attach our script to the `AppManager` object and connect all the objects that follow:

1. With `AppManager` selected, click and drag the `ApplicationManager.cs` file to the Inspector window and drop it:

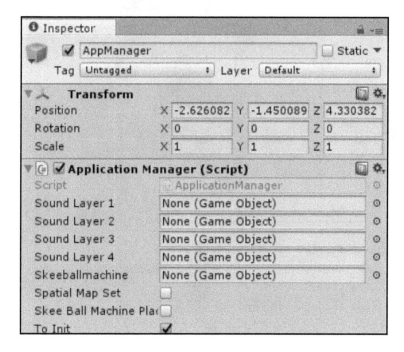

You will notice that we have a bunch of empty Game Object slots; let's fix that.

2. With `AppManager` selected and displayed in the Inspector, click on the lock at the top of the Inspector; this will make the `AppManager` remain the object in Inspector no matter what you click in the Hierarchy or Project views.

3. Selecting the object **Layer 1** in the Hierarchy view, drag it to the **Sound Layer 1** slot:

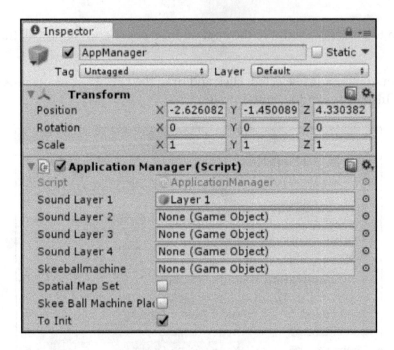

4. Repeat step 3 for layer 2, layer 3, and layer 4.
5. Now, drag the skee object to the `Skeeballmachine` slot of the `AppManager` object.
6. Now, you can click on the lock again to unlock it.

When you finish these steps, you should have an `AppManager` object that looks like this; note that this object is an unseen object, so position does not matter:

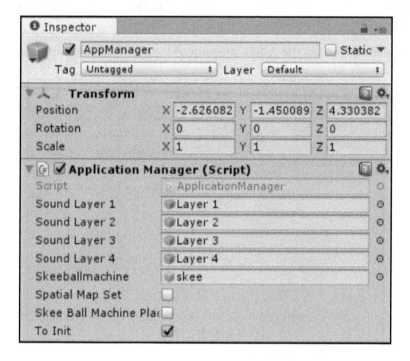

So let it be written... so let it be done...

Now, we will need to set up our **Keyword Manager** so that we can wire in our voice command; this can be accomplished in just a few simple steps:

1. We need to click on the **Add Component** button under our application manager:

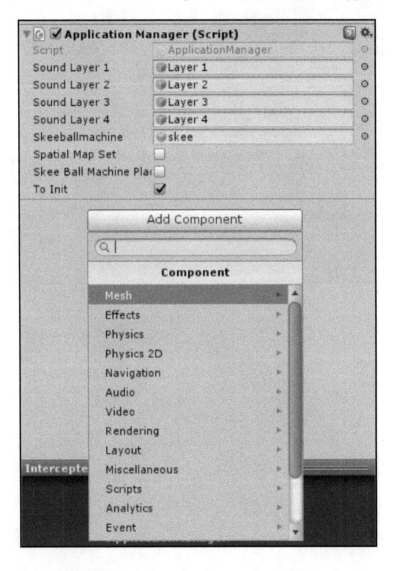

2. Type `Keyword` into the search box and select **Keyword Manager**:

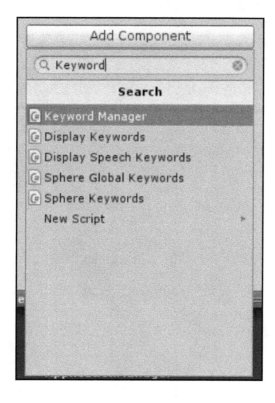

3. In the **Keyword Manager**, expand the **Keywords and Responses** option and replace the 0 with a 1:

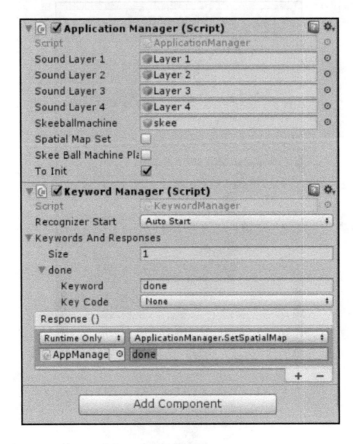

4. In the element 0 keyword put the word done.
5. In the **Response** section, click on the plus symbol.
6. Drag the AppManager object to the new slot that has just appeared under Response.
7. Now, click on **No Function**, select **ApplicationManager**, and then select **SetSpatialMap** (string).
8. Then, type done in the empty box.

When you are done, this is what your new **Keyword Manager** should look like.

The home stretch

For the final part of this chapter, we will set up our `PlaceSkeeBallMachine` class, which will allow us to airtap the collider of the Skeeball machine. It will then move with our view until we find a good spot for it; airtap again and everything start from the beginning.

I have included a copy of the `PlaceSkeeBallMachine` script file in the `Chapter6Downloads.Zip` file. This is a heavily modified version of the `TapToPlace` script that comes with the HoloToolkit. Of course, as usual I recommend that you type it out. Now, let me add you do not have to type all the comments unless you want to. I recommend that you put in comments that help you keep up with how it works, in your head. Normally, comments are designed for people who already know how to write code, not people learning to code. Jargon, while useful for the future, can take some time wrapping your head around, and therefore it slows down the learning process. Word it how it makes sense to you.

Now, we will attach the script file to the appropriate object and set it up:

1. Expand the **skee** object and locate the **TapToPlaceCollider**. Select it to see it in the Inspector:

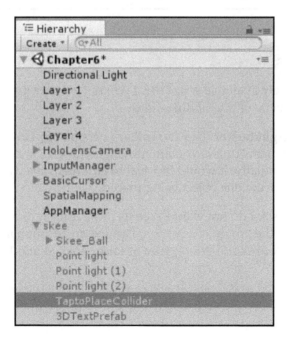

2. Select the `PlaceSkeeBallMachine.cs` file in the Assets view, drag it to the `TaptoPlaceCollider` object, and drop it:

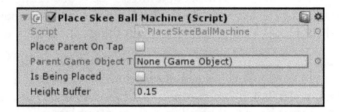

3. Select the `skee` object in the Hierarchy view, and without releasing the mouse button, drag it to the **Parent Game Object Tap** field. Then, select the **Place Parent On Tap** box:

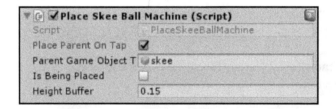

Code matters

So, `TapToPlace` is a freely available script file. I will not go over the entire script; however, I do want to point out some of my modifications.

For one, I added the **height buffer**. The TapToPlace version of placement does not really allow for vertical adjustments unless you are moving up a wall, and I like to have some height adjustments. Eventually, it would be ideal to add this via a dynamic process; but in this project, we only have the one object being placed.

After the spatial map is set, I do not want to see its mesh appear except when placing the Skeeball machine. So, in the `OnInputClicked`, I added an additional bool that I wanted a hard set either the `DrawVisualMeshes` is true or false. Also, at line 110, you can see another simple use of a Singleton: `ApplicationManager.Instance.skeeBallMachinePlacementSet = true;` this will turn on the sounds.

After that, we immediately turn the `DrawVisualMeshes` to `false`. Those are really all the important changes.

Let us enjoy our hard work

Now, it is time to do a run through.

If you click on the play button, you should see the spatial map appear. If you navigate around, you can find my living room--it is a large room with a 45-degree corner and a couch:

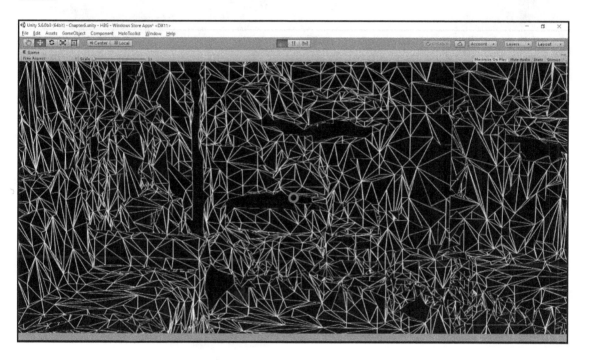

Click on this room somewhere or say `Done` and the mesh should disappear and the Skeeball machine will appear:

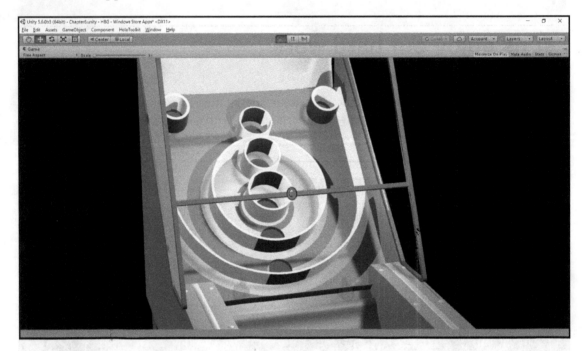

Click on the Skeeball machine and it will begin moving with your cursor, and the mesh will reappear:

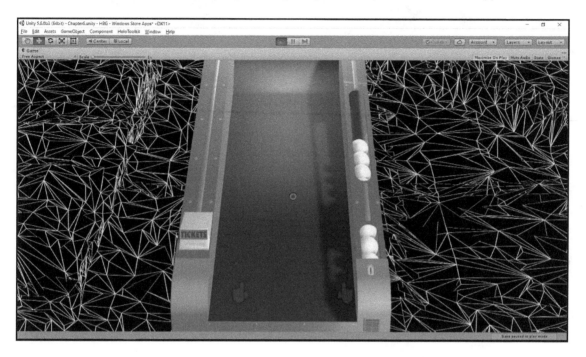

Once you airtap again, the mesh will disappear and the sounds will be activated.

Congrats on making it this far.

Summary

In this chapter, we learned about Spatial Mapping, what its purpose is, how it works, and how to get it working inside our own applications. We touched upon design patterns a bit in the context of what we are working with.

We pushed much farther into the game we started working on in the previous chapter. We analyzed a lot of the code we were using in the process. We used ideas from the previous chapters, further reinforcing the knowledge gained.

7
The Tools of the Trade

In this chapter, we will look into the idea of persistence, or the ability for a hologram to reappear in the same spot every time we open our application. We will learn to use **World Anchors**, the **World Anchors Manager**, and the **World Anchor Store** and see how they facilitate persistence.

While World Anchors are not really complex, we will learn about some of my trials and errors that occured in the process. Then, we will spend some time going over the best practices laid out by Microsoft.

We will then continue fleshing out our application by adding a scoreboard and a few in-game menu options, such as start and reset options. In the process, we will also build a simple debug information window ourselves. This is so that we can test and determine what is going right and what is going wrong.

Persistence

Defined as *continuing to exist or endure over a prolonged period,* persistence is a word that seems a perfect fit for its function in the holographic world. The primary goal of persistence, as it pertains to holograms, is to help create consistent experiences that the users can come to rely on being where they are supposed to be.

Think of it like a save game system for video games; however, instead of saving your character's location and how many bullets he has left, it saves the current positions of the holograms around your house.

Why are persistent holograms necessary?

Imagine that you have this great new smart house system that uses your HoloLens to control everything. However, it is controlled with panels and other objects that you put around your home. You get home from a hard day's work and set everything up. You put your HVAC thermostat in the hallway to the bedrooms. You then set up a sprinkler system timer and put that on the wall in your garage. You keep going, and spend hours putting everything where it goes, making sure that it's all set up exactly how you like.

The next day you come home from work excited, put on your HoloLens and see that suddenly everything is gone. You walk around angrily looking for your hologram controls, and then remember that there is a voice command to find certain panels. You speak the command, and the arrow that points toward the direction appears. You walk through the house following the arrow; you pause suddenly as you realize the arrow is pointing you out the front door.

You head out the door and continue to follow the arrow to your neighbor's yard. You look up, while thinking to yourself "what is going on?" Just at that moment, you see a corner of one of your panels sticking out of the wall of your neighbor's house. Your head explodes (I'm sure I mean this figuratively...pretty sure).

In most cases, creating a consistent experience for your users will be a big part of the holographic process. So, how do we fix this problem of persistence?

Coordinate systems

The simple answer is **spatial coordinate systems**. You likely just had a flashback to high school math classes, possibly with a little heavy breathing, which is an appropriate response. However, anyone who works on 3D applications deals with rigid virtual coordinate systems on a constant basis; they are essential for making a 3D program work, be it a game or the new mixed reality fitness simulator.

Coordinate systems are consistent in the computer world. If your coordinates are broken down so that 1 unit is equal to 1 meter in a 3D application, you know that when you move a character to the 40th unit, you are 40 meters out. This, unfortunately, is not the case in the real world. So, while we do have the geographic coordinate system, which is a combination of longitude, latitude, and elevation, we don't have an accurate way to translate that into a mobile computer in real-time.

Global Positioning System (**GPS**) is one common option, an option that has been left out of the HoloLens. The problem with GPS--making it completely justifiable to be left out--is that it is not very accurate. Often, GPS can vary by 15 ft-25 ft, which would be terrible for a world-scale device such as the HoloLens. These devices, being designed for the indoors, could not function with that level of imprecision.

So, instead of using a highly inaccurate system, Microsoft went with one whose--while still somewhat inaccurate--imperfections are far smaller in scale: World Anchors.

World Anchors

Most coordinate systems are absolute in nature. This means that 1 meter is always 1 meter. If you plot a point at 0.2 inches by 1.7 inches on a graph, you know the distance will be 1.5 inches. As previously explained, there are a lot of benefits of absolute measurement systems. However, without a way to measure in absolutes on a large scale and convert that to a mobile digital system, Microsoft had to find a different solution.

Some systems are relative, which means that they plot positions in relationship to other objects in the system; this type of system works better on a larger scale.

World Anchors or spatial anchors use a coordinate system that is primarily relative. With the HoloLens, the sensor array is always working, though it can be less than accurate at times. Lighting, the color of your fixtures, and furniture affect the scanning process. Sometimes, things get moved around and changed, and this can factor into the process as well.

World Anchors use the mesh generated from the spatial mapping process to determine the relative positions of items. However,they also use the other holograms in the area as points of reference, using your position for priority. In other words, if you put one hologram in your living room near your couch, the mesh data that makes up that general area of the spatial map is used as the reference for that hologram's placement.

Now, if you go and place five more holograms, they now all have parts of the mesh they are using for relative positioning information, but are also now looking at the position of the other objects in the area.

The closer the holograms are to the user determines their priority to accuracy. If changes in the Spatial Mapping happen and lead to the need to shift positions, generally the major shifts will happen farther away from the user.

World Anchor system

The system that Microsoft has devised to make and manage World Anchors is relatively simple. For the longest time, the process was made up of the **World Anchor Store** (**WAS**), as well as the World Anchors themselves.

Knowing when to save, load, delete, and attach a World Anchor could be a little confusing at first. Knowing that an object that has a World Anchor attached to it and cannot be moved added a layer of complexity.

A recent addition to the HoloToolkit, the **World Anchor Manager** (**WAM**), really simplifies the whole process down to this:

- Supplying a name
- Telling the manager to remove the anchor when you want to move an object
- Telling the manager to attach a new one when you are done moving an object

It is helpful to know and understand the system that is in place, even if the World Anchor Manager mostly controls it now. With that in mind, we will quickly break down the World Anchor Manager's functions:

- Managing the World Anchor Store: So, mostly everything
- Attaching an Anchor: WAM handles checking whether the anchor exists in the store and loads that anchor or names and saves a new one
- Removing an Anchor: This deletes the World Anchor component attached to the game object and then deletes the anchor from the store

Now, let's get back to our project.

Some quick upkeep

We need to get set up so that we can get rolling through the rest of the chapter.

First, open Unity and do the *New Chapter Shuffle*, as I am now calling it. Save the final version of the `chapter6` scene as `Chapter7.unity`. I will have a `Chapter7downloads.zip` for any important files, but as always, I recommend that you type it out to learn it.

Once you are loaded up with our fresh `Chapter7` file, you should see something that looks like this:

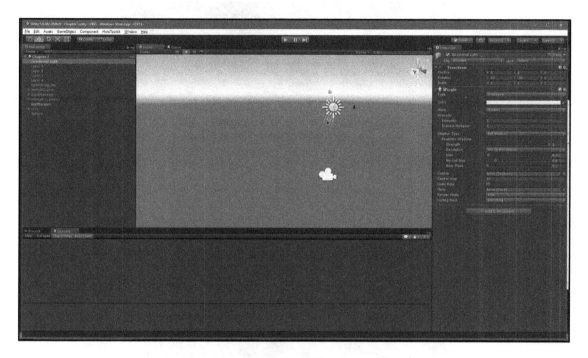

If you look in the Hierarchy view, you should see the Sphere object is inactive. Select it and press the *Delete* key; we don't need it.

So, when I finished the last chapter and started working on this one, I realized one thing I did was a bit inefficient. I had a separate Collider object instead of using the Collider that was already present on our root object. I had my reasons for it, but in the end, that would make some of the steps going forward too complicated. So, we will fix that really quick by adding a Collider to our root object.

Expand the skee object and select the **TaptoPlaceCollider**, then press the *Delete* key:

Select the **skee** object. This is what you should see in the **Inspector** window:

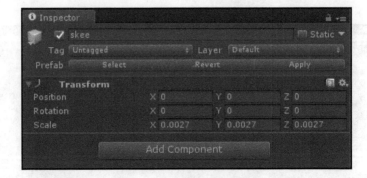

Click on the **Add Component** button, type B into the search bar, and click on **Box Collider** in the list:

Look at the **Box Collider** component. We will adjust the center and size elements of this component as follows:

- **Center**: X: -152 , Y: 39, Z: -335
- **Size**: X: 304 , Y: 463 , Z: 1189:

What we just did was adjust the size and placement of the collision box. You may note that the collision box is a bit larger than the object it is surrounding, that is on purpose. This collision box will only be used when we are initially placing it. Once placed, we will code it to turn off.

Now, let's attach the code we will be working with our object. With the **skee** object still selected, click on the **Add Component** button again. Type `Pla` into the search box and select the **PlaceSkeeBallMachine** script:

With setup out of the way, we are ready to go.

World Anchor code

Here, we will implement World Anchors. We will go through what we add line by line and learn what everything means. Just to set expectations, this next section is almost entirely code-based.

In our fields and properties area, we need to add the two lines that are at **11** and **12 in the picture below**. Depending on how you have your own code written, these numbers may not line up exactly, but should be close; this screenshot shows you the code that surrounds it to give reference points:

```
8    public class PlaceSkeeBallMachine : MonoBehaviour, IInputClickHandler
9    {
10
11       public string skeeBallAnchorName = "SkeeBallMachine01";
12       WorldAnchorManager wAnchorManager;
13
14
15       [Tooltip("Place parent on tap instead of current game object.")]
16       public bool PlaceParentOnTap;
17
18       [Tooltip("Specify the parent game object to be moved on tap, if the immediate parent is not desired.")]
19       public GameObject ParentGameObjectToPlace;
```

In the first of the two lines, we are creating a string to give our anchor a name.

The second line will be used to get a reference to our WorldAnchorManager Singleton, which we will set up next, in our Start() function.

From this screenshot, you need line **40** and then lines **48-55**; lines **43-46** should already be there:

```
38       protected virtual void Start()
39       {
40           wAnchorManager = WorldAnchorManager.Instance;
41
42           spatialMappingManager = SpatialMappingManager.Instance;
43           if (spatialMappingManager == null)
44           {
45               Debug.LogError("This script expects that you have a SpatialMappingManager component in your scene.");
46           }
47
48           if(wAnchorManager != null && spatialMappingManager != null)
49           {
50               wAnchorManager.AttachAnchor(gameObject, skeeBallAnchorName);
51           }
52           else
53           {
54               Destroy(this);
55           }
56
57
58
59
```

The first thing we add, at line **40**, is the wAnchorManager reference to the WorldAnchorManager we just talked about.

Lines **48-55** check whether `wAnchorManager` is not null and that `spatialMappingManager` is not null. If these two conditions are met, we use our reference to the `WorldAnchorManager` to attach and anchor to our **skee** object. We are also assigning the name stored at `skeeBallAnchorName`.

One common way to reference a `gameObject` in code, but which can be confusing to new scripters, is as follows:

- **gameObject (notice the lower case g)**: This is the actual game object you are attached to.
- **this.gameObject**: This is the same as `gameObject`.
- **this**: This is a reference to the specific mono behavior attached to the current game object. If you have three components assigned to an object and want to delete one of those three without affecting anything else, `this` is the one to use.

In the update function, we just have one small change. Here, we add the height buffer that we created in the preceding chapter and apply it to the not parent version of the class, on line **102**:

```
93      if (PlaceParentOnTap)
94      {
95          // Place the parent object as well but keep the focus on the current game object
96          Vector3 currentMovement = hitInfo.point - gameObject.transform.position;
97          ParentGameObjectToPlace.transform.position += new Vector3(currentMovement.x, currentMovement.y + heightBuffer, currentMovement.z);
98          ParentGameObjectToPlace.transform.rotation = toQuat;
99      }
100     else
101     {
102         gameObject.transform.position = new Vector3(hitInfo.point.x, hitInfo.point.y + heightBuffer, hitInfo.point.z);
103         gameObject.transform.rotation = toQuat;
104     }
105 }
```

`hitInfo` is the result of a raycast being sent from the user's head. We are using that result to position the object where the user is looking at. We are replacing the `Vector3` `hitInfo.point` with a new `Vector3` that is the same refactored out to an individual axis and adding the height buffer to y.

Now, in our `OnInputClicked` function, we will be changing two lines--one to attach an anchor and one to remove an anchor; simple enough:

```
109        public virtual void OnInputClicked(InputClickedEventData eventData)
110        {
111            // On each tap gesture, toggle whether the user is in placing mode.
112
113            IsBeingPlaced = !IsBeingPlaced;
114
115            // If the user is in placing mode, display the spatial mapping mesh.
116            if (IsBeingPlaced && !placed)
117            {
118                spatialMappingManager.DrawVisualMeshes = true;
119                wAnchorManager.RemoveAnchor(gameObject);
120
121            }
122            // If the user is not in placing mode, hide the spatial mapping mesh.
123            else
124            {
125                placed = true;
126                ApplicationManager.Instance.skeeBallMachinePlacementSet = true;
127                spatialMappingManager.DrawVisualMeshes = false;
128                wAnchorManager.AttachAnchor(gameObject, skeeBallAnchorName);
```

First on, line **119**, we will need to add `wAnchorManager.RemoveAnchor(gameObject)`. This translates to tell the `AnchorManager Singleton` to remove the anchor from the `gameobject` this script is attached to.

Line **128** is exactly the same as what we used at line **50** with the caveat of being in response to a click, as opposed to the start of the script.

ApplicationManager changes

OK, we now have a few changes to make in the `ApplicationManager`. Previously, we used the `SetActive(true)` call to turn our Skeeball machine on and off; this is less than optimal for working with the `WorldAnchor` system.

Instead, we will add two new functions: **HideSkeeMachine** and **ShowSkeeMachine.** Add everything you see from line **26** (the last line of the `Start()` function) to line **46**:

```
25              InputManager.Instance.PushModalInputHandler(this.gameObject);
26              HideSkeeMachine();
27          }
28
29      void HideSkeeMachine()
30      {
31          foreach (Transform child in skeeballmachine.transform)
32          {
33              child.gameObject.SetActive(false);
34          }
35
36
37      }
38      void ShowSkeeMachine()
39      {
40          foreach (Transform child in skeeballmachine.transform)
41          {
42              child.gameObject.SetActive(true);
43          }
44
45      }
46
```

Both of these functions will use a `foreach` loop to cycle through all of the child objects of the **skee** object. Each child it finds will then have `SetActive` set to `true` or `false`, depending on whether we want it on or off.

Next, move your cursor down to the `Update()` function and delete the lines selected in the following screenshot:

```
48      void Update () {
49
50          if (spatialMapSet)
51          {
52              skeeballmachine.SetActive(true);
53              if (toInit)
54              {
55                  //this is the first time through only
56                  skeeballmachine.transform.position = Camera.main.transform.position;
57                  skeeballmachine.transform.position += new Vector3(skeeballmachine.transform.position.x, -1.25f, 3.0f);
58                  //we have finished the initiallization of the skeeball machine set the toInit flag to false
59                  toInit = false;
60              }
```

Replace them with `ShowSkeeMachine()`.

A few more quick changes

So, we have a few more steps and then we can see these changes in action.

Select the **skee** object and change its **Transform** to X: 0, Y: -1.25, and Z: 3, as follows:

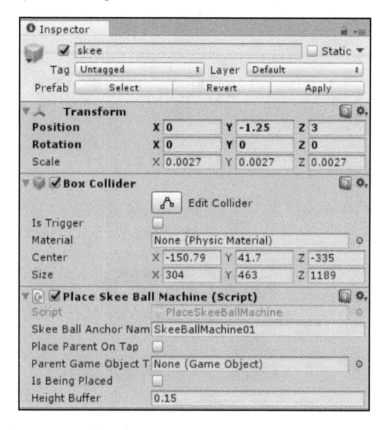

Select your **AppManager** object and click on the *gear* symbol next to the
WorldAnchorManager and click on **Remove Component**:

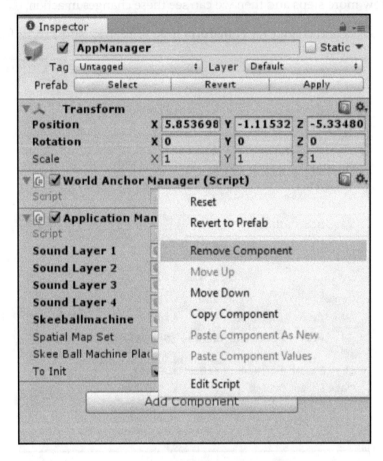

In the Hierarchy view, Click on **Create** and select **Create Empty;** name the object Managers.

Select the `Managers` object. In the **Inspector**, click on **Add Component**, type `worl` in the search box, and select **World Anchor Manager**:

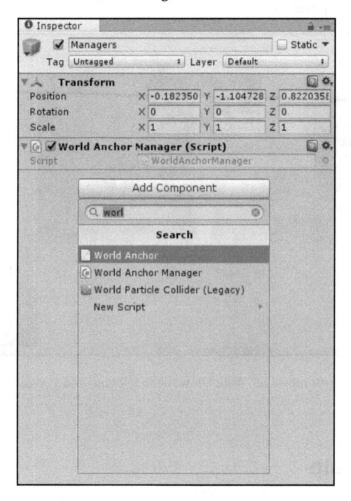

Now, it is time for the test. Click on the play button in the **Editor** and look around the spatial map. Find a spot and click on the mesh. The Skeeball machine will appear; now, click on it to pick it up and move it:

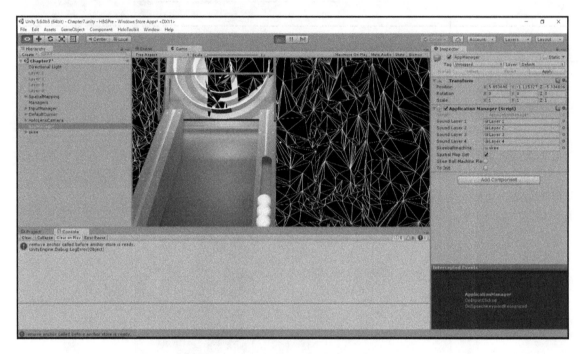

Wait! What is that error message? Well, allow me to tell you, and you can learn a lesson from my pains.

Seeking help

In the process of writing this chapter, I hit an absolutely stopping roadblock. Apparently, there were three things going on that were keeping World Anchors from working. The problem with three separate mysterious issues and only one error message is that it can create a domino effect of failures. You get into the cycle of changing things and getting no positive effect, so you change other things. You may have fixed one issue, but it still doesn't work, so you change it again. It can be very frustrating.

After many, I mean many, hours of making changes, checking versions of software and searching Google for answers, I finally came across the first answer, World Anchor Store does not work in the Unity Editor, as I said.

So, in order to not bore you with all the insane details, the very last thing we changed in the last section was the final puzzle piece. All said, I am lucky I did not pull all of my hair out.

My point in telling you this is threefold:

1. Do not hesitate to search for an answer. Most of the time someone has come across your problem before you did, and there is an answer if you just look for it.
2. When that fails, ask. There are many development communities on the Internet, and most people in those groups will not talk down to you as they answer your question in the most nebulous way they can.
3. Sometimes, you will have to find the answer on your own. When that is the case, you need to have the necessary tools.

The simple answer was "the `WorldAnchorStore` does not work in the Unity Editor." And at this point, there is no fix for it. On the other hand, if you build, compile, and deploy, it works perfectly fine. So go try it out before moving on to the next section where we will learn an easy way to avoid the pains I went through.

The in-game debug window

We will dig into debugging and profiling your application in the final chapter of this book; this section won't be about that. This will be a simple textbox that gets attached to the camera. To keep it simple, we will headlock it.

The reason we do this is that when we need to test certain conditions, we get an immediate response without having to linger over our computer.

To keep this in the scope of this section, we will create our own statements when we need to. Again, I will show you.

The prefab

First, you need to look in the Project View and drill down into the **HoloToolkit | UI | Prefabs directory** like we have before, select it, then click and hold the **3DTextPrefab,** and drag it to the **Hierarchy** view:

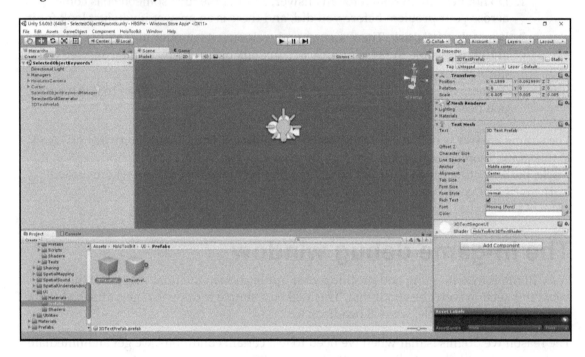

Now, select the prefab, and in the **Inspector**, click on the small donut next to the words missing font, then select the **Arial** font:

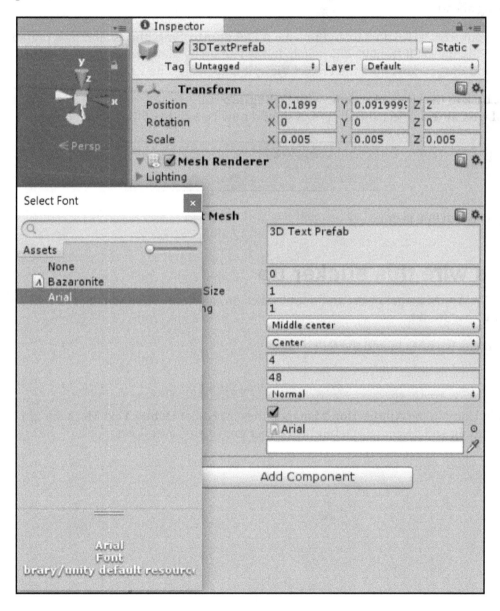

With that done, click back on your Hierarchy view ensuring that 3DTextPrefab is still selected and press *Ctrl + D* to duplicate that prefab. That is for the next section--just a little thinking ahead.

Select your first 3DTextPrefab and rename it **DebugInfo**. Since this is already a prefab, we need to disconnect it from its old prefab. In the Hierarchy view, select the **DebugInfo** object again and drag it down into the Project View; it will create a new prefab.

Now, back in the Hierarchy view, with **DebugInfo** still selected, drag the object onto the **HoloLensCamera** object and drop it; it should now be a child of the camera object:

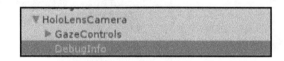

Now, construction is done.

Let's wire this sucker up

Select the **AppManager** object and double-click on the ApplicationManager script to open it up in Visual Studio.

Once there, we need to add the following:

```
public TextMesh debugTextMesh;
public string debugInfoString = "DebugInfo:";
```

Back in Unity in the **Application Manager**, the empty slot **Debug Text Mesh** should appear; drag and drop your **DebugInfo** object to that slot, as follows:

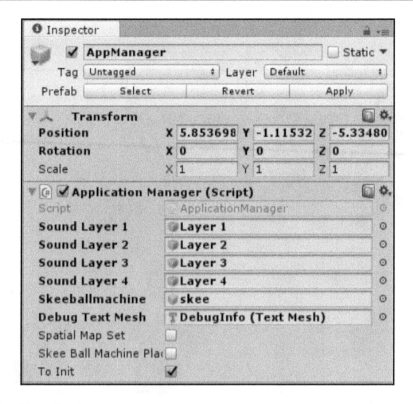

Great, one last line of code.

Move down to the first empty space in the `Start()` function and add `debugTextMesh.text = debugInfoString;`.

This connects our string to our prefab textbox.

Move or hide the other two 3DTextPrefabs and click on the play button; you should see something like this:

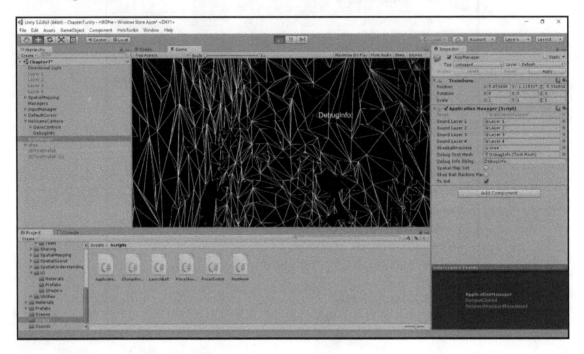

If you move it around, it will stay with you. If you don't need it, you can always turn it off in the editor and turn it on when you want.

Now that we have our makeshift debugger, let's finish this chapter with our last section and try out our debug window in the process.

In-game menu

In this section, we will reinforce some of our previous lessons while we add something that we need to our project. We will also learn how to add debug messages to our new system here.

Remember when I had you hit the duplicate command in the last section? Well, that was step one for this section taken care of already.

 Always think ahead when you can; avoid getting painted into corners.

OK, so here we will make a few changes to our **3DTextPrefab** to work as a menu button. Then, duplicate it one more time.

So, we will attach our buttons to the Skeeball machine. In order for the button to be clickable, we need to add a collider to it.

Creating the menu items

With the 3DTextPrefab selected in the **Inspector**, select **Add Component** and go to Physics 2D and select **Box Collider 2D**:

1. Now, change the text of the **TextMesh** component to Start.
2. Change the **Name** to StartBtn.

2. Change the **Character size** to 4.

3. Here is what yours might look like:

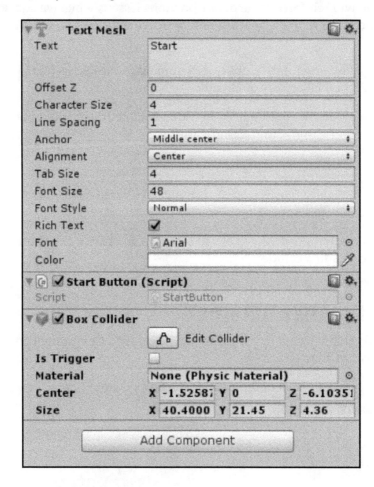

5. Now, click on the **Edit Collider** button. You might notice an issue. If you did everything in the preceding order, your collider is much smaller than your word; this is a quick and easy fix:

6. Click on the gear icon of the **Box Collider** component and click on **Reset**:

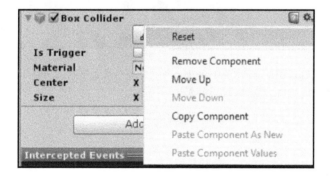

It is fixed now.

In your Hierarchy view, click and drag **StartBtn** down to your project view to create a unique prefab. Select **StartBtn** again in your Hierarchy view and press *Crtl + D* to duplicate **StartBtn**.

Rename the new button **OptionsBtn**. Now, click and drag **OptionsBtn** in the exact same way to create a prefab. Change the text of OptionsBtn to Options.

Setting up to code

This is a short and sweet section. We will find good positions for our menu prefabs before attaching them to the Skeeball machine.

Using whatever method is comfortable with you, select our prefabs and move them to look approximately like this:

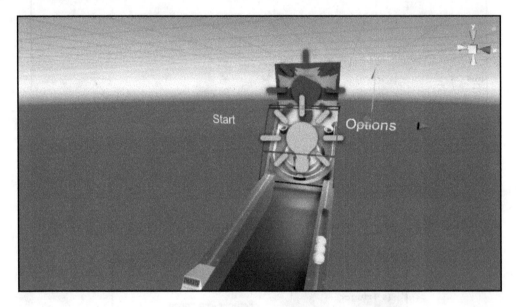

Once you have your **StartBtn** and **OptionBtn** prefabs where you like them, select both in the Hierarchy view and drag them to the **skee** object.

Now, they will come and go with the Skeeball machine.

Time to code

We don't actually have a game to start just yet, and we don't have options. So, what we will do is set up the buttons to send a message to our debug window and tell us if that has been clicked.

Our debug window is attached to a Singleton, so we can easily access it from anywhere in the code using `ApplicationManager.Instance.debugInfoString =`. Application Manager is the Singleton, Instance is the directline to application manager and debug **InfoString** is a connection to the text we want to change. Whatever is on the other side of the equal sign will be put into our debug window.

Simple, right?

OK, so now we need to select the StartBtn object and click on **Add Component,** click on **New Script,** type `StartButton`, and press *Enter*. Now, double-click on it to open it in Visual Studio.

Here is the entirety of the script file. We are using the HoloToolkit input module to handle the air-taps.

When an air-tap happens, we send the message `\n Start Button Clicked`.

Please note the += sign and the \n. The += sign means that we are taking the string that is there and adding to it, while the \n means new line:

```
1   using System.Collections;
2   using System.Collections.Generic;
3   using UnityEngine;
4   using HoloToolkit.Unity.InputModule;
5   using System;
6
7   public class StartButton : MonoBehaviour,IInputClickHandler {
8
9
10      // Use this for initialization
11      void Start () {
12
13      }
14
15      // Update is called once per frame
16      void Update () {
17
18      }
19
20      public void OnInputClicked(InputClickedEventData eventData)
21      {
22
23
24          ApplicationManager.Instance.debugInfoString += "\n Start Button Clicked";
25      }
26  }
27
```

Create an `OptionButton` script for your `OptionsBtn` object and use this exact same code from line **8** to line **25,** with the exception of replacing `\n Start Button Clicked` with `\n Options Button Clicked`.

Now, if you run the application and click on the start and option words, you should see something like this; great work!

 If you are having issues getting the program to recognize your clicks, ensure that your buttons are far enough away from the Skeeball machine. It has a big bounding box.

Summary

So, in this chapter, we learned about persistence, World Anchors, and all the other parts needed to make them work. We got World Anchors working in our project so that when we leave our Skeeball machine somewhere, it will be there when we get back.

We learned about building a simple debug information window so that we can find issues without having to stand around the computer. Of course, the trade-off is that far less information is revealed.

Finally, we started creating a menu system for our project and used it to test out our debug window.

Wow, we made it through. We are a few steps closer to rolling Skeeballs and getting some points. That is coming soon, but first we will talk about sharing the experience with others in Chapter 8, *Share What You've Got*.

8
Share What You Have Got

In this chapter, we will discuss the subject of **Holographic Sharing**--a term meant to describe shared or networked experiences on the HoloLens. The ability to not only see holograms but to be able to interact with them socially is what makes mixed reality stand above all the other post-reality incarnations.

This technology can and most likely will be a great boon to every facet of our lives, from work and entertainment to learning and socializing. That is, of course, if we as developers do our job perfectly, and make the right software.

In order to achieve these shared experiences, we will have to take a few steps into the deep end of the pool and learn a little bit about a subject that is a little above the beginner level-- *computer networking*.

Do not worry though; this primer will only scratch the surface of the topic.

Networking

Networking can seem a bit scary. Due to the massive amount of devices that we own today that can be connected on some level, this can be an immense topic. Besides Wi-Fi, Bluetooth, Ethernet, and cellular, there are so many different ways for devices to connect and communicate with each other and us.

Fortunately for us, Microsoft has spent the time and effort to make the process of building a shared experience much easier than it would be otherwise, without years of network code under your belt. However, we must get our hands a little dirty to get it all figured out.

You must walk before you can run, so before we walk or run down that winding road, let's talk about the basics first.

What is a network?

On the simplest level, a computer network is created whenever two computers are connected to each other in such a way that allows them to communicate with each other. Of course, that used to strictly mean computers and telecommunication devices. Now, it can mean a wide range of devices, from refrigerators and other household appliances to cars.

The two primary types of network that we deal with on a day-to-day basis are as follows:

- **Local Area Network (LAN)**: The Wi-Fi router and physical Ethernet connections at home are examples of LANs. If you are a gamer, you have likely heard the term *LAN party*, which is a good use of a LAN.
- **Wide Area Network (WAN)**: This is a network that would allow someone in Seattle to communicate with someone in Italy. The Internet as a whole is considered a WAN, though it is a far less common term.

While computer networks have many different configurations, one of the most common networks is the **client-server model**. This network configuration allows a software developer to build a client application that runs on a user's computer or phone. Whenever the user uses the software, whether they know it or not, they are connecting to the server provided by the software company and offloading the heavy processing or file storage to a server on the network. This lets the client software weigh in at a far smaller size and as a result is far less CPU intensive. The downside is that unless contingencies have been made, the software will not work without the server.

This network model is the one we will use for this chapter. Microsoft has provided a service that can run on your computer as a server. When anyone on your network loads up software via the HoloLens or other UWP options, it will go through the process of automatically connecting to that software.

Making the Skeeball game a shared experience

For our purposes, we will not be making a full-fledged game. We will essentially simulate a Skeeball game. We will keep this simple; we will make a score and a way to score points. When a player plays a round, there will be a way to reset the game. If multiple people want to play, they can just take turns, exactly like they would if they were standing in an arcade.

Quick setup

As usual, you will need to load the previous chapter's finished project and save the scene as `Chapter8.unity`. Don't forget to switch the scenes in the **Scenes In Build** section of the **Build Settings** window:

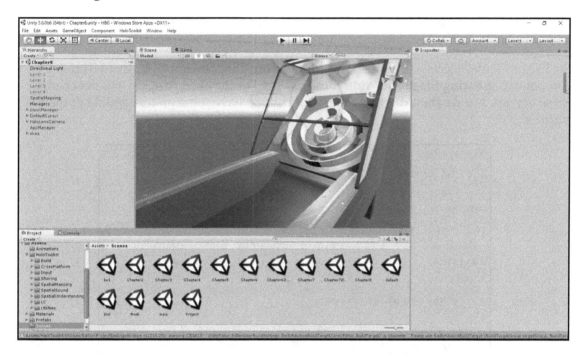

Your window should look something like the preceding screenshot.

Alright then, let's do this.

A very simple first step

The HoloLens networking system that we will be working on has been designed for the **HoloToolkit**--Unity by Microsoft and a few community members. If the goal was to do a good deal of heavy lifting, then our mission is accomplished. A single Prefab does all the initial setup we will need.

So, let's put the sharing Prefab in the project and then learn about what it does:

1. Go to your **HoloToolKit | Sharing | Prefabs** directory in the **Project** window.
2. Now, drag and drop the **Sharing** Prefab into your **Hierarchy** view, anywhere under the skee object.

Great! Pretty simple as first steps go. Now that we have it in our project, let's take a look and see what it does.

So, like all GameObjects it of course has a **Transform**. Other than that, it has two other components, **Sharing Stage** and **Auto Join Session**. For the most part, we will not change these options, but we should go over them so that you have some understanding of their purpose:

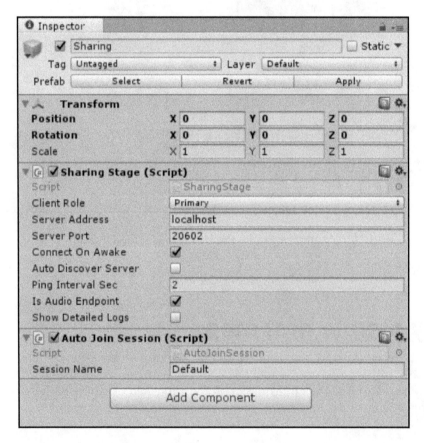

The following list explains all of the options from the preceding screenshot:

- **SharingStage:** A component designed to manage the core networking for our application. It handles the auto discovery, error logging, and session and session user management, among other things.
- **Client Role:** This has two options, **Primary** and **Secondary**. The **Primary** option connects directly to a session server which is an executable that comes with the HoloToolkit. The **Secondary** option connects to a **Primary**. It is a far simpler implementation that cannot manage the session. We will leave our set as **Primary.**
- **Server Address:** This is the IP address of the server. Internet-savvy people will understand what this means. This will be the IP address of the computer running the server software.
- **Server Port:** This is the port that goes along with that IP address. Generally speaking, most programs that use Internet connections tend to find a port range and stay there.
- **Connect On Awake:** Should this component attempt to connect to the server the moment it starts or should it wait till you say go?

- **Auto Discover Server:** This is switched off by default. This option implements a system of listeners actively looking for a server to appear on your local network.
- **Ping Interval Sec:** This tells the **Auto Discover** feature how often to ping in its search efforts.
- **Is Audio Endpoint:** This determines whether the app will be providing audio input or output.
- **Show Detailed Logs:** This is a very useful tool when you are trying to track down an issue; I keep it on all the time.
- **AutoJoinSession:** Normally, when joining games or other applications on a network, there is a login process, rooms, and user rights. This class handles that work on its own.
- **Session Name:** This is the name the software will be looking to match during the process of trying to connect. In our case, change the name from **Default** to **HBG**.

Too much information

When it comes to network-connected 3D applications, there is about 25 years of knowledge on the subject before now. For the most part, that 25 years of experience is game development. With the recent move of mixed reality out of complete obscurity, comes along a use for 3D applications and 3D models that do not require logging into Xbox Live to yell at seemingly entitled children.

When you are playing a 3D game by yourself, the computer is handling all the incoming data and responding to it at real time. It can track the position, rotation, and scale of all the objects in the scene, all while playing sound effect that responds to certain events happening and also doing a numerous number of other things.

When you do something that creates an object, it does not require much for the computer to track and update all the various properties associated with that object.

In a multiuser, real-time 3D application or game, there can be anywhere from 2 to 32 people using it at the same time; the standard forms of object creation do not do what we need.

In this case, the server computer is receiving updates from all the users at once, and then has to sort through each of those messages. The server then sends out or broadcasts update responses to each object that it is trying to manage.

So, if you are playing a first-person wargame and as you run by a barrel, it gets shot and explodes, the server is receiving the input from all the players and then broadcasting relevant information to each relevant object. This kind of knowledge can help understand this whole process a bit better.

Spawning our Skeeball machine

Different systems handle object instantiation in different ways. For the single-user version of the project that we have created over the past couple of chapters, we did not use spawning or instantiating at all. We have had the object turned off, and would turn it on only when certain conditions are met. Before we continue, we need to correct that. Let's perform the following steps:

1. In the **Hierarchy** view, select the **skee** object.
2. Click on the **Apply** button in the **Inspector** just to be sure.
3. With the object still selected in the **Hierarchy** view, right-click on the object and click on the **Delete** option.

Now, we need to set up our system that will allow us to spawn in our `skee` Prefab; we will use a component with the name **Prefab Spawn Manager**:

1. With the **Sharing** object selected in the **Hierarchy** view, click on the **Add Component** button in the **Inspector**.
2. Type `Pref` into the search bar and select **Prefab Spawn Manager**, as follows:

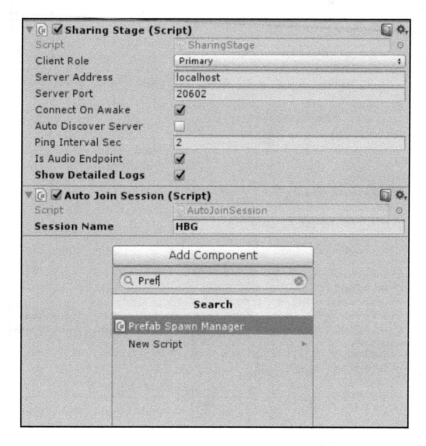

Now, let's put in the information we need to get this working:

1. Click on the arrow next to the **Spawnable** Prefabs.
2. Put the number `1` in the size box and press the *Tab* key.
3. Type `SyncSpawnedObject` into the **Data Model Class Name** box.
4. Click on the small donut past the Prefab box.

1. Select **Skee**. Ensure that it is the object in the Prefabs directory; you will notice the object path in the window under the **Select GameObject** box, as shown in the following screenshot:

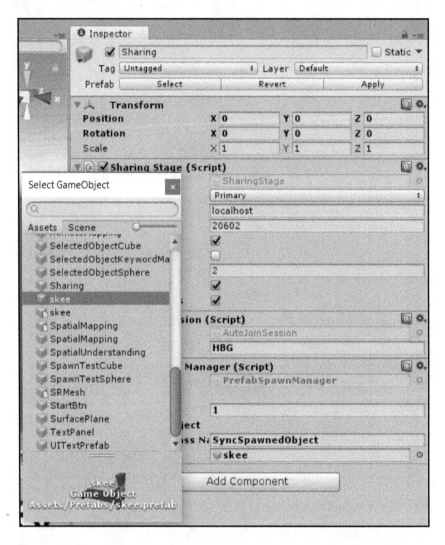

The SyncSpawnedObject class in a sense converts data into a format that allows the system to track and broadcast or synchronize the information out to various clients.

In the **Project** view, go to the **Prefabs** directory and select the **skee** object:

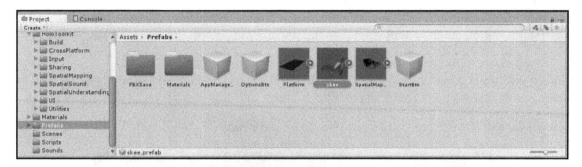

We need to add components to the object. Using the **Add Component** button again, add `DefaultSyncModelAccessor`; this works with the `SyncSpawnedObject` to update the transform information among clients. Then, add `ImportExportAnchorManager`. This handles world anchors between clients.

That's it for the **skee** Prefab in this chapter.

It's not really backtracking if it was the plan

With that part done, let's have a quick talk. I have mentioned previously in this book that there are many ways to offer a similar solution. Some work better for one situation and less for another. With that in mind, we will partially rewrite the `ApplicationManager` class in this chapter to better work for our needs now.

In the end, it will basically do the same thing as it did before. The few features we will add to it could have been easily added to the `ApplicationManager` from `Chapter 7`, *The Tools of the Trade*, but where is the fun in that?

Most of the work in this class will be done in the `Update ()` function. This other approach will allow better and more visible flow control down the line. Up to this point, we just have a few simple if statements running the flow. We will be changing that to a switch statement, a rather long one.

After changing `ApplicationManager`, we will add a new class to our `AppManager` object called `SyncSpawnSkee`. This class is the one that actually spawns in our Skee machine.

Application manager

OK, as I mentioned, since this is our application or game manager when we get to the point of making this a game, we will need it to handle scoring and all the other elements that make a game a game.

So, first we will go in and delete what we no longer need. In the next series of screenshots in this section, all the highlighted text is what is being deleted.

For off, let's delete the `bools` that we will no longer need:

```
20
21          public bool spatialMapSet = false;
22          public bool skeeBallMachinePlacementSet = false;
23          public bool toInit = true;
24
```

In our `Start()` function, delete the method call, as highlighted:

```
// Use this for initialization
void Start () {

    InputManager.Instance.PushModalInputHandler(this.gameObject);
    HideSkeeMachine();
}
```

In the `Update()` function, delete everything that used the `bool` variables we have just deleted in the previous sections:

```
50
51          if (spatialMapSet)
52          {
53              skeeballmachine.SetActive(true);
54              if (toInit)
55              {
56                  ShowSkeeMachine();
57                  //we have finished the initiallization of the skeeball machine set the toInit flag to false
58                  toInit = false;
59              }
60          }
61          else
62          {
63              skeeballmachine.SetActive(false);
64          }
65
```

Here is more of `Update()`:

```
48
49          debugTextMesh.text = debugInfoString;
50  
51          //if the skeeball machine placement is set then we want to run all of the layers of sound.
52          if (skeeBallMachinePlacementSet)
53          {
54  
55              soundLayer1.SetActive(true);
56              soundLayer2.SetActive(true);
57              soundLayer3.SetActive(true);
58              soundLayer4.SetActive(true);
```

Finally, we need to get rid of this `bool` call in our `SetSpatialMap()` method:

```
73      void SetSpatialMap()
74      {
75  
76          spatialMapSet = true;
77          SpatialMappingManager.Instance.DrawVisualMeshes = false;
78          InputManager.Instance.PopModalInputHandler();
79  
80      }
```

With these out of the way, we now need to look at the additions. In this case though, as we go, we will talk about what they do:

```
11          public GameObject soundLayer1;
12          public GameObject soundLayer2;
13          public GameObject soundLayer3;
14          public GameObject soundLayer4;
15  
16          public GameObject skeeballmachine;
17          public GameObject sharingPrefab;
18          public GameObject spatialPrefab;
19  
20          public TextMesh debugTextMesh;
21          public string debugInfoString = "DebugInfo:";
```

As a manager object, `AppManager` needs to have a quick access to almost everything in a scene. Here, we are exposing three new `GameObject` to the editor so that `AppManager` can turn them on or off as needed.

Directly under our new Prefab `GameObject` comes the heart of this change. As I mentioned, we are using a switch to control the flow of everything.

Enums

We will use an *enum* or *enumerated type* to keep up with each state that we want to switch through. Here, we have an enum structure with multiple states in it, such as `SharingInit`, `ConnectingToServer`, `SpatialMapping`, `MapComplete`, `PlaceSkeeMachine`, `PlaceSkeeMachineComplete`, `StartGame`, `EndGame`, and `Reset`.

The beauty of the enum structure is that while each element, as far as the computer is concerned is elements 1 - 9 (or 0-8 since I have the = 0 after the first one), but to you or me as a programmer, it can be hard to keep up with which state number 6 is as opposed to `PlaceSkeeMachineComplete`.

```
23
24     public enum AppState
25     {
26         SharingInit = 0,
27         ConnectingToServer,
28         SpatialMapping,
29         MapComplete,
30         PlaceSkeeMachine,
31         PlaceSkeeMachineComplete,
32         StartGame,
33         EndGame,
34         Reset,
35     }
36
37     public AppState myAppstate;
38
39
40     // Use this for initialization
41     void Start()
```

An enum has many uses, and while it is not the most efficient means of producing code, it is very easy for a person to read and understand what is happening.

Let's say we want an enum for the states of my music system volume; it would look something like this:

```
enum MusicVolume
{
Loud,
Medium,
Soft,
Mute,
}
```

We would create a copy of it like this:

```
public MusicVolume myMusic;
```

We can use the preceding code to change the current state like this:

```
myMusic = MusicVolume.Soft;
```

Then, we can use it to do things with it, as follows:

```
if (myMusic==MusicVolume.Soft){
//change music volume to 2
}
```

You get the idea. As you will see in the next section, though, one great use of an enum is switch.

Updating the Update() method

In this section, we will change the `Update()` method, and then using a `Switch` statement, change the overall flow of our application.

About the only thing that will not change in the update is the debugTextMesh line at line 70, we are using it a bit more as you will see shortly.

A switch statement is like a gate controller. The programmer calls `switch` (with a variable) with a number of case statements or potential outcomes. Depending on the value of the variable determines which gate opens up.

For instance, using the `MusicVolume` given in the preceding section as an example:

```
Switch(myMusic)
{
case MusicVolume.Loud:
{
```

```
//make the volume loud
}
break;
case MusicVolume.Medium:
{
//make the volume medium
}
break;
}
```

You could think about it like a road intersection with only one path out. While not great for roadways, it can be amazing when you are trying to direct the flow of traffic:

```
66        // Update is called once per frame
67        void Update()
68        {
69
70            debugTextMesh.text = debugInfoString;
71            switch (myAppstate)
72            {
73                case AppState.SharingInit:
74                {
75                    sharingPrefab.SetActive(true);
76                    myAppstate = AppState.ConnectingToServer;
77                    debugInfoString = "\n" + myAppstate;
78                }
79                break;
80                case AppState.ConnectingToServer:
81                {
82                    //need a test to determine that the user is connected.
83                    myAppstate = AppState.SpatialMapping;
84                    debugInfoString = "\n" + myAppstate;
85                }
86                break;
87                case AppState.SpatialMapping:
88                {
89
90                    spatialPrefab.SetActive(true);
91                    debugInfoString = "\n" + myAppstate;
92                }
93                break;
94                case AppState.MapComplete:
95                {
96                    SyncSpawnSkee.Instance.SyncSpawnSkeeBallMachine();
```

Also, some more lines of code:

```
90                        spatialPrefab.SetActive(true);
91                        debugInfoString = "\n" + myAppstate;
92                    }
93                    break;
94                case AppState.MapComplete:
95                    {
96                        SyncSpawnSkee.Instance.SyncSpawnSkeeBallMachine();
97                        myAppstate = AppState.PlaceSkeeMachine;
98                        debugInfoString = "\n" + myAppstate;
99                    }
100                   break;
101               case AppState.PlaceSkeeMachine:
102                   {
103                        debugInfoString = "\n" + myAppstate;
104                   }
105                   break;
106               case AppState.PlaceSkeeMachineComplete:
107                   {
108                        debugInfoString = "\n" + myAppstate;
109                        soundLayer1.SetActive(true);
110                        soundLayer2.SetActive(true);
111                        soundLayer3.SetActive(true);
112                        soundLayer4.SetActive(true);
113                        myAppstate = AppState.StartGame;
114                   }
115                   break;
116               case AppState.StartGame: { debugInfoString = "\n" + myAppstate; } break;
117               case AppState.EndGame: { debugInfoString = "\n" + myAppstate; } break;
118               case AppState.Reset:
119                   {
120                        debugInfoString = "\n" + myAppstate;
121                   }
122                   break;
123               default:
124                   {
125
126                   }
127                   break;
128           }
129       }
```

In the two preceding screenshot, you can see the new version of Update(). We are now using the enum myAppstate to test against nine states. As certain combinations of conditions are met, we can control the flow.

In some cases, I have what is a series of dominos, meaning that one enum state is changed inside another case. There is a definite argument for this not being efficient. All of the statements that are in cases which are connected together in such as way could all be in the same case.

That is absolutely correct. Also, depending on the complexity of the decision, this could be controlled with a series of `if/else` statements. However, as a program grows and becomes more complex, not only can I add more to each state and case, but I can easily add more states to the enum itself. I can create all new paths for the flow to follow with minimal effort.

You may also notice that some of the states have no code at all other than our `debuginfo`, `StartGame` and `EndGame`. These states are here simply for planning ahead, for when we need them. Soon.

```
139    public void OnInputClicked(InputClickedEventData eventData)
140    {
141        if (myAppstate == AppState.SpatialMapping)
142        {
143            SetSpatialMap();
144        }
145
146    }
```

These final two functions in our ApplicationManager are mostly the same, but they have been changed to test against the condition set by my AppState enum, another very useful feature of the enum

```
148    public void OnSpeechKeywordRecognized(SpeechKeywordRecognizedEventData eventData)
149    {
150        if (myAppstate == AppState.SpatialMapping)
151        {
152            switch (eventData.RecognizedText.ToLower())
153            {
154
155                case "done":
156                    SetSpatialMap();
157                    break;
158            }
159        }
160    }
161 }
162
```

It is also worth noting that there will be an error message that pops up until we write the `SyncSpawnSkee` class, which will be done in the next section.

Now, if we go back and look at our `AppManager` object in the **Inspector**, we can see the new entries that we need to change. We will wire this up in a bit, but first we need to write the class that will oversee spawning our network-friendly Prefab.

These changes will break another class, so we need to fix that real quick. Let's follow the following steps:

1. Open `PlaceSkeeBallMachine.cs`.
2. Search for `ApplicationManager.Instance.skeeBallMachinePlacementSet = true;` in line 126.
3. Select and delete that line.

Filling in the blanks

In this section, we will finally make sure that our network code can understand our object by spawning it with network-friendly code. Instead of turning our skee object on or off based on certain conditions, we will spawn it into the game using the `PrefabSpawnManager`.

The `PrefabSpawnManager` class takes a Prefab and converts it into data types that can easily be translated across a network. This makes for a far more efficient use of objects:

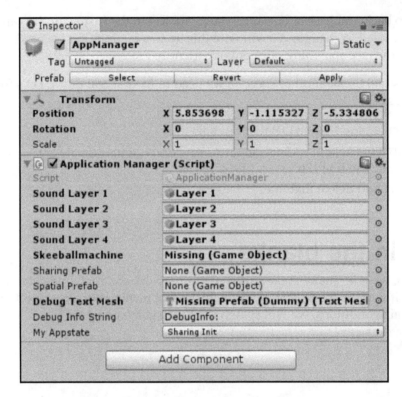

To begin, click on that **Add Component** button shown in the preceding screenshot. Scroll down to **New Script**, type `SyncSpawnSkee` in the box, make sure that **C Sharp** is selected, and click on the **Create and Add** button.

Double-click on the file you have just created, and when it opens, type this short section of code into the editor:

```
using HoloToolkit.Unity;
using HoloToolkit.Sharing.Spawning;
using UnityEngine;

public class SyncSpawnSkee : Singleton<SyncSpawnSkee>
{
    // public GameObject SpawnParent;
    public GameObject skeePrefab;
    public GameObject skeeMachine;
    public PrefabSpawnManager SpawnManager;

    public void SyncSpawnSkeeBallMachine()
    {

        SyncSpawnedObject spawnedObject = new SyncSpawnedObject();
        Vector3 position = skeePrefab.gameObject.transform.position;
        SpawnManager.Spawn(spawnedObject, position, skeePrefab.gameObject.transform.rotation, null, "skee", true);
        ApplicationManager.Instance.skeeballmachine = spawnedObject.GameObject;
        skeeMachine = spawnedObject.GameObject;
        skeeMachine.transform.parent = null;
        skeeMachine.name = "skee";  //spawnedObject.GameObject.name = "skee";

    }
}
```

In the `SyncSpawnSkeeBallMachine()` method, we first create a `SyncSpawnedObject` called `spawnedObject`. We then get the position to spawn the object. In this case, we are using the actual position stored in the Prefab itself.

Next is our actual spawn line:

```
SpawnManager.Spawn(spawnedObject, position,
skeePrefab.gameObject.transform.rotation, null, "skee", true);
spawnedObject = Our Prefab;
position = the position to spawn the object;
skeePrefab.gameObject.transform.rotation = the prefabs rotation;
null = parent to assign to the object;
"skee" = baseName;
True = isOwnedLocally;
```

After that, we link it up so that the `ApplicationManager` has a direct reference to the `spawnedObject`. We then get a reference to the `spawnedObject` inside this class, so we can make sure that the object does not have a parent and change the object name to `skee`. The system takes the basename and applies it to a process so that this comes out:

```
"skee - 23481325423 - ff39457315fh- fneu2941".   I wanted something simple.
```

Alright, now that we have all of our coding done, it's time to wire up the object that we have just set up and see if this thing works:

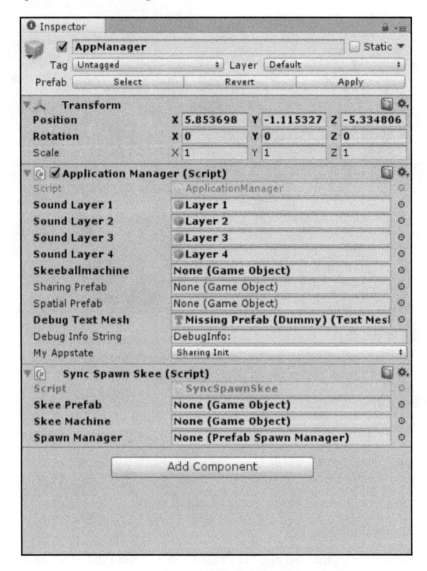

Yeah, that is a lot of missing stuff. Not a problem. This should not take more than a few minutes to fix. First and foremost, skip the Skeeball machine; that will be filled in dynamically.

Next, use the following steps to fill in the missing details of the **Application Manager**:

1. For the **Sharing Prefab**, drag the **Sharing** object from the **Hierarchy** view to this field.
2. For the **Spatial Prefab**, drag the **Spatial Mapping** object from the **Hierarchy** view to the field.
3. If for some reason you are getting the missing Prefab error for the **Debug Text Mesh**, refer to the preceding chapter for that.

Lastly, use the following steps for SyncSpawnSkee:

1. Drag the skee Prefab from the Project view to the skee Prefab field.
2. Drag the Sharing object from the Hierarchy view to the Spawn Manager field.

That is it.

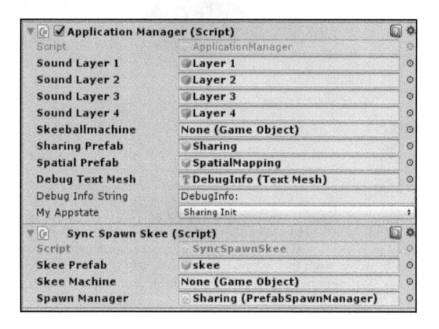

Yeah, it does look like it's missing something, but as I said, some of it is handled dynamically:

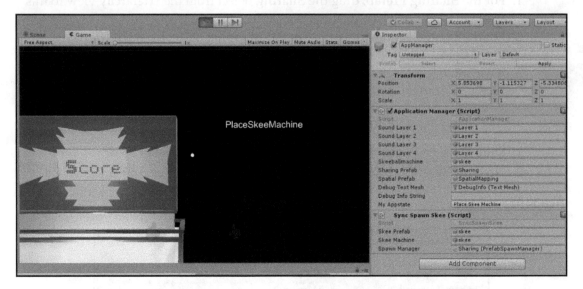

The payoff

Would you now like to see our hard work in action? What we did here was very simple in effect, but not easy to see by ourselves. There are a few methods I have been able to test something like this with:

- **Two instances of Unity on the same computer**: This is likely one of the quickest ways. Take your development directory and move it somewhere else on the computer. With your main project opened, run a second instance of Unity and open the project from this second directory. As you run through the various clicks in the program and move the machine around, you will see it move in the second instance.
- **Two computers running Unity**: Very much like the previous point, except you do not have to press the *Alt* + *Tab* keys to see it in action.
- **HoloLens and computer**: This is another option; it probably takes about the same amount of time in terms of iteration as the second option. When you move the machine through the HoloLens, you can see it moving around on the computer. Funnily enough, if you move it on the computer, it does not do anything on the HoloLens. This appears to be a problem with the world anchors in the editor.

- **HoloLens and HoloLens**: Well, it is not easy to test it like this, by myself, though I have tried. The constant swapping of HoloLens is mighty bothersome. Also, one issue, apparently, the system being not in place does not automatically sync up the spatial mapping of the other, or some other issues are happening. When you get both HoloLens up and past the spatial map, the two Skeeball machines are in different places. When either is moved, you can see them both move but they just happen to start in different places.

Summary

Network programming is not easy in the slightest. It can be rather frustrating in my experience. Once it works, though, not only does the accomplishment feel great, typically you have learned about 50 things in the process that you will hopefully use.

In this chapter, we touched on the bare minimum that we could do to get a working network capable program. While the effect was minimal, so was the work.

In the next chapter, we will use a bit of everything we have learned to finish making our Skeeball game. We will use physics and some more advanced inputs, such as manipulation and navigation, to make a way to fire our ball like a pinball machine.

We will even finally make our scoreboard work by having triggerable game objects that respond when hit by our ball objects.

9
Putting It All Together

In the last eight chapters, we learned a great variety of ideas and approaches to problem-solving using Visual Studio and Unity for HoloLens. We are rapidly approaching the end of our journey. Don't let your guard down just yet, though; you know what they say, it's always darkest before the dawn.

We will spend most of the time in this chapter reinforcing many of the ideas that we have already learned throughout this book, with the overall goal being to walk away with not only the framework of a proper game, but also a greater understanding of the whole process.

Our main Prefab

In this chapter, we will make some major changes to our `skee` Prefab. Some of them are simply organizational, while others are there to fill out the elements that we need to make this a complete game.

If you followed the tutorials up to this point, after Chapter 8, *Share What You Have Got*, you should have something that looks like the following screenshot:

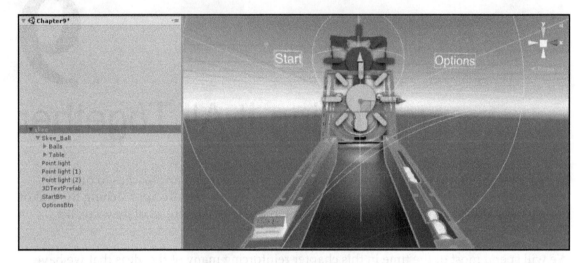

As seen in the screenshot, the **Skee_Ball** object in the **skee** hierarchy is the largest and most difficult. It holds nearly all the mesh data for the SkeeBall machine. Fortunately, we don't really need to deal with that, so we can just pass that mess by. Then, we have our three point-lights sitting next in the list. After that, we have our scoreboard, 3DTextprefab, very lazily named, and our **Start** and **Options** button.

The organization system

While our current setup is simple enough to look at and gives a general idea of how each piece functions, it lacks a certain level of polish in terms of organization to keep the tutorial easy to follow. As projects get larger and more complex, unless you can hold every element of a program in your head, this lack of organization can cause major headaches down the road.

Without getting into a long list of filing system best practices, just remember that, in the end, the point of organization is to keep the project maintainable and extendable.

With that in mind, along with the many other changes that we will be making, we will also be keeping an eye on better organization. By the end of this chapter, the **skee** Prefab will look like this:

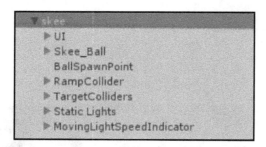

Let's take a moment to break down the specific organization system I am using here. We will address each section and what its purpose is:

- **UI**: All our user interface elements, such as TextMesh objects and buttons, will be children of this parent.
- **Skee_Ball**: There are a few minor changes to this section, which we will talk about in a bit. Otherwise, this does the exact same thing it did in the previous version of the Prefab.
- **BallSpawnPoint**: Here, we have our Spawn Point for the ball when the start button is pressed.

- **RampCollider**: So, there was a problem with this model that caused the physics to go a bit haywire. To fix this problem, we have to add a collection of colliders that fits the model and delete the original collider. In the following image, green lines represent the collider for the selected objects:

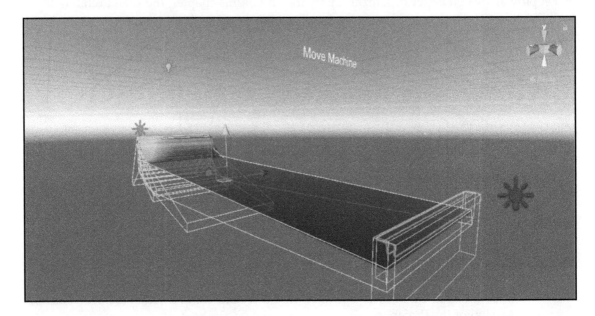

- **TargetColliders**: We also use colliders in order for the GameBalls to score points but, unlike the RampColliders, we do not want GameBalls to physically react to hitting these colliders. With a simple tick of the `IsTrigger` option, we now have a collider that when the ball hits it and leaves, the player's score will go up and then the ball is destroyed:

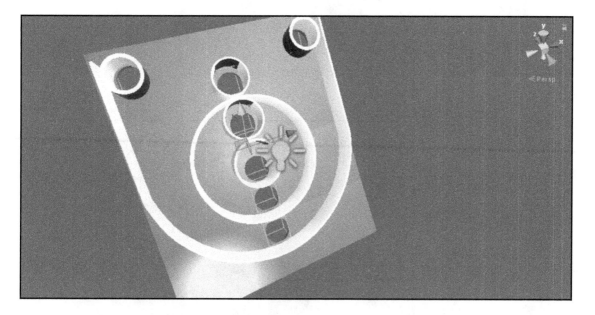

- **Static Lights**: These are the lights that we have had from the beginning of this project. They are just now in a designated place.
- **MovingLightSpeedIndicator**: This system is how we can determine the speed that is applied to the ball when an air-tap is registered.

The reorganization

In this section, we will set up our Prefab's new structure. This can be important if you decide to have a life-sized SkeeBall machine in your home and want to make it even better. Really, who doesn't want a life-sized SkeeBall machine in their home, especially one that they can make disappear with the flick of a few fingers.

Alright, it's time to do the new chapter shuffle. This should be a process you can do in your sleep by now:

1. Load the last version you have of your `Chapter8` scene.
2. Save the scene as `Chapter9`:

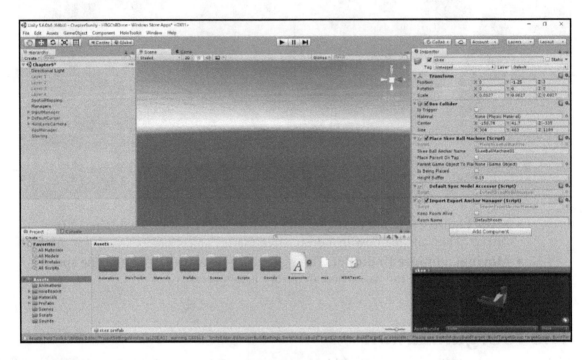

Now, let's move on to reorganizing our Prefabs in an effort to keep things clean, as we mentioned earlier. It will help us understand what is coming up much easier:

1. In your Project view, navigate to the `Prefabs` directory and select `skee`, drag it to your **Hierarchy** view, and drop it. Once you see the SkeeBall machine in your scene view, click on the arrow next to it to expand its hierarchy:

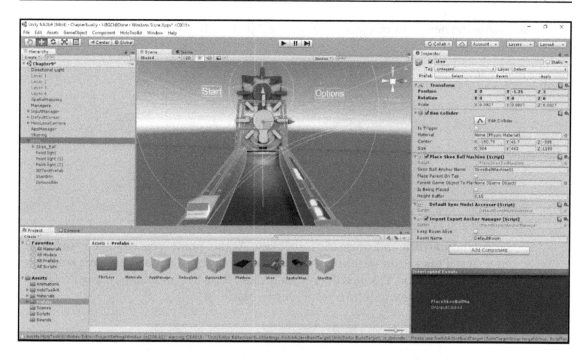

Here's the space we are focusing on for a while:

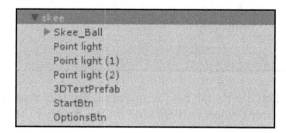

2. Right-click on the parent **skee** and select **Create Empty**.

3. Name the new GameObject `UI` and drag it just under the parent object:

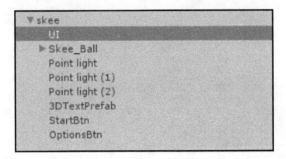

4. Rename **3DTextPrefab** to `ScoreBoard`.

5. Select the**StartBtn** and press the *Delete* key. At this point, you will get a warning message, **This action will break the Prefab instance. Are you sure you wish to continue?**; click on **Yes**. It will only be broken for a few moments. Your Prefab in the **Hierarchy** view will turn from blue to black:

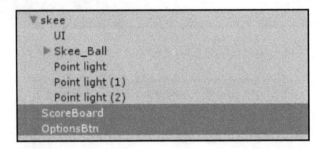

6. You have broken the Prefab for the moment, but this is easily remedied by selecting the parent object and clicking on the **Apply** button in the **Inspector**:

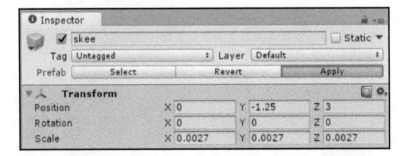

7. Now, go back to the **Hierarchy** view, select **ScoreBoard** and **OptionsBtn**, and drag both the objects to the UI object:

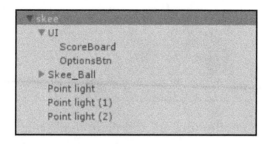

Now we need to do the same thing for our point lights, but we will use a slightly different way to get there:

1. With **skee** selected in the **Hierarchy** view, click on the **Create** button and select **Create Empty Child**:

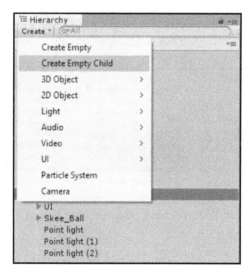

2. Select the newly created child, called **GameObject**, and name it **Static Lights**:

3. Select **Point light**, **Point light (1)**, and **Point light (2)** in the **skee** hierarchy:

4. Drag them to the **Static Lights** object and release:

We now have everything that was in the scene currently organized. Now, it is time to begin adding things that were not in the previous chapter, and we will start with something a bit different.

Importing the RampColliders

If you have ever worked with Unity in a team setting, especially in a source control environment such as GitHub or BitBucket, you may have run into issues like overwriting each other's work. It can be hard to avoid this situation at times. Prefabs are one of the safeguards against killing each other's work.

In this section, we will import a Prefab and put it inside our main Prefab. This allows us to update part of a Prefab with little hassle. Once it's in, it should align perfectly and be ready to go.

The RampColliders object was made as a result of a physics error that was happening with the project. In response to the error, I turned off the mesh collider on the ramp object and created five objects layered in a way that attempts to mimic the curve of the ramp, as pictured earlier in this chapter.

If you have all the associated project files downloaded, locate them. If not, you should download them now and have them ready. Follow the given steps:

1. Click on the **Assets** button in the main menu:

2. Click on the **ImportPackage** option:

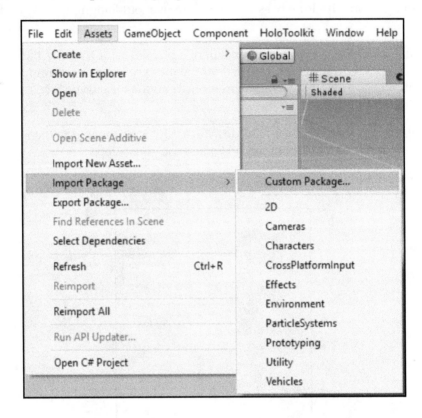

3. Click on **Custom Package....** When the open file window appears, navigate to the location you have the downloads for this book. Then, select **rampcolliders.unitypackage**:

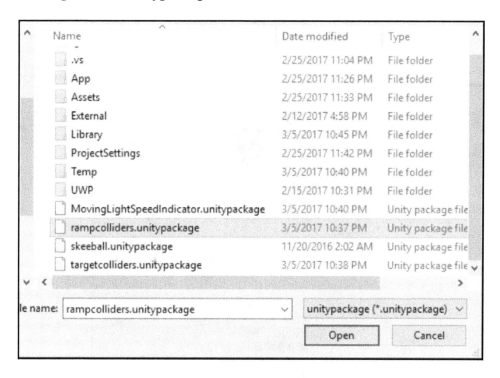

4. When the **Import Unity Package** window appears, ensure that the **RampCollider.prefab** is the only thing with a check mark next to it and click on the **Import** button:

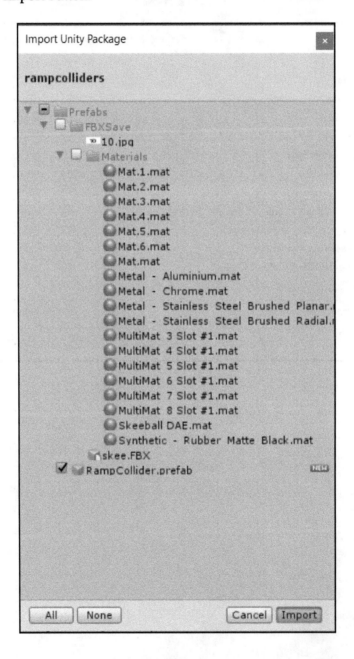

5. Now if you go to your Project view and look in the Prefabs directory, there should be a new object called **RampCollider**:

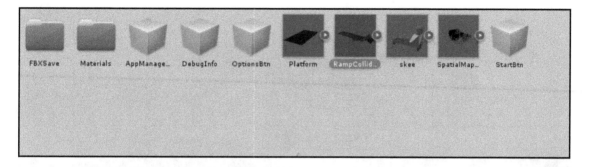

6. Click on the **RampCollider** object, drag it to the **skee** Hierarchy, and drop it. Ensure that it is a child of **skee**, not a grandchild:

7. If you have done everything correctly and you click on the **RampCollider** parent object, you should see a (green) wireframe similar to the one in the picture:

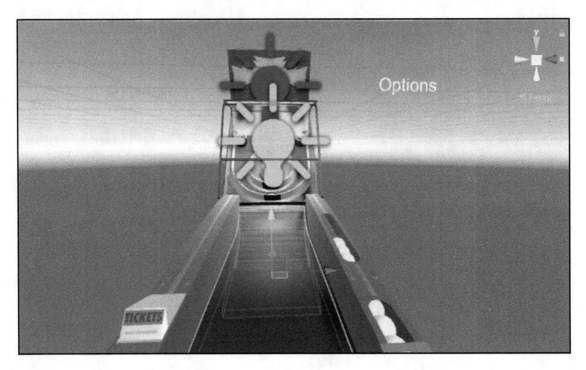

When bounding boxes collide

So, we have accomplished the organization and simple importing processes. That wasn't much of a challenge, was it? Well, now it is time for something with a little more substance.

In this section, we will build seven trigger colliders so that our application will register a score when they are hit by the balls. We will then write a simple script that tells the application manager to change the score based on the trigger that was hit.

To start, we need somewhere to put our collection of collider boxes. As we did with UI and Static Lights earlier in the chapter, create an empty child object of **skee**, called `TargetColliders`.

The **Mesh Renderer** of a Unity GameObject is what determines the visibility of that object. It stores the materials and lighting information. In my experience, I have found that building an actual mesh object and then removing or turning off the Mesh Renderer produces better results in terms of collisions.

The scoring system in our game will be the classic 10, 20, 30, 40, 50, 100. We will start with 10 and build and copy till we are done. Look at the following steps:

1. Right-click on the **TargetColliders** GameObject in the **Hierarchy** view.
2. Click on **3D Object**.
3. Then, select **Cube** as the type of **3D object** to create:

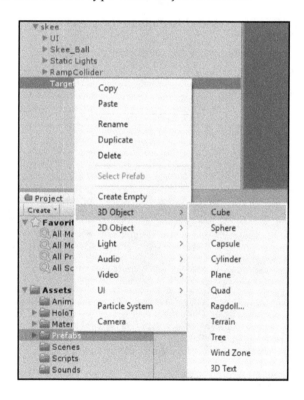

4. In the Inspector, change the object's name to `10Collider`:

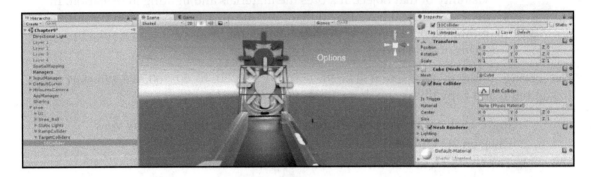

5. In the Inspector view, we need to change the transform of the object, as follows:

- **Position X**: `-155.2 Y: 65.7 Z: -43.99997`
- **Rotation X**: `35.86 Y:0 Z:0`
- **Scale X**: `31 Y:31 Z: 31`

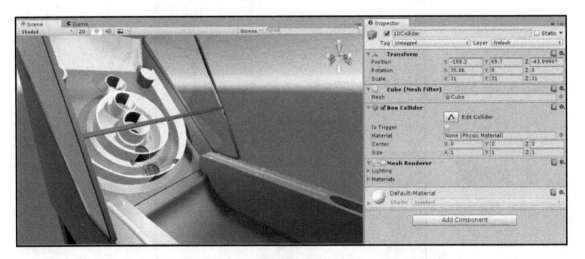

6. Click on the checkbox labeled **IsTrigger**:

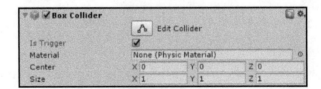

7. Uncheck the checkbox that says **Mesh Renderer**:

Who wants to score?

Now we have an invisible collision box waiting for something to hit it. Unfortunately, without a script to tell it how to respond, it will do nothing when it is triggered. Let's fix that by following these steps:

1. In the Inspector, click on **Add Component** near the bottom of the **Component**:

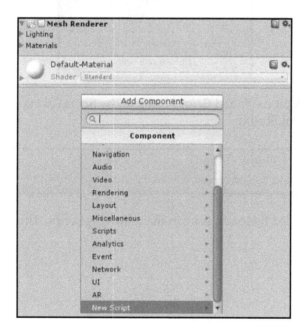

2. Name the **New Script** ScorePoints:

3. Double-click on the faded **ScorePoints** in the **ScorePoints** component. This will load up Visual Studio:

4. Once Visual Studio loads, type in the following script. This is a very simple script:

```
1   using System.Collections;
2   using System.Collections.Generic;
3   using UnityEngine;
4
5   public class ScorePoints : MonoBehaviour {
6
7
8       public int scoreValue;
9
10      // Use this for initialization
11      void Start () {
12
13      }
14
15      // Update is called once per frame
16      void Update () {
17
18      }
19
20      void OnTriggerEnter(Collider other)
21      {
22          ApplicationManager.Instance.score += scoreValue;
23      }
24      private void OnTriggerExit(Collider other)
25      {
26          Destroy(other.gameObject);
27      }
28  }
29
```

5. Let's go over the code and see exactly what it does:

- On line eight, we declare a public integer, called **scoreValue**. This is where we will store the numeric value for each trigger. A 50-point trigger will have a scoreValue of 50.

- Unity has a few events associated with colliders, although they are not part of the collider class technically.

- OnTriggerEnter, when another object collides with the object this script is attached to, this method is called. It also sends a reference to the object that collided with it. What we are doing here is calling our ApplicationManager singleton to add the scored amount to the total.

- `OnTriggerExit` runs when the triggering object leaves its collider. In our case, we destroy the `other.gameObject` or the ball that hit it when that happens.

6. If you go back to Unity at this point, you will get an error message. Currently, there is no variable in ApplicationManager called score. So, let's alleviate that really quick.

7. Open up `ApplicationManager` in Visual Studio. Somewhere around line 23, add the following line directly after:

    public string debugInfoString = "DebugInfo:";

    public int score = 0;

```
public class ApplicationManager : Singleton<ApplicationManager>, IInputClickHandler, ISpeechHandler
{
    public GameObject soundLayer1;
    public GameObject soundLayer2;
    public GameObject soundLayer3;
    public GameObject soundLayer4;

    public GameObject skeeballmachine;
    public GameObject sharingPrefab;
    public GameObject spatialPrefab;

    public TextMesh debugTextMesh;
    public string debugInfoString = "DebugInfo:";

    public int score = 0;
```

8. Alright, now that error is out of the way; if you click on the **10Collider** object, you should see a newly formed **Score Value** = **0** in the **ScorePoints** component:

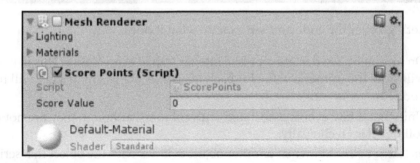

9. Well, since this is the **10Collider** object, we need it to equal 10. Type that into the box:

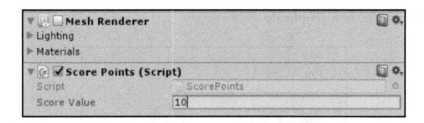

- Alright! That one down, six to go, but the rest are just duplicates.

10. Select the **10Collider**, right-click on it, and click on the **Duplicate** option:

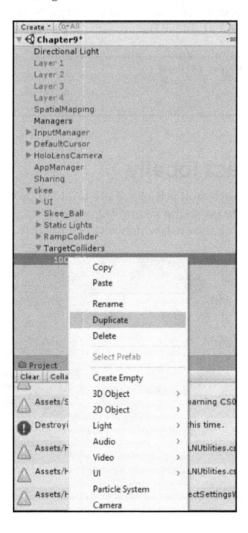

11. Rename the new **Duplicate** `20Collider`:

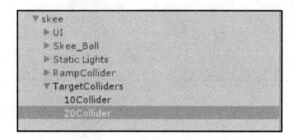

12. Now, change its score value to the equivalent of its name. Repeat this process for colliders 30, 40, 50, 100, and 100:

Think globally act locally

Unless you have changed the default settings, there is a high probability that if you look at your scene view to attempt to move the second trigger to its appropriate spot, you will see the Transform Gizmo pointing upward, which is very similar to the following screenshot:

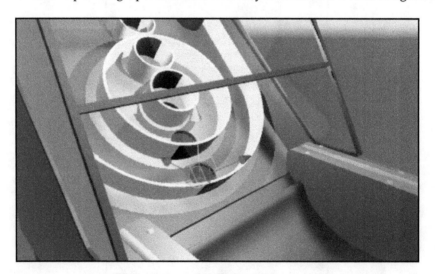

Our object is on a 40-degree angle, but our Transform Gizmo is aligned with the world. This movement configuration will cause a few headaches in the process of positioning the other TargetColliders:

Fortunately, sitting on the Unity toolbar is the answer. The Transform Gizmo toggles. Simply by clicking on the right button and changing the option from **Global** to **Local,** you see your Translation Gizmo align to your object:

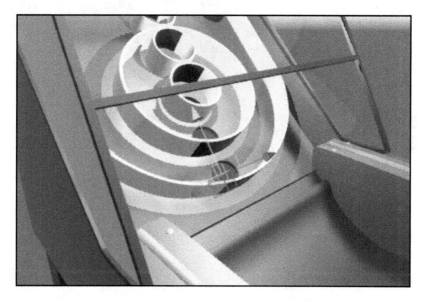

Now move the `20Collider` to its appropriate hole using the Green Gizmo arm:

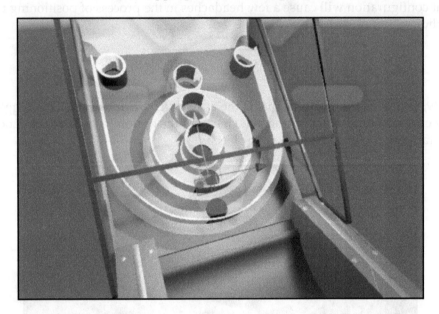

With that out of the way, repeat this process for 30, 40, 50, 100, and 100; duplicate, rename, adjust to the appropriate `scoreValue`, and move the collider to its correct spot. When you are finished, it should look something like this:

Finishing the Prefab

We have a few things left before we can wrap this Prefab up in a bow. The Spawn Point for the SkeeBall, speed indicator, and the SkeesPawner (start button) all need to be added. So, let's get it done.

Ball Spawn Point

Here, we will create an object to use as the Spawn Point for our SkeeBalls. It's a pretty quick and straightforward process; let's look at the steps to accomplish this:

1. Right-click on the **skee** object, select **3D Object**, and click on **Sphere:**

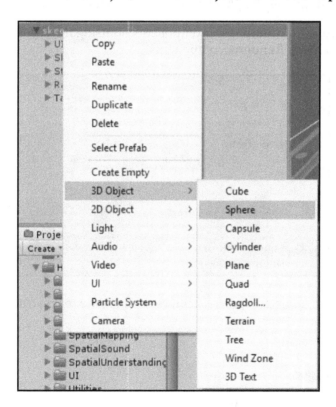

2. Name the newly created sphere **BallSpawnPoint**.

3. Set the **Transform** component to the following settings:

- **Position X** = `-153` `Y` `=` `2.800006` `Z` `=` `-780.4`
- **Rotation X**= `0` `Y` `=` `-90` `Z` `=` `0`
- **Scale X** = `30` `Y`= `30` `Z` `=` `30`

If you are curious as to why we are rotating the object, the reason is that we need our object to spawn with its forward vector facing down the ramp; this way the object goes the correct direction when we apply force to it. The reason we must do this is due to a problem with the machine model that is being used. Likely it was created in a program with a different coordinate system and as a result, it is rotated 90 degrees. The simple change of rotating our object to 90 degrees simplifies the physics calculations that come later.

Now uncheck the boxes to turn the two components off using the checkboxes for the **Sphere collider** and **Mesh Renderer** components:

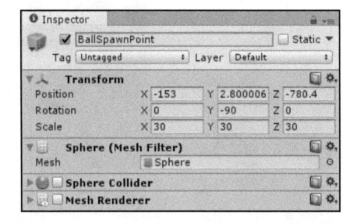

With that, we have a completed Spawn Point. Now, it is time to create the object that will spawn our ball Prefab.

SkeeSpawner

In the flow of the program, once we have the machine placed how we want, we need a start button, which we deleted earlier. If you have ever played one of these games in the real world, how did you start the machine? You did so by putting a quarter or token in the machine. With that in mind, does it not make sense to use the coin slots as the start button? Well, that is what we will do.

In this case, we will only need an empty game object with a collider. We will fit that object around the coin slots so that the user can click on the coin slots to start the game.

When you are in the flow of creating a project, there are definitely different approaches you can use. For instance, we can easily create a box, attach it to the Prefab, move it to the correct location, and so on. However, it seems better to me that if we have an object in this project already, or even in the very Hierarchy of objects we are using, that is very similar to our needs, it will be a better solution than creating a new object from scratch.

Here, we will take the colliders we created for the targets and repurpose them for our needs to make a **Start** button/SkeeBall Spawner. Let's take a look at the following steps:

1. Select the **10Collider** object, right-click, and hit **Duplicate**:

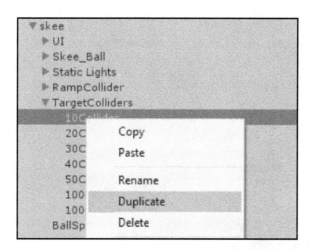

2. Rename the object `SkeeSpawner` and move it to the **UI** section of the Prefab.
3. Set the object's transform position to X = -33.96297, Y = -6.33325, and Z = -822.9261.
4. Set its X rotation to be 0 and its X, Y, and Z scales to be 37.
5. In the objects **Box Collider**, turn the **IsTrigger** checkbox off.

3. Finally, remove the **ScorePoints** component by right-clicking on the gear icon of the component and selecting the **Remove Component** option:

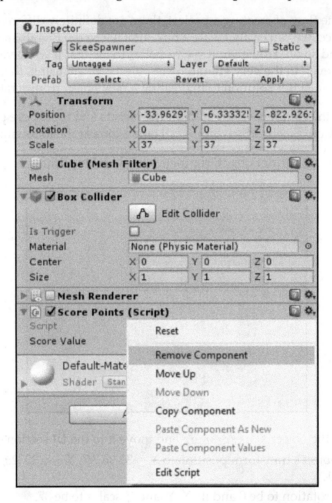

7. Now, as we have done before, click on **Add Component** | **New Script**.
8. Type SkeeSpawner in the box and click on **Create and Add**:

9. Now, double-click on the newly created component to bring it up in Visual Studio:

```
using HoloToolkit.Unity.InputModule;
using System.Collections;
using System.Collections.Generic;
using UnityEngine;
using System;

public class SkeeSpawner : MonoBehaviour, IInputClickHandler {

    public GameObject spawnPoint;
    public GameObject skeeballPrefab;

    public void OnInputClicked(InputClickedEventData eventData)
    {
        ApplicationManager.Instance.startButtonClicked = true;


    }

    // Use this for initialization
    void Start () {

    }

    // Update is called once per frame
    void Update () {

    }
}
```

10. Replace the code in the fresh SkeeSpawner with the preceding script. First, we have a reference to the Spawn Point we created in the last section. Secondly, we have a reference to our **Gameball** Prefab, which we will be creating soon. Lastly, we are using the HoloLens InputModule to react to the OnInputClicked event. If the button gets clicked, the ApplicationManager is informed by having a bool set to true, which the application manager reacts to and then immediately sets the bool back to false.

11. Open up your ApplicationManager script in Visual Studio and add this at or around line 23:

```
20          public TextMesh debugTextMesh;
21          public string debugInfoString = "DebugInfo:";
22
23          public bool startButtonClicked;
24          public int score = 0;
```

12. If we look at the `SkeeSpawner` object, the **SkeeSpawner (Script)** component now has two input boxes waiting for GameObjects.
13. Drag the **BallSpawnPoint** to the field next to **Spawn Point**.
14. The other field is looking for our **Skeeball Prefab**, which we have not yet made, so we will have to address this in a bit:

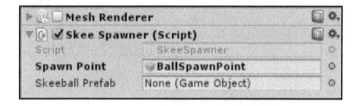

Onward and upward as they say.

Speed indicator

When I was working on building this project, since we cannot actually throw a ball up the ramp, I tried a few other approaches and control schemes to let the player get the ball from one end of the ramp to the other. I tried to set up a pinball-style air-tap and hold scheme, a double-tap measuring the timing of the two taps to determine the strength of the throw, and a few others as well.

My reason for not sticking to any of the earlier versions was that each one required the user to be looking at the ball, and generally by the time the user looks up, the ball is just starting to land or is already in a hole in some cases.

When you play SkeeBall in real life, you look at the target board the whole time, not the ramp. I decided that I wanted to use a control scheme that mimicked that. So, I landed on this solution.

At the end of the ramp, there is a light moving back and forth, transitioning in color from green to red. Depending on the color and position of the light when the user air-taps, it determines the amount of force that is applied to the ball when it is released.

This allows the user to look at the holes they are aiming for and therefore the experience feels a bit more authentic. Now, let's go through the steps to make this work:

1. In the skee **Hierarchy**, create an empty game object called **MovingLightSpeedIndicator**.

2. Set its **Transform** information to match the following image:

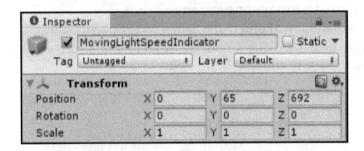

3. As a child of that object, create another empty GameObject, called **LightPos**, with the following **Transform** information:

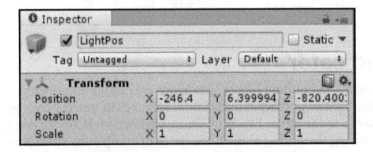

4. Create another empty GameObject as a child of **MoveLightSpeedIndictator**, called **LightPos2**, with the **Transform** information, as follows:

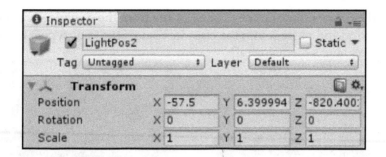

5. The last object we need to create for this branch of the hierarchy is a **Point light**. Set its **Transform** and light component fields to match the following image. The color we are using for this light is R = 0, G = 255, and B = 0:

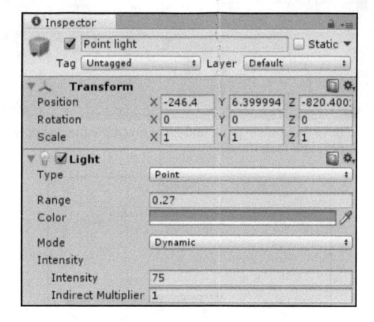

6. Finally, click on **Add Component | New Script** with the **Point light** object still selected.

7. Type `BounceObjectToPoints` in the name field and click on **Create and Add**. Now, double-click on the name to open it in Visual Studio.

7. Grab the `BounceObjectToPoints.cs` file from the downloads package and either copy and paste it into the class in Visual Studio or type it out manually (for reference, here's a screenshot):

```
1   using HoloToolkit.Unity;
2   using System.Collections;
3   using System.Collections.Generic;
4   using UnityEngine;
5
6   public class BounceObjectToPoints : Singleton<BounceObjectToPoints>
7   {
8
9       public GameObject lightPoint1;
10      public GameObject lightPoint2;
11      public float moveSpeed = 2.0f;
12      public float pauseTime = 0.5f;
13      public float maxSpeed = 900;
14      public float minSpeed = 500;
15      public Color startColor;
16      public Color endColor;
17      float previousX;
18      bool notMoving;
19
20      Renderer rend;
21      Light thisLight;
22      public float currentBallSpeed;
23
24      enum MoveState { StartPos, Moving, EndPos, Return }
25      MoveState myMove;
26
27
28      void Start()
29      {
30
31          rend = GetComponent<Renderer>();
32          thisLight = GetComponent<Light>();
33
34      }
```

8. Once you have the code in place and have saved the file, the options for the class should appear and look like this:

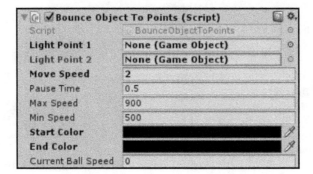

10. Drag and drop each of the **LightPos** objects over and change the rest of the fields to match the following image:

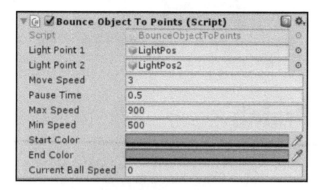

So, if you did type it all out, you might be curious as to what it all meant. Well, let me tell you. The big-picture idea is that we are using two GameObjects as transform references. We have an enumeration, called `MoveState`, with four states: `StartPos`, `Moving`, `EndPos`, and `Return`.

In the `Update()` method of our light object, we have a switch looking at two of those `MoveState`: `StartPos`, and `EndPos`. Each of those cases calls a coroutine, Lerps, short for Linear Interpolation, the object from either position A to B or from B to A.

`Vector3.Lerp` linearly interpolates between two vectors.

After the switch section, we have two lines of code that are important.

The first is our means of setting the current speed. Using a `MapScale` function, we can map our `maxspeed(900)` and `minspeed(500)` to the local X `position(-245.1f to -57.5f)` of the Point Light:

```
currentBallSpeed = MapScaleFloat(transform.localPosition.x, -245.1f,
-57.5f, maxSpeed, minSpeed);
```

The second line uses the same `MapScaleFloat` method to map the maximum and minimum speed of the ball from `0.0f` to `1.0f`. The return value of this method is used as the value for the red color. The way this function is being used creates a `1.0f` to `0.0f` range. In the green element of the color, we have the same method with the exception that maximum and minimum speed are switched, creating a low to high range:

```
thisLight.color = new Color(MapScaleFloat(currentBallSpeed, maxSpeed,
minSpeed, 0.0f, 1.0f), MapScaleFloat(currentBallSpeed, minSpeed, maxSpeed,
0.0f, 1.0f), 0f);
```

The rest of the `Update()` method is using the x position from the current frame instead of the previous frame to determine which move state should be active.

Now that we are done with the skee Prefab, for now, we can move a few steps closer to a playable project. Next up, we have the actual GameBall that will be using the speed that we set up just now.

GameBall Prefab

The final object we need to make our game an actual game is our ball. In this section, we will create a sphere, add a couple of classes and a rigid body, apply a material, and then turn the object into a Prefab. This will be short and sweet. Let's follow the given steps:

1. Start off by creating a sphere and ensuring that it is not a child of anything in the **Hierarchy** view.
2. Rename the sphere to **GameBall**.
3. Set its **Position** to 0,0,0 and its **Scale** to 0.07,0.07,0.07:

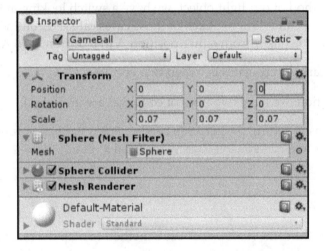

1. In the Project view, right-click on the Materials folder. Click on **Create** and then click on **Material**.
2. Name the new material GameBall and set the **Albedo RGB** values to 255,255,0--a very bright yellow.

2. Select the **GameBall** material in the Project view, drag it on top of the **GameBall** object, and drop it:

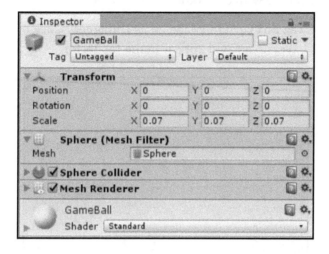

Now we have a yellow sphere sitting on top of the camera, which we cannot quite see. Now we need to add some code and a component before we can turn this into our game object. First though, we need to take a moment to look at **Tag** and **Layer**.

Tags and Layers

Tags are systems that allow us, as developers, to categorize objects in a scene. When situations arise where we need a reference to objects of a particular tag, we can use commands such as the following:

```
GameObject.FindObjectsWithTag("SomeTag");
```

This makes it really easy to locate objects of certain types.

If you look directly under the name of the object in the Inspector, you will see the dropdown for Tag.

We have two Tags currently in our project, and we need to add three more. It is worth noting that while the order is more important for Layers than Tags, in my experience, it can matter at times.

Layers allow for easy filtering. With Layers, if you need the camera to ignore certain objects or need your lights to only affect the ground, it's rather easy. In our case, we will use Layers so that objects will not collide with each other:

1. Click on the **Tag box** currently labeled as **Untagged**. Click on **Add Tag**.
2. The **Tags & Layers** page will appear in the **Inspector**:

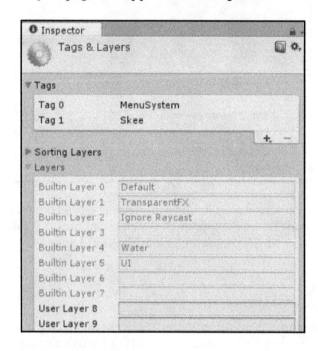

3. We need to use the + button to add three Tags in this order:

- **ScoreBoard**
- **SkeeBall**
- **SpawnPoint**

4. While we have this page open, we need to add two layers as well:

- **User Layer 8** - SpatialMapping Collision
- **User Layer 9** - needs to be SkeeBall

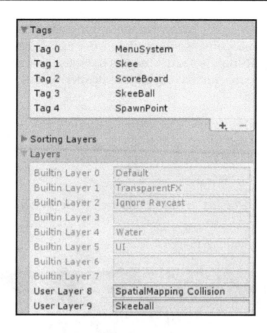

5. Now, select the `GameBall` object again and select SkeeBall for its Tag and SkeeBall for its Layer using the drop-down menus below the name.

6. Now, click on **Add Component** | **New Script** and create a class called `IgnoreSpatialMappingLayer.cs`.

7. Add this single line of code to the `start()` method:

```
1   using System.Collections;
2   using System.Collections.Generic;
3   using UnityEngine;
4
5   public class IgnoreSpatialMappingLayer : MonoBehaviour {
6
7       // Use this for initialization
8       void Start () {
9
10          Physics.IgnoreLayerCollision(8, 9);
11
12      }
13
14  }
15
```

I ran into scenarios where spatial mapping artifacts would pop up, and though we could not see them, they were causing odd physics issues, such as the ball hitting the spatial map as the map sat inside the ramp, or would not allow the machine to be laid out properly. This very simple solution fixed that.

In order for this to function correctly though, the children of the spatial map needed to be on the same layer as the parent object. So, we will create a quick and simple script that will iterate through each child of the spatial map object and change its layer.

8. With the `SpatialMapping` object selected, click on **Add Component**. Click on **New Script,** type `ChangeLayerOfChildren`, and then click on **Create and Enter**.

9. Now type out this quick piece of code:

```
void Update()
{

    if (ApplicationManager.Instance.ThrowBall)
    {
        throwDirection = Camera.main.transform.forward;
        throwForce = BounceObjectToPoints.Instance.currentBallSpeed;
        rb.AddForce(throwDirection * throwForce);
        ApplicationManager.Instance.ThrowBall = false;

    }
}
```

Simply put, we check whether the layer that the attached object is using is the one we want (8 - SpatialMapping Collision).

After the `if` statement, we manually set the objects layer to the one we want. Then, check the children of the object using a `foreach loop`, at which point we set the layer for each child.

ThrowBall.cs

With the GameBall selected, click on **AddComponent** | **NewScript** and create the `ThrowBall.cs` class. Grab this file from the downloads. We will not put the whole thing here, but we will go over the important area of the script:

Here, in our `Update()` function--remember that it's called every frame--
`ApplicationManager.Instance.ThrowBall` is checked. If that bool is true, this code is
executed:

- `throwDirection` is a variable set by the current forward vector of the camera or
  your position. Simply put, the angle you are pointing to determines the angle the
  ball will be thrown in.
- `throwForce` is a variable set by our `BounceObjectToPoints` class, based on the
  current location of the speed indicator light.
- Using the rigid body, we apply the force `throwDirection*throwForce`.
- As soon as we have sent the ball off, we set the `Throwball` **bool** back to false.

Now we need to add a rigid body so that the Unity physics engine can do its work.

With the **GameBall** still selected, click on **Add Component** | **Physics** | **RigidBody**. We can
leave these setting at the default. We have everything done on our **GameBall**, and we need
to turn it into a Prefab.

Click on the **GameBall** object, drag it down to the Prefabs folder in the Project view, and
release it. Once you see the **GameBall** in the Prefabs directory, delete the GameBall object
from the Hierarchy view.

Finishing touches

Now that we have our GameBall Prefab and our layers and Tags are set up, we can finish
our `skee` Prefab by carrying out the following mention changes:

- **skee**: Click on the root **skee** object. Change its tag to **Skee** and its layer to
  SpatialMapping Collision. When the dialog asks if you would like to change the
  children as well, choose **No, this object only.** The reason for this choice is that
  some of the children need to have different collision options.
- **ScoreBoard**: Go to **skee** | **UI** | **ScoreBoard** and change the tag to **ScoreBoard**.

- **SkeeSpawner**: Go to **skee | UI | SkeeSpawner** and drag the **GameBall** Prefab from the Project view to the **SkeeBall Prefab** box in the **SkeeSpawner** component:

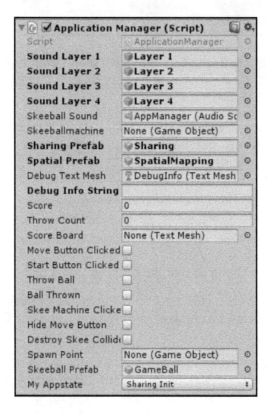

- **BallSpawnPoint**: Change the Tag to **Spawn Point** and Layer to SkeeBall.

With that, select the root **skee** object and hit **Apply** in the **Inspector**. This will save all the changes that have been made. Once that is accomplished, select skee in the **Hierarchy** view again and hit the *Delete* key.

Updating Placeskee ballMachine

We need to update and add some new functionalities to Placeskee ballMachine. Mostly, we will change the update function to respond to AppState.PlaceSkeeMachine, AppState.PlaceSkeeMachineComplete, and AppState.StartGame.

We will also change our **Options** button by renaming it to `MoveBtn` and then making it change whether the user is moving the machine or not. Let's carry out these steps:

1. Open up the `Placeskee ballMachine.cs` file and add the following line around line 28:

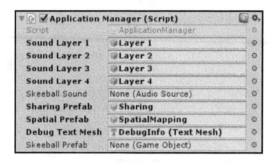

2. Save the file and head back to Unity for a moment.
3. Find **skee|UI|OptionsBtn**.
4. Rename it to **MoveBtn**.
5. Now, drag the object from the **Hierarchy** view to the **Move Button** field of the `Placeskee ballMachine` GameObject.

Now, we need to go back to Visual Studio and ensure that `Placeskee ballMachine` still has focus. We will change the `Update()` method by adding three new `if` statements.

Directly inside the function, before the existing code in the `Update()` method, add lines 74 to 101:

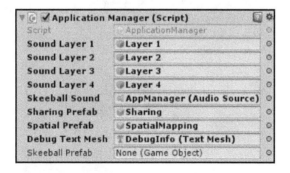

It's time for a quick rundown of the changes we made:

- In the first `if` statement, we check to see whether the `ApplicationManager` has set the bool `destroySkeeCollider` to true, which means we are getting rid of the outer collider on the machine. If that bool is set to `true` in the application manager, then we destroy the collider attached to this GameObject.
- The second `if` statement checks to see whether the `AppState.PlaceSkeeMachineComplete` is the current `myAppState`. If it is, we stop drawing the **SpatialMapping** visual mesh and attach a **World Anchor** to the object.
- In the final `if` statement, we are repeating parts of the last two `if` statements and then setting our move button text to an empty string to make it go away. Then, we set the `AppState` to `WaitForInput`. There were scenarios where we would reach this state without having reached the previous if statements, so this is very bad, but there's a quick fix for that issue.

Now, in the `OnInputClicked()` function down at line **141**, we need to change it so that the object will only accept input at certain times. In this case, the only time this object should react to a click at all is if the `AppState` has been set to `PlaceSkeeMachine`. Fortunately, this is rather effortless. We simply add an `if` statement to check whether the AppState of ApplicationManager is currently `PlaceSkeeMachine`. This should be the first code inside the method. Then, we add a } at the end:

```
141    public virtual void OnInputClicked(InputClickedEventData eventData)
142    {
143        // On each tap gesture, toggle whether the user is in placing mode.
144
145        if (ApplicationManager.Instance.myAppstate == ApplicationManager.AppState.PlaceSkeeMachine)
146        {
147            if (!IsBeingPlaced)
148            {
149                IsBeingPlaced = true;
150            }
151            else
152            {
153
154                IsBeingPlaced = false;
155            }
156
157            // If the user is in placing mode, display the spatial mapping mesh.
158            spatialMappingManager.DrawVisualMeshes = true;
159            wAnchorManager.RemoveAnchor(gameObject);
160
161        }
162    }
163
```

ApplicationManager

Okay, this class has become a bit of a monster, but we have built upon the changes we made previously using the enum and switch to make the process a bit smarter and to plan ahead to add things such as keeping score and setting throw limits, as well as other things.

With that in mind, the script is too large to go over every line, so grab the version in the `Chapter9` downloads package and copy it to your current version. We will spend some time going over the core changes and additions in the next chapter.

Once you have the code copied and saved, the application manager will suddenly look a bit less unruly. One problem that can arise with writing code for Unity is protection levels. Public variables have a slightly different function in Unity than they do in plain C#.

Action makes sound

Now, before we get into the core of the new `ApplicationManager`, we need to add another component to the `AppManager` object.

While I like the atmospheric sounds that play when the game begins, it needs something else for when the ball is thrown. Let's add that now:

1. With **AppManager** selected, click on **AddComponent | Audio | AudioSource**.
2. Get the `skee.wav` file from the downloads package and put it in your `Sounds` directory.
3. Drag the `skee.wav` file to the **AudioClip** field of the **AudioSource** component and drop it.
4. Then, change the **Spatial Blend** from 2D to 3D.

With the new audio source added to the object, we now need to get a reference to the Application Manager component. How are we going to do that? They are on the same object. Maybe the answer is just too obvious that people think it's a trick question, but really you just drag the application manager object from the **Hierarchy** view to the open field in the Application Manager component.

Once you do that, the appropriate class will appear in the field, as you can see in the **SkeeBall Sound** slot:

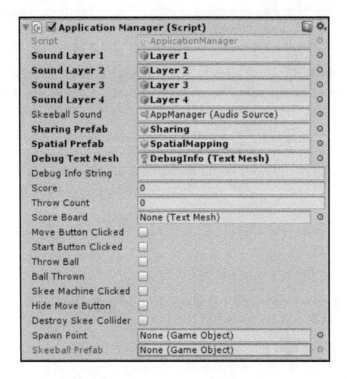

Oh, and ensure that there's only one slot left to fill.

In the Prefabs directory, select the **GameBall** Prefab and drag it to that last slot in the **Application Manager (Script)**, called **Skeeball** Prefab.

Also, while we are here, delete the text in the **DebugInfoString** field and replace it with `Air-Tap` once the Spatial Mapping is complete, to continue. We will be using `3DTextPrefab` for instructions in the final application.

Some quick house cleaning

If you were to test the application at this point, it should run and do everything we have set out for it to do, with one exception. If you start to play the game itself, for some reason the GameBall will not move more than a few inches. This is a problem with the SkeeBall machine model itself--a problem that I have fixed and made downloadable. You will need to import to get the full working effect of the project.

Before we do that, we need to clean out a few script files and move the important ones to the correct directory.

First, let's get rid of the stuff we do not need. If any of the following files are in your scripts directory, delete them:

- ChangeRectColor.cs
- LaunchBall.cs
- MasterPermission.cs
- PowerSwitch.cs
- RectAnim.cs
- StartButton.cs

After that purging (assuming that you did not already move scripts from this chapter to the scripts folder), you should have the following:

- Application Manager.cs
- OptionsButton.cs
- PlaceSkeeMachine.cs
- SyncSpawnSkee.cs

Now you should have six files in your Assets directory, (again, assuming that you did not already put them in your Scripts directory). Select and drag them to your scripts folder. Unity will take a quick moment to recompile and link up with objects:

- BounceObjectToPoints.cs
- ChangeLayerOfChildren.cs
- IgnoreSpatialMappingLayer.cs
- ScorePoints.cs
- SkeeSpawner.cs
- ThrowBall.cs

Replacing the main Prefab

Alright, now we will import the working skee ball machine into your project:

1. Look in the downloads for `skeemachine9.unitypackage`.
2. Click on **Assets** | **Import Package** | **Custom Package**.
3. Then, select the `skeemachine9.unitypackage` and let it import everything it suggests.
4. Once it has finished importing, ensure that all the important connections made through it are intact. I have run into multiple situations where the connections broke and, of course, you have no idea till the application is not working.

Here's a rundown of the potential problem areas to check and the appropriate GameObjects that should be there:

- **AppManager GameObject** | **SyncSpawnSkee> Skee Prefab**: skee
- **AppManager GameObject** | **Application Manager component** | **SkeeBall Prefab**: GameBall
- **Skee** | **UI** | **SkeeSpawner** | **Spawn Point**: BallSpawnPoint
- **Skee** | **UI** | **SkeeSpawner** | **SkeeBall Prefab**: GameBall
- **Sharing** | **PrefabSpawnManager** | **Prefab**: skee

Regardless of whether all those connections made it through or you had to manually fix them, you are ready to build and test out the SkeeBall game. If for any reason you cannot get it to run either in the editor or on the HoloLens in the downloads package, there is a file called `HoloLensBeginnersGuideChapter9Final.rar`. Just extract the `Assets` folder on top of your `Assets` folder and allow it to overwrite everything.

Ideally, if this is the case, the next chapter should help you find the solution without having to resort to such actions, but I do understand that people get impatient to try things, so I have offered a cheat here.

Summary

We covered a lot of ground in this chapter, and that ground was far and wide. We started off by reorganizing our main Prefab to make change and iteration a bit more organized and easier to maintain. We imported a section of a Prefab and put it into our current Prefab, replacing the colliders.

We moved from there to setting up our scoring system, first creating trigger colliders and then a script that will respond with a score update and then delete the ball that touched it. We also learned a bit about using global versus local transforms.

Next up, we set up a Spawn Point to use it as a reference for the GameBall in our entire world. We set up a start button on the skee ball machine where the coin slot should be.

As we continued, we dug into the speed indication system, learned how to programmatically animate a light moving between two GameObjects, and then use its position to determine the color of the light, while at the same time determining the speed of the ball.

Next up, we created our GameBall Prefab and worked with Tags and Layers to help simplify some elements of object selection and selective responses to objects in the scene. With a `RigidBody` component and a few lines of code, we learned how to set the angle and apply force to our object. While we did touch on the Application Manager at the end of this chapter, it was only the start.

In the next chapter, we will break the entire Application Manager down into its important parts so that we all can understand it. Once we have made it through that, we will learn about debugging and optimization, and many of the tools available to us through both Unity and Visual Studio.

10
Fixing Problems

Issues will arise as you make your way through your own projects and when they do, it helps to know as many approaches as possible to help you find a solution. Between **Visual Studio** and **Unity**, there are numerous ways to tackle such problems when they show up.

In this chapter, we will dig into debugging. Now, what we worked on in Chapter 7, *The Tools of the Trade*, was a valid way to debug, but that was one of the many ways. We will look at a collection of ways to find entirely different levels of information for those times when there is a bug you just can't squash.

While the details may be outside the scope of beginner development, we will also touch lightly on concepts such as optimization and profiling. Many of the tools we use for the process of debugging will work for optimization as well. The hope here is that you walk away armed with enough knowledge to try and learn.

That said, before we get into either of those subjects, we still need to take a solid look at our Application Manager. As part of the work for Chapter 9, *Putting It All Together*, this class became far more robust. We will now take a little time to go over the class in its entirety.

The Application Manager

As we have talked about previously, the **Application Manager** is the engine that makes everything else run. It handles flow control and the triggering of most of the events. It does this through the use of an **Enumerator** type, or **enum**, and a **switch** statement. For those two elements to do their job, there is a supporting cast of variables and methods.

Seeing it all at once

When developing an application, it often helps if you can hold all the moving pieces in your memory. As your experience grows, you will learn various systems and understand how they work together, and while you may not know every variable by heart, that feat will eventually not be as daunting as it sounds.

Diagramming your application can go a long way to help you understand the flow of your project from the word go. If used from the planning stage, you will tend to write code that is cleaner and easier to manage.

Let's take a top-to-bottom view of our Application Manager in a diagrammatic format known as a **mind map**. This type of diagram lets you map out all the important elements and even connect the associations, if you so choose. In this case, we are aiming to keep it simple, that is, without any associations:

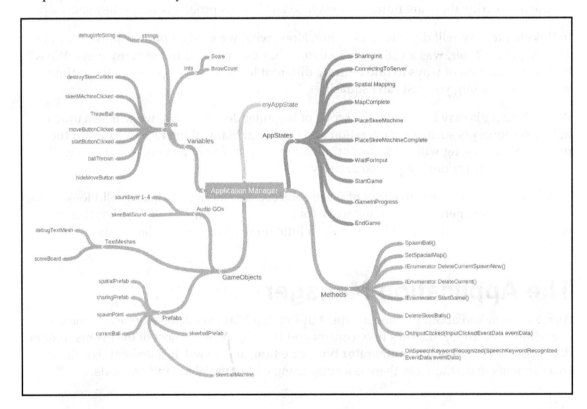

It can be argued that **UML** or **Unified Modeling Language** is a better choice for planning application development, and I would agree, but with these caveats. First, a mind map is a great place to gather your raw ideas and plan your steps before moving them to a UML diagram. Second, mind maps are far easier to digest for beginners, so they are the right choice for this project.

In the preceding example, we can see a breakdown of all the variables and GameObjects, all the enum states, and the methods used to create the experience. This is a simple snapshot of our application. While we cannot see that `IEnumerator StartGame()` calls the `DeleteSkeeBalls()` method, enables the `ChangeLayerOfChildren` component on the spatial map, or sets the AppState to `gameInProgress` when it is finished, having this overall view can be a simple way to compartmentalize the workflow.

What does our Application Manager do?

With the basic overview out of the way, let's get into the heart of our code. We will go through every line of code, though we will only lightly touch some areas.

First, start with the using statements:

```
using System;
using System.Collections;
using System.Collections.Generic;
using UnityEngine;
using HoloToolkit.Unity;
using HoloToolkit.Unity.SpatialMapping;
using HoloToolkit.Unity.InputModule;
```

We can access additional functionality outside that of standard C# and .NET libraries through `using` statements.

Let's move forward with the declaration of `ApplicationManager`:

```
Class Declaration
public class ApplicationManager : Singleton<ApplicationManager>,
IInputClickHandler, ISpeechHandler
{
```

This is the declaration of `ApplicationManager`. We declare it as a Singleton which, in this case, is a product of `using HoloToolkit.Unity;`. The HoloToolkit team took the time to implement the Singleton design pattern.

Normally, there is a construction process for creating a Singleton, but the HoloToolkit team decided to simplify it. This class also implements the `IInputClickHandler` and `ISpeechHandler` interfaces, which allow us to use air-tap and keyword controls. The Singleton pattern restricts its own existence to a single instance. One effect this has is providing an access point on a global level for other classes to use. In our case, having a single Application Manager Singleton to control the flow of the whole process keeps our program easy to follow.

Next, we have our variable declarations. These are our references to various GameObjects in the scene and prefabs, followed by the string, ints, and bools that we will use throughout our application:

```
public GameObject soundLayer1;
public GameObject soundLayer2;
public GameObject soundLayer3;
public GameObject soundLayer4;
public AudioSource skeeballSound;

public GameObject skeeballmachine;
public GameObject sharingPrefab;
public GameObject spatialPrefab;
public GameObject spawnPoint;
public GameObject skeeballPrefab;
GameObject currentBall;

public TextMesh debugTextMesh;
public TextMesh scoreBoard;

public string debugInfoString = "";

public int score = 0;
public int throwCount = 0;

public bool moveButtonClicked;
public bool startButtonClicked;
public bool ThrowBall;
public bool ballThrown;
public bool skeeMachineClicked;
public bool hideMoveButton;
public bool destroySkeeCollider;
```

Following our variables is our Enumerator type declaration `AppState`. In the declaration, we define ten different states, which will be set as 0-9, due to the first one being declared as 0:

```
public enum AppState
{
    SharingInit = 0,
    ConnectingToServer,
    SpatialMapping,
    MapComplete,
    PlaceSkeeMachine,
    PlaceSkeeMachineComplete,
    WaitForInput,
    StartGame,
    GameInProgress,
    EndGame,
}
```

Here, we declare our `AppState` variable, `myAppState`:

```
public AppState myAppstate;
```

Now it is time to create out methods; we will start with the two standard Unity methods: `Start()` and `Update()`. Unity has a collection of others, but these two will always be in any `cs` file we create from Unity. The `Start()` method is called on the frame that the associated object is enabled.

In our `Start()` method, we start simple. In order to accept an air-tap without the need to have a focused object, we are using `PushModalInputHandler`. This is so when the application finishes scanning the room, the player's air-tap does not require an object to be the focus:

```
void Start()
{
    InputManager.Instance.PushModalInputHandler(this.gameObject);
}
```

Next, we have our `Update()` method and the majority of this class. `Update()` is called by the Unity Engine every frame.

We will cover this block by block. If you look through the code, you will note `#region` statements. These statements make it easy to keep important code focused, while hiding code that is finished or of lower priority at the time:

```
void Update()
{
```

```
#region   IfStatements
if (scoreBoard != null)
{
    scoreBoard.text = score.ToString();
}
```

Here, in the first `if` statement, we are checking to ensure that our `scoreBoard` object is not null and then we update the board with the current score. Convert the score integer to a string in the process:

```
if (moveButtonClicked && myAppstate != AppState.PlaceSkeeMachine)
{
myAppstate = AppState.PlaceSkeeMachine;
moveButtonClicked = false;
}
```

In the second `if` statement, we are checking to see whether the move button has been air-tapped and that the current `myAppstate` is not `Appstate.PlaceSkeeMachine`. If those conditions are not met, we move on. Otherwise, we move into the `PlaceSkeeMachine` state:

```
if (startButtonClicked)
{
    myAppstate = AppState.StartGame;
    startButtonClicked = false;
}
```

The final statement in the block is waiting on the `startButtonClicked` bool to be true, which occurs when the player air-taps the coin slot on the machine. When that happens, the `AppState` is changed to `StartGame` and the game begins:

```
#endregion
```

Now we have reached our switch statement; this is the biggest block of code in the project and we will cover it case by case.

It is worth noting that due to this switch statement being in the `Update()` function when a particular state is active, the code for that state will run repeatedly until the state is changed. This can cause issues. To resolve this, most of the states make a change and then change to a different state:

```
#region   Switch
debugTextMesh.text = debugInfoString;
   switch (myAppstate)
{
    #region Connection and Spatial Mappng stuff
```

```
case AppState.SharingInit:
    {
        sharingPrefab.SetActive(true);
        myAppstate = AppState.ConnectingToServer;
    }
    break;
```

This state activates the `sharingPrefab` and then changes the state to
`AppState.ConnectingToServer`:

```
case AppState.ConnectingToServer:
    {
        //need a test to determine that the user is connected.
        myAppstate = AppState.SpatialMapping;
    }
    break;
```

After Chapter 8, *Share What You Have Got*, I stopped using the server due to testing issues
and time, so currently the only thing this case does is to go to `AppState.SpatialMapping`:

```
case AppState.SpatialMapping:
    {
        spatialPrefab.SetActive(true);
    }
    break;
```

This case is again simple. It sets the `spatialPrefab` to active. Having it constantly
`SetActive(true)` is not optimal by any means, but does not interrupt the flow:

```
case AppState.MapComplete:
    {
        SyncSpawnSkee.Instance.SyncSpawnSkeeBallMachine();
        skeeballmachine =
GameObject.FindGameObjectWithTag("Skee");
        spawnPoint =
GameObject.FindGameObjectWithTag("SpawnPoint");
        scoreBoard =
GameObject.FindGameObjectWithTag("ScoreBoard").GetComponent<TextMesh>();
        debugInfoString = "If you need to move the Skeeball \n
Machine, select the Move Machine menu \n option. Otherwise, Air-Tap the \n
Red Coin Slot.";
        myAppstate = AppState.WaitForInput;
    }
    break;
```

In a Unity scene, objects and prefabs cannot be linked to each other. So, in order to get references to a prefab that was just spawned, we have to use various types of search function.

In this state, which is activated when the user air-taps after the spatial map is finished:

- We spawn the `Skeeball` machine
- We assign the `Skeeball` machine a variable using the `Skee` tag we assigned to it to help find the variable
- We assign the `spawnPoint` for the `gameBall` to the `spawnPoint` variable in the same manner
- The scoreboard's `TextMesh` component is assigned to the scoreboard variable
- `debugStringInfo` is updated with instructions for the user
- Finally, the `AppState` is changed to `AppState.WaitForInput`

```
case AppState.PlaceSkeeMachine:
    {
        // Plae SkeeballMachine.cs should be working right now.
        debugInfoString = "Air-Tap on the Skeeball \n Machine
to move it. \n Once you find a spot \n you like Air-Tap again \n to place
the machine.";
        if (moveButtonClicked)
        {
            myAppstate = AppState.PlaceSkeeMachineComplete;
            moveButtonClicked = false;
        }
    }
    break;
```

In this case, the user is actively moving the Skeeball machine around with their gaze. We change the variable `debugInfoString` to give the user instructions and then wait for the user to hit the `moveButton` a second time. When the user does hit the button, we change the state to `PlaceSkeeMachineComplete`, as shown in the following code:

```
case AppState.PlaceSkeeMachineComplete:
    {
        debugInfoString = "";
SpatialMappingManager.Instance.GetComponent<ChangeLayerOfChildren>().enable
d = true;
    }
    break;
```

In the `PlaceSkeeMachineComplete` state, we set the `debugInfoString` to an empty string and then enable the `ChangeLayerOfChildren` component of the `SpatialMappingManager`:

```
case AppState.WaitForInput:
    {
    }
    break;
```

There is nothing in the `WaitForInput` state; this is an idle state that is activated while we wait on the player to click on the start button, as shown in the following code:

```
case AppState.StartGame:
    {
        StartCoroutine(StartGame());
    }
    break;
```

The `StartGame` case runs the `StartCoroutine()`, as shown in the following code:

```
case AppState.GameInProgress:
    {
        if (ballThrown)
        {
            if (throwCount <= 10)
            {
                StartCoroutine(DeleteCurrentSpawnNew());
                skeeballSound.Play();
                ballThrown = false;
                throwCount += 1;
            }
            else
            {

                StartCoroutine(DeleteCurrent());
                ballThrown = false;

                myAppstate = AppState.EndGame;

            }
        }
    }
    break;
#endregion
```

This case is where the game logic happens, which is really simple. If the `ballThrown` bool becomes true, it verifies that the `throwcount` is not 10 or more. If that is the case, the ball is thrown in the `ThrowBall` class, so this case runs a Coroutine that counts to 3, deletes the ball, and spawns a new one. Then, it triggers the sound effect, increments the `throwcount`, and resets the `ballThrown` trigger. If `ballThrown` is 10 or greater, a Coroutine that counts to 3 and deletes the ball runs. This time, the ball is not respawned. The `ballThrown` trigger is reset and the `AppState` is set to `EndGame`:

```
#region EndGame
        case AppState.EndGame:
        {
            soundLayer1.GetComponent<AudioSource>().volume = 0.2f;
            soundLayer2.GetComponent<AudioSource>().volume = 0.2f;
            soundLayer3.GetComponent<AudioSource>().volume = 0.2f;
            soundLayer4.GetComponent<AudioSource>().volume = 0.2f;
            debugInfoString = "Game Over";
            myAppstate = AppState.WaitForInput;
        }
        break;
        #endregion
        default:
        {

        }
        break;
    }
```

In the `EndGame` case, all the atmospheric sounds are set to a much lower volume, the `debugInfoString` is set to `Game Over`, and the `AppState` is set back to `WaitfrInput`:

```
#endregion
    }
```

With `Update()`, the hard part is out of the way; the rest of this should be a breeze. `SpawnBall()` instantiates a ball into the game world and assigns it to the `currentBall` variable, as shown in the following code:

```
void SpawnBall()
    {
        currentBall = Instantiate(skeeballPrefab,
spawnPoint.transform.position, spawnPoint.transform.rotation);

    }
```

The primary reason for this assignment is that the ball can be deleted when it is not needed. Let's call the `SetSpatialMap()` method:

```
void SetSpatialMap()
{
    SpatialMappingManager.Instance.DrawVisualMeshes = false;
    InputManager.Instance.PopModalInputHandler();
    myAppstate = AppState.MapComplete;

}
```

`SetSpatialMap()` is called when the user air-taps to confirm that the spatial map is complete. We set the visibility to `false`, then we pop the `ModalInputHandler` off the stack, and set the `AppState` to `MapComplete`.

`Pop` and `Push` are terms that come from assembly programming. In assembly, you are working directly with processor registers that work using a stack. **Last In First Out -- LIFO** is how a stack works. `Push` is adding something to the stack, `Pop` is taking something off the stack. One thing this does afford us, as developers, is the ability to order changes in the various input modes:

```
IEnumerator DeleteCurrentSpawnNew()
{
    yield return new WaitForSeconds(3.0f);
    Destroy(currentBall);
    Debug.Log("Push-DeleteCurrntSpawnNew");
    InputManager.Instance.PushModalInputHandler(this.gameObject);

    yield return new WaitForSeconds(0.5f);
    SpawnBall();
}
```

This method is an `IEnumerator` type, or a Coroutine as it is commonly referred to. What makes this different from your typical method is that it has the ability to be paused, a very useful ability in this type of programming. Here, we wait for 3 seconds and then destroy the `currentBall`. We then push a new `ModalInputHandler` onto the stack, wait for half a second, and call the `SpawnBall()` method, as shown in the previous code.

```
IEnumerator DeleteCurrent()
{

    yield return new WaitForSeconds(3.0f);
    Destroy(currentBall);

    yield return new WaitForSeconds(0.5f);
    myAppstate = AppState.EndGame;
```

```
    }
```

This is similar to the preceding WaitForSeconds() method in that it waits for 3 seconds and deletes the currentBall. This time though, it waits for half a second and sets the AppState to EndGame, as shown in the following code:

```
    IEnumerator StartGame()
    {
        yield return new WaitForSeconds(1.5f);
        debugInfoString = "";
SpatialMappingManager.Instance.GetComponent<ChangeLayerOfChildren>().enable
d = true;
        if (currentBall != null) { DeleteSkeeBalls(); }
        throwCount = 0;
        score = 0;

        if (soundLayer1.activeInHierarchy)
        {
            soundLayer1.GetComponent<AudioSource>().volume = 1f;
            soundLayer2.GetComponent<AudioSource>().volume = 1f;
            soundLayer3.GetComponent<AudioSource>().volume = 1f;
            soundLayer4.GetComponent<AudioSource>().volume = 1f;
        }
        else
        {
            soundLayer1.SetActive(true);
            soundLayer2.SetActive(true);
            soundLayer3.SetActive(true);
            soundLayer4.SetActive(true);
        }
        SpawnBall();
        Debug.Log("Push-StartGame");
        InputManager.Instance.PushModalInputHandler(this.gameObject);
        myAppstate = AppState.GameInProgress;


    }
```

There is one last Coroutine to start the game: it waits for 1.5 seconds, sets the debugInfoString to empty, and then enables the ChangeLayerOfChildren. As there should not be any game balls active at the start of the game, it checks whether currentBall is not null and if that condition is true, it deletes the ball.

Throwcount and score are both set to 0. The ambient sounds are all turned to 1.0f and set to active. The SpawnBall() function is called. Once more, we push the PushModalInputHandler method and set the AppState to GameInProgress:

```
    public void DeleteSkeeBalls()
```

```
    {

        List<GameObject> skeeballs = new
  List<GameObject>(GameObject.FindGameObjectsWithTag("SkeeBall"));
        if (skeeballs != null)
        {

            foreach (GameObject go in skeeballs)
            {
                Destroy(go);

            }
        }

    }
```

This method creates a collection known as a List, searches the scene for any active objects with the SkeeBall tag, and then iterates through the list deleting each object:

```
public void OnInputClicked(InputClickedEventData eventData)
{
    Debug.Log("OnInput");
    if (myAppstate == AppState.SpatialMapping)
    {
        SetSpatialMap();
    }
    if (myAppstate == AppState.GameInProgress)
    {
        Debug.Log("Pop-DeleteCurrntSpawnNew");
        InputManager.Instance.PopModalInputHandler();
        ThrowBall = true;
        ballThrown = true;
        Debug.Log("ThrowBall is true");
    }

}
```

Whenever there is an air-tap, this method is called. Depending on the current AppState, it will function differently. If this AppState is SpatialMapping, the method calls SetSpatialMap. If the AppState is Game In Progress, we pop the current PopModalInputHandler() method from its stack and then trigger both ThrowBall and ballThrown by setting them to true, as shown in the preceding code.

```
public void OnSpeechKeywordRecognized(SpeechKeywordRecognizedEventData
eventData)
    {
        if (myAppstate == AppState.SpatialMapping)
```

```
        {
            switch (eventData.RecognizedText.ToLower())
            {

                case "done":
                    SetSpatialMap();
                    break;
            }
        }
    }
}
```

In the final method, we are checking for speech; when the word **done** is recognized and the current `AppState` is `SpatialMapping`, the `SetSpatialMap()` method is called.

With that, we have covered the entire `ApplicationManager` class. My hope is that, even if you have no intention of ever writing code, now you can look at that code and have a solid understanding of what is going on under the hood. With some time and patience, you can eventually make changes that work and possibly even write your own code one day soon.

Always keep in mind that most programmers start off modifying other people's code. It's a modern rite of passage.

Now, it is time to learn how to fix the problems that arise when we can't see every consequence to the code we write. It is time to learn about debugging, what it is, how it can help us, and what tools are available to make it easier.

Debugging

Once we get our projects to a place where we can run them, we will begin testing the software, looking for errors, and attempting to find solutions to correct these errors. Debugging is the name given to the process of finding and getting rid of the problems in our software. This process can be accomplished in numerous ways, from simple console warnings to using far more elaborate software. We will go over all the options we have with the Visual Studio and Unity setup.

The primary categories of errors that occur can be broken down into the following:

- **Syntax errors**: These types of bugs do not affect us in the testing phase because if they occur, we cannot test; the application will not run at all.
- **Logic errors**: Infinite loops, index out of range errors.
- **Arithmetic errors**: In my mind, this is a subcategory of logic errors. When the math is wrong, the application will behave erratically and it can be painful to track down the problem.
- **Resource or Runtime errors**: These are access violations or errors that occur during the execution of a program.
- **Null pointers**: An error that occurs when we are trying to access the members/methods of a null object.
- **Performance errors**: Attempting to use more processing power than the device is capable of producing.

One of the benefits of using C# as our language is that it is a very smart language. C# falls into the **Common Language Runtime** or **CLR** standard. Just-in-time compilation is compilation done during program execution or runtime. CLR is a standard that brings with it many benefits, including memory management, garbage collection, smart exception handling and thread management. Due to the benefits of CLR, the preceding error list is not a lot more elaborate.

This section will cover many different tools and, as such, this will not be in the tutorial form as the rest of this book has been, well mostly. This is more about informing you of the options and a few lessons I have learned along the way.

Bring the black flag

While it would be nice if there was a magic wand to wave and all the bugs were gone, it just doesn't work that way...yet. For now, we must manually find the bugs, then and only then can we take them out. If programming is a path you plan to go down for the long term, strap in and get ready, debugging is a process that you will spend a large majority of your time doing.

Traditional applications tend to benefit from debugging systems, while games and, by extension, 3D applications for HoloLens or other head-mounted-displays and mobile devices have lacked the ability to use the low-level tools effectively, at least until recently.

Generally, with 3D applications or non-traditional hardware, we would end up having to create the tools we use to hunt down the problems we had. This is not uncommon for any kind of development, but just more common in this space. These high-level solutions are typically visual in nature, but can also be a basic console logger like the one we made in `Chapter 7`, *The Tools of the Trade*. I ended up using it a lot when I was working my way through the rest of the application.

The tests we need to get feedback on can be as simple as an object turning red or green when certain conditions are met, or seeing the constant value of a variable as conditions are changed throughout the execution of the application. We will start on this level in Unity itself and the Inspector panel.

Inspector

Quick and customizable feedback is one of the key elements of quick and accurate bug squashing. Unity has made a tool that can allow a developer to plan for the problem areas and have the tests in place to ensure that everything goes as smoothly as possible.

Before we can really utilize the **Inspector**, we need to know a few other things about the scripts that we make in Unity. To start off, we will look at Unity Property Attributes.

Unity Property Attributes

When a variable is set to public, as opposed to private, in C#, with Unity it is exposed to the Inspector, which allows real-time changes. In most cases, this is great; it is exactly what we want to quickly create feedback.

There are cases though, for instance, using Singletons or creating static classes, in which we need variables that are to be set to public, but we do not want them to be changed in the editor. These are cases where other classes need to change the variables.
Let's have a look at our **Application Manager**:

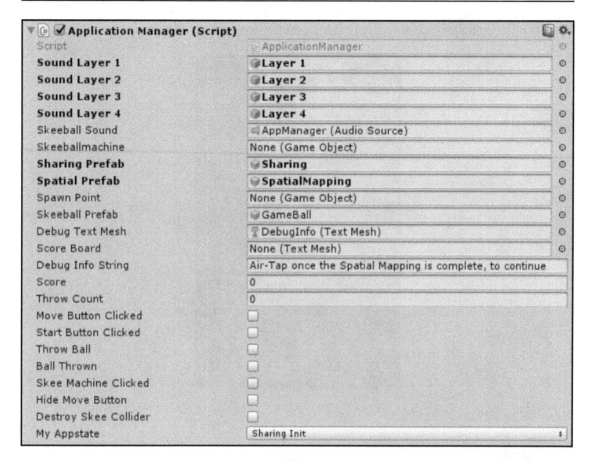

If you look at our **Application Manager** at the moment, it is an absolute mess. As you can see, the long-term effect of using a bunch of public variables is a component in Unity with a large number of fields that we do not need to see. It can be a rather ugly and indiscernible mess.

The first property attribute we will look at directly affects this mess by allowing us to hide public variables that we do not need edit access to: **[HideInInspector]**. By simply using this attribute for each variable we want to be hidden, we can clean up our mess quite quickly.

For example, consider that our ugly looking component uses the following:

```
[HideInInspector]
public GameObject soundLayer2;
[HideInInspector]
public GameObject soundLayer3;
[HideInInspector]
public GameObject soundLayer4;
[HideInInspector]
public AudioSource skeeballSound;

[HideInInspector]
public GameObject skeeballmachine;
[HideInInspector]
public GameObject sharingPrefab;
[HideInInspector]
public GameObject spatialPrefab;
[HideInInspector]
public GameObject spawnPoint;
[HideInInspector]
public GameObject skeeballPrefab;
GameObject currentBall;

[HideInInspector]
public TextMesh debugTextMesh;
[HideInInspector]
public TextMesh scoreBoard;

public string debugInfoString = "";
```

It can become this in minutes:

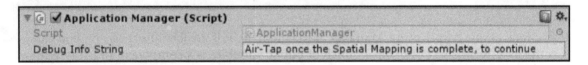

Of course, this is an extreme example.

Aside from **[HideInInspector]**, there are a couple of other *property attributes* that can allow us to clean up our class a bit without having to hide everything.

- **[Space]:** It allows us to put blank space between groups of fields
- **[Header("HeaderName")]:** It allows us to name those groups for an easier way to discern the mass of objects

After a few minutes of adjustments, we now have something that is easy to read:

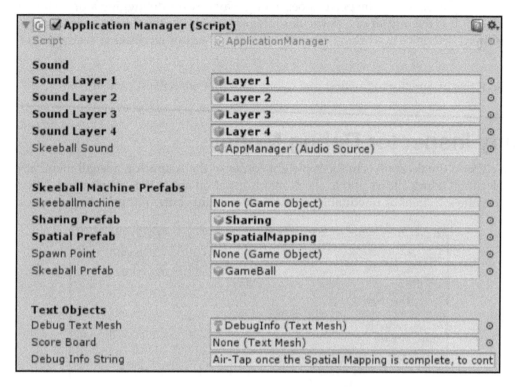

As the Inspector moves towards debugging:

```
[Header("Sound")]
public GameObject soundLayer1;
public GameObject soundLayer2;
public GameObject soundLayer3;
public GameObject soundLayer4;
public AudioSource skeeballSound;
[Space]
[Space]

[Header("Skeeball Machine Prefabs")]
public GameObject skeeballmachine;
public GameObject sharingPrefab;
public GameObject spatialPrefab;
public GameObject spawnPoint;
public GameObject skeeballPrefab;
GameObject currentBall;
[Space]
```

So, now you may be asking what this has to do with debugging. Well first, being able to choose what you see in the Inspector goes a long way toward debugging a problem on a high level. If it is the output of a particular integer or whether the timing of getting a **GameObject** reference is working correctly, instant in -editor feedback is really good to have.

Second, it ties in directly to the first real debug tool that we will talk about.

Unity Inspector Debug Mode

If you click on the three lines in the top-right corner of the **Inspector**, a small menu appears, and selecting **Debug** allows you to see more information about the components. It does show private variables as uneditable, so that is a great attribute of this **Debug** option:

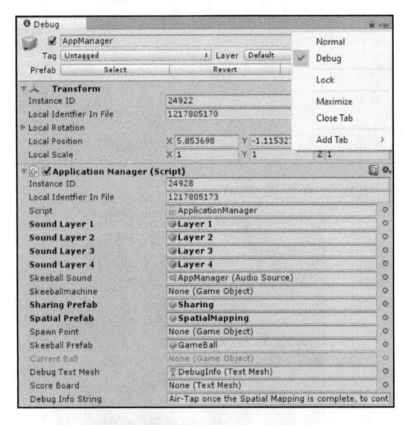

Now, this is really a tool for debugging custom editor controls and windows, but this can absolutely be put into your tool belt for the right occasion.

The range of tools available to us to find the problems that will occur is indeed wide. From the most basic of tracking variables in the Unity interface down to Visual Studio Graphic, debugging allows you to break down every individual draw call to find and fix really deep problems.

Debug.Log/Console window

Unity's console window is there so often that you almost take it for granted. I know I nearly forgot about it as a debug option. However, the power level and ability of this window is added to `Debug.Log ("Pop-DeleteCurrntSpawnNew")`. It comes with a stack to read as well; while not quite what you will get out of a full-fledged debugger, this does not require tracing every line of code. I know, doesn't that sound like fun.

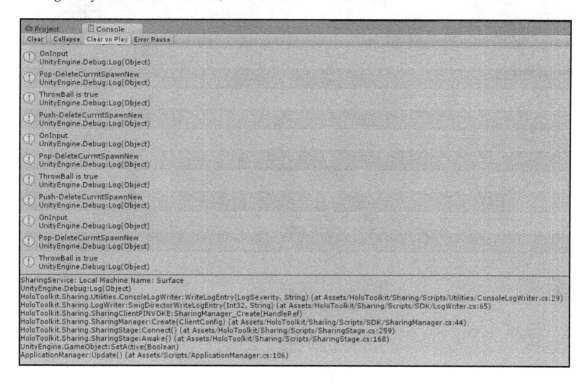

Visual Studio Debugger

Speaking of tracing every line of code, a lesson that I have had to learn and relearn a couple of times over the years is that sometimes when you are really stuck, the best thing you can do is set a breakpoint, a point in the code that tells the debugger to stop execution, set up to watch a specific variable, and start stepping in and out of methods.

It was not that long ago that I had spent 6 hours with no luck trying to figure out an issue. I set up the Visual Studio Debugger and watched the call stack for a single pass through and noted an odd occurrence--it was fixed in 3 minutes. Seriously, 3 minutes after hours of beating my head against a wall--I can be stubborn at times.

Let's have a look at the `currentBallSpeed` variable:

Here's another example. I was having issues with the speed of the game ball and wanted to see what is happening with the `currentBallSpeed` variable. I set a breakpoint on the line after the `currentBallSpeed` was updated, then I set a watch for that variable. I them ran the program on my HoloLens and connected the debugger. At this point, I just let it hit the breakpoint and hit continue again. This process was pushing it further one frame at a time, so I could see the numerical value for the speed the ball was moving. I noted that the value was correct in terms of the direction it was going, but I also noted that the number was jumping nearly 100 per frame; there was not enough resolution. This explained a few issues I had noted. Now those issues are addressed.

It doesn't matter what debugger you stick to as your go-to option; you must familiarize yourself with this debugger and the process. It can be a life saver. That said, at times it can be slight touchy about working with HoloLens. Sometimes it is amazing, other times a trial.

Profiling and fixing performance

Profilers, while they are technically still debuggers, are designed to debug a different element and from a completely different perspective. A profiler is a much lower-level debugging system that is looking at performance and what is attributed to the performance as it stands during execution.

Like standard debuggers, these tools can easily give you insights that lead to finding solutions to high-level problems, but will generally help you determine why your application is running at 14 FPS instead of 60.

HoloLens Developers Portal

There is a tool built right into HoloLens that does a great job of letting you see how your application is running. It displays SoC (system-on-chip) power, system power, Frame Rate, GPU, CPU, input/output, network, and memory. On most of the HoloLens projects I work with this, as this is the first test to perform when performance is not great.
Let's take a look at **System Performance**:

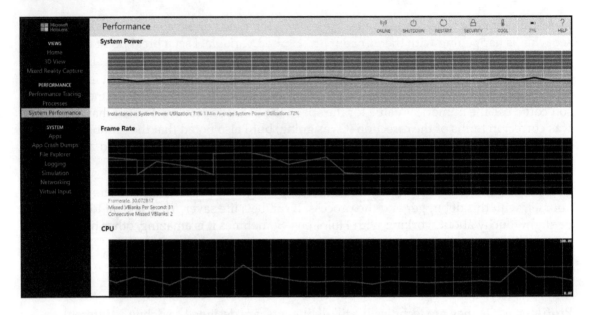

This can be accessed from any PC on the same network by pulling up a browser and typing the device's IP address into the browser address bar. This is one of the few debugging and profiling tools that does not seem to affect the performance of the application.

HoloToolkit FPS prefab

Much like our old `DebugInfo` prefab, being able to see our frames per second in the game can be a great benefit to hunting down problems that occur. Also, considering that it's just a drag and drop away, there is no reason everyone should not run it until a project is finished.

To install this into our project, do the following:

1. Drill down into your **HoloToolkit | Utilities | Prefabs**
2. Select **FPSDisplay** and drag it out to your **Hierarchy** view.

After performing these steps, the following screen would appear as shown:

This prefab has **TagALong** and **Billboard** attached, so you do not need to attach it to anything in particular. One thing to consider when using the **FPSDisplay** is that the total FPS will be down one frame because of the work the counter is doing.

Unity Profiler

The Unity Profiler looks at the hardware in use and how it is being used. At the same time, it is using the application that is running and breaking it down into method calls. It breaks each method call down to a percentage of use, as well as memory allocation and other elements.

In the following screenshot, you can see the skeeball game running and how the methods are being broken down to use percentages:

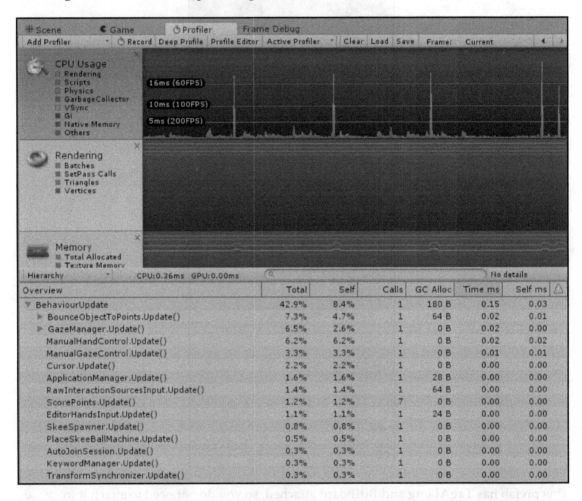

This can be really useful for finding a method that is taking up way more process than it should be.

Visual Studio performance profiler

Microsoft has a profiler that operates somewhat similar to the Unity profile, but it digs in a bit deeper, well at least that seems to be the case for HoloLens. Much like the Unity profiler, this one allows you to drill down to specific function calls, but the level of detail that this profile can see is rather jaw dropping:

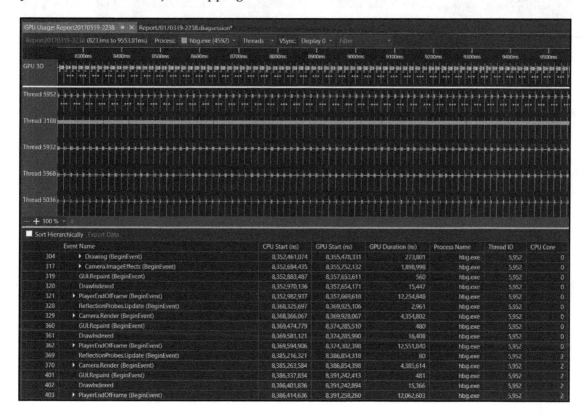

Here, we have the GPU threads for about a second of the profile:

This is what the CPU did in the same session:

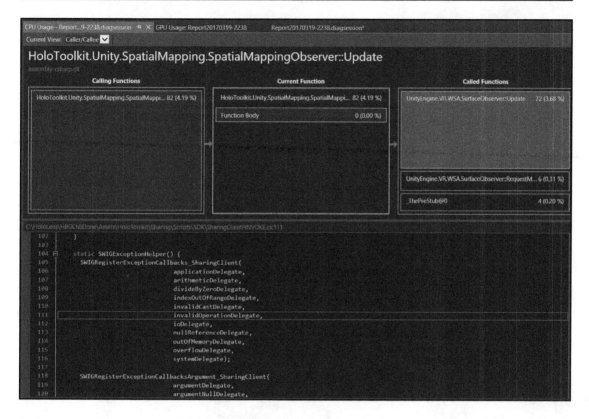

This profiler lets you drill down into the specific classes that were in use at a given moment.

I really do not see how you can get much deeper than this, but apparently you can. It is just from a different perspective--a frame.

Unity Frame Debugger

Unity's lowest level tool is the **Frame Debugger**. This tool breaks down a segment of time into frames. Then, you can look at each draw call at a specific frame:

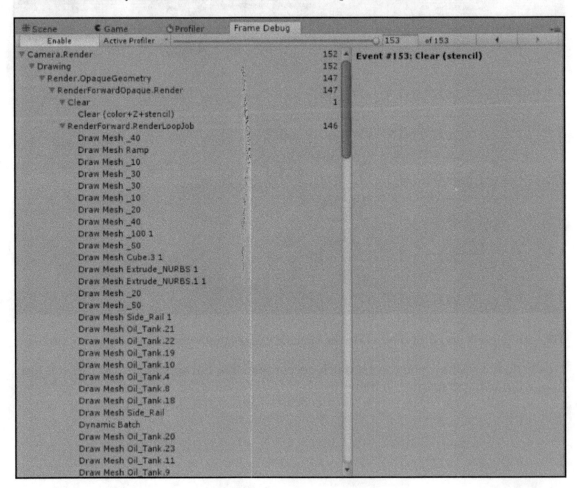

With the game view open, you can select objects in the list and see them appear. If you ever had any questions about a render pipeline and how it composites, this can answer a lot of questions.

With that, we go to the last tool in the list, and an even lower-level tool.

Visual Studio Graphics Debugger

Much like the Unity Frame Debugger, this profiler then breaks down to individual frames. However, the big difference between the Unity and Microsoft versions is that this drills down to the DirectX level, which is about as low as you go without going to assembly language and machine code:

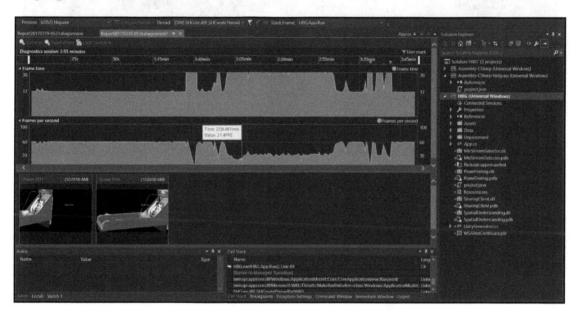

Much like the other debuggers, you can break down the program to the various method calls to help find problems. However, this tool is designed around debugging visual problems:

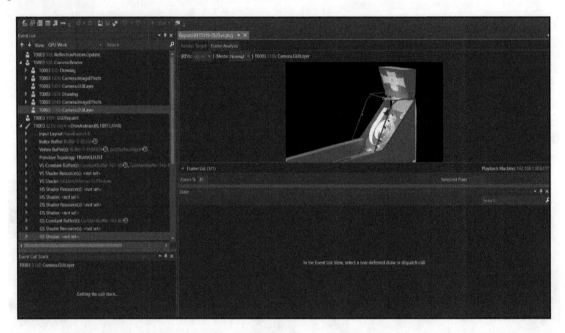

You can select specific frames and break down a captured moment to the draw calls and even the stencils and light calls:

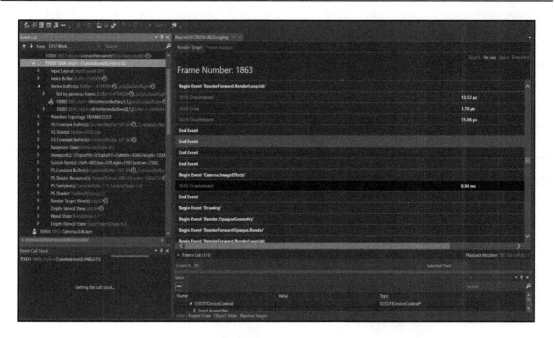

These are really amazing tools, and maybe one day I can use them to figure out how to get 60 frames a second with HoloLens. In all reality, these low-level tools will likely only be used by processor manufacturers and the creators of new 3D engines trying to understand why their backfaces are not culling correctly. Generally speaking, we will stick to the Visual Studio Debugger and may jump into a basic profiler from time to time to try and learn what is taking up so much processing time. Looking at our game In this section, we will look at a few options that can be looked at to fix the problems with this project.

Currently, if you have gone through this project step by step, you are, like me, likely getting 22 frames per second when you play the game on HoloLens. In the HoloLens world, minimum recommended performance is **60 FPS**. This number is needed to maintain the illusion that holograms really exist in the world. This goal is a very tall order; 30 is the norm and 45 is pushing it in my experience. Light probes One issue I am currently clearly aware of is due to the change to the quality settings. With the light probes set at 2 instead of Microsoft's recommended 0, and the number of lights in our scene, we are shaving 8 frames per second off. It just looks so bad without it.

There are a few options to potentially fix this:

- Of course, bite the bullet and change the light probes setting to 0
- Take out some of the lights in the scene
- Bake static lighting into the scene
- Alternatively, make our speed indicator an object that changes colors instead of using lights

Unity Profiler Taking a quick run through the Unity Profiler showed me that over 80% of the processing is in `HoloLensWaitOnGPU`, which means it is happening on the GPU itself. Now, let us have a look at the **Profiler**:

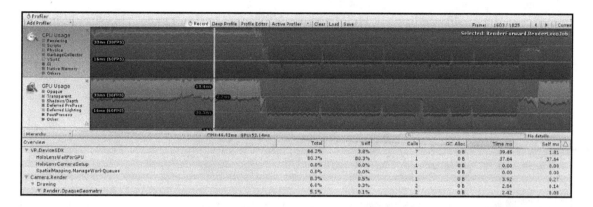

Looking at the **Timeline** reinforces that idea in the **Main Thread**:

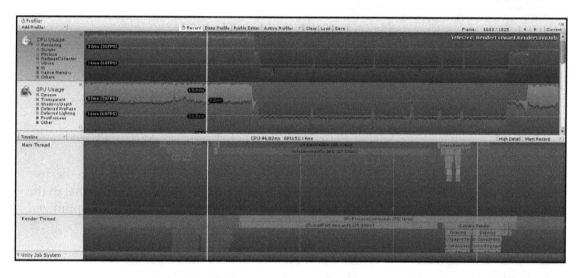

Selecting the GPU to dig down, we can see that 57.3% of the processing is happening in **Graphic.PresentAndSync** | **Device.Present**. From all accounts, this has to do with **VSync** or **Vertical Sync**.

In our case, the quality settings of HoloLens has **VSync** set to **don't sync**. This should not be affecting us, so let's try looking elsewhere:

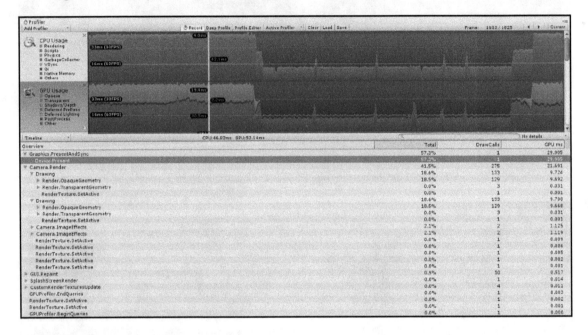

Looking at the **CPU:46.02msGPU:52.14ms** shows us that we are GPU bound. This means that we have a graphics bottleneck on our hands slowing us down; now I know that in the case of this project, the Skeeball machine is a high poly model that has not been optimized, so that's the culprit--the answer to our mystery.

Often when dealing with these types of graphics, bottleneck models being too high in detail can definitely be a problem. Another big issue that can arise is the correct use of shaders.

In our case, HoloLens is considered a mobile device and should be treated as one. I looked at our use of materials and noted that all of them, aside from two, were set to standard. As we are on HoloLens, we should be using HoloLens/StandardFast. Now, this change will not likely fix our issue but will possibly give us a 1 or 2 FPS return.

One potential solution to use, if this was a normal Unity project, would be going to Quality and changing many of the settings:

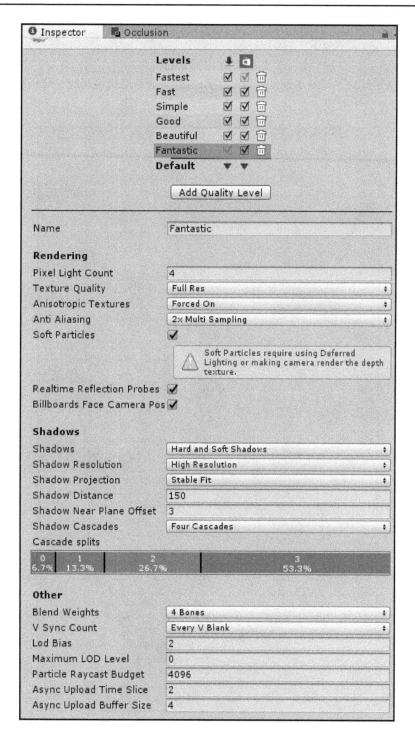

In many cases, a slow project is quickly and easily brought back up to speed by making a few adjustments. Now, this should only be considered a band-aid; in the end, you will have to do what is being done in the chapter to run the project efficiently. However, in the case of HoloLens, you are stuck with debugging and optimizing because all the quality settings are turned down to begin with:

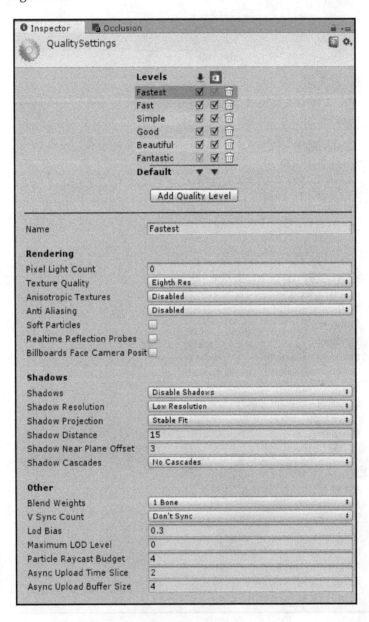

Simplygon

Simplygon is a polygon reduction tool, one that I have used with great success in a few projects. It can be used to simply reduce the triangles in an object like we would use in this particular project, or it can be used to create **level of detail** (**LOD**) models. These are series of single models that contain fewer and fewer triangles as you get further away. These are more ideal for big game projects than what may be done in a HoloLens project. Simplygon was recently acquired by Microsoft, so hopefully, it will be integrated into the workflow eventually.

Summary

It appears that we have reached the end of this road. Thanks for coming along with me on this journey. I really hope I reached my goal of getting my readers to a point that allows them to jump in and get their feet wet with holographic development. Between HoloLens and the new Windows mixed reality headsets that will be hitting the street in just a few short weeks, there will be many opportunities to create all kinds of software.

What I aimed to help you learn was a wide range of ideas, but focused on a single project. I tried to avoid the fluff and stick to what mattered. I tried to keep the perspective of someone that was new to this and approach it from a way that would have helped me get farther faster. Of course, people learn in different ways. If I have left questions unanswered, please look me up on the various social media outlets. I will be happy to try to help when time permits.

Sometime around the release of this book, expect a GitHub repository to appear with the final version of this project in it. I would love to see people add to this project and improve it.

Index